The Gehlen Memoirs

The Gehlen Memoirs

*The first full edition of
the Memoirs of
General Reinhard Gehlen 1942–1971*

Reinhard Gehlen, *1902–*

Translated by David Irving

Collins
St James's Place, London, 1972

William Collins Sons & Co Ltd
London · Glasgow · Sydney · Auckland
Toronto · Johannesburg

First published in Great Britain 1972
© Reinhart Gehlen, Berg, Germany, 1971
© William Collins, London, 1972, and World Publishing Company,
    New York, 1972
First published in a shorter edition by v. Hase und Koehler
Verlag, Mainz, Germany, 1971

ISBN 0 00 211293 0

Set in Monotype Times
Made and printed in Great Britain by
William Collins Sons & Co Ltd Glasgow

To my colleagues in the Service

Contents

8   *Contents*

Illustrations

Introduction

As a young officer I stubbornly refused to learn any foreign language beyond what I had picked up at school, so that there could be no risk of my being posted to military Intelligence work within the General Staff, let alone to the secret service itself. Like all my comrades in the long years of the history of the German General Staff, I yearned for the day when I would be given an active command of my own. Yet it was precisely in this dreaded field of human endeavour that I was fated to find my métier – and, I say with gratitude, my fulfilment – analysing the enemy's position, and working with the Intelligence services.

In the milestones of a person's life we can of course see reflected the broad trends of his epoch: in him we can detect the *Zeitgeist*, the spirit of the age, just as we can recognise the scars left behind by the particular circumstances of his era – war, expulsion from native soil, national collapse and defeat. But we can also see something of the inner bearing of the man that will stamp him as a soldier, and – more than that – a General Staff officer. In my own view, the mundane milestones in my own life are not worth committing to the pages of this book. My childhood, my education, my entry into the Reichswehr, my commissioning as a lieutenant at the end of 1923, and then my service in various positions in the line and at staff level – there is little in all that to distinguish me from a thousand other General Staff officers. I do not expect others to be interested in my works until my appointment on 1 April 1942 as head of that branch of the army's General Staff known as *Fremde Heere Ost*, or 'Foreign Armies East'.

It is this, the latter segment of my life, that prompts me, and I would claim justifies me as well, in publishing my memoirs. From that day my life took a unique turn. From 1 April 1942 onwards I was in a position of extreme responsibility, exerting a growing influence on Intelligence work that was of the utmost importance for the security of my country.

The essence of secret Intelligence work, apart from the need to know everything, is an ability to follow historical trends and project them into the future. We all know how clearly and accurately those rare statesmen with the gift of vision can perceive the developing trends of history perhaps fifty years in advance. How much more possible it must be to do so over a shorter period, if one has a thorough knowledge of the factors determining any given situation and the future trends.

Admittedly, this kind of knowledge does not fall like manna from heaven. It is pieced together from a large number of individual facts which have to be assayed and correlated with one another on the basis of a solid general knowledge and absolute cognisance of one's own situation and that of one's partners, as well as of the potential and actual enemies. To achieve this painstaking result, one needs an apparatus of high-grade specialists, skilfully organised and trained and closely attuned to one another. This is the task of the foreign Intelligence service, and that is why, as the British, for example, have found out, it must be regarded as the most important instrument for the marshalling of the raw materials of foreign policy.

In the Anglo-Saxon world, as in the Soviet Union, there is in consequence no debate about the need for such a service, nor over the special character imposed upon such an agency by the uniqueness of its task. Particularly in Britain, to work for it is hardly regarded as disreputable, on the contrary, it is considered a proof of particular trustworthiness. It is a gentleman's business, and one that enjoys the esteem of the people. It is not a backstairs trade or a James Bond adventure. Alas, in Germany the importance of such a high-grade instrument has never been recognised by the general public. This was shown most noticeably by the publication in 1971 of a series of articles in *Der Spiegel*, on the Federal Intelligence Service which I had created. The many major and minor errors in the articles may well have aroused some doubts as to the seriousness with which the articles should be taken, but this does not detract from the fact that in no other country would it be possible for such a tasteless, indiscreet and inaccurate series to have been published about a government agency. After all, an Intelligence service needs a measure of screening from public scrutiny if it is to do its job properly. Only the parliamentary sub-committees concerned with its supervision should have any powers of inspection.

This may give rise to misunderstandings, particularly in this age of 'absolute' freedom of the press. But the consequences otherwise may well be that a sinister aura will begin to surround the Intelligence service, and this can only be harmful to the service in its already thankless work. The lack of understanding can have such repercussions that the accomplishment of its job is made less certain, and the objects it is set are not attained. From my years of experience and from repeated exchanges of views with leading members of other allied Intelligence services, I know that in stating these bald facts I am neither exaggerating nor expressing an opinion not shared by others. This, more than anything else, has persuaded me to commit my memoirs to paper, so far as they relate to the development of the German Intelligence service since 1945.

At the same time I wish to express my gratitude to my many civilian and military colleagues in the service. Without their perpetual understanding and assistance, all our efforts would have been in vain, and my work in particular would have been without success.

Prologue
From Hitler's bunker to the Pentagon

As a brigadier-general of the German army and chief of one of its most important Intelligence branches, controlling all army Intelligence work on the eastern front, I had never imagined that, late in August 1945, I would find myself seated with a number of my former staff-officers in the comfortable bucket-seats of an American Air Transport Command DC3 flying the standard of a three-star US army general, on my way to Washington DC.

We must have seemed an unlikely group to be crossing the Atlantic at that time. We had been given only three days to obtain the necessary civilian clothes to replace our Wehrmacht uniforms, and to lay hands on such suitcases as we could before departing for the United States; for on no account were we to be recognisable as former soldiers. Fitting us out in plain clothes was no easy matter in a Germany pulverised from one end to the other by air raids and the general ravages of war. I had had to beg and borrow to obtain the most urgent items from my friends. It was an even taller order to get hold of suitcases at such short notice, and in the end we had to improvise with the most motley collection of receptacles – Colonel Stephanus, one of my Intelligence officers attached to an army command, had had to ram his few effects into an empty violin case. Perhaps people who saw us took us for members of a string sextet – unless they had happened to notice that we were embarking on the personal aircraft of General Bedell Smith, Eisenhower's chief of staff. This precaution would make it possible for us to travel without attracting too much attention, or so the Americans thought; for the aeroplane was normally used only by the general. Secrecy was necessary because the Russians had begun to ask their recent allies where General Gehlen was. The charade remained successful, despite the fact that, when we touched down for a brief refuelling stop in mid-Atlantic on the Azores, we found the local community drawn up in a guard of honour to welcome Bedell Smith, whom they not unreasonably took to be aboard the aeroplane. None of us had ever been to the United States before, but though we were curious as to what lay ahead, the mood was anything but exhilaration.

Thirty-six hours of flying lay ahead. I reflected on the events of the last few months. It was five months or more since I had last seen Hitler: on 27 February 1945 Colonel-General Heinz Guderian, the Army's chief of staff, had taken me with him to the Bismarck room of the Reich Chancellery in Berlin, where the Führer still held his war conferences. The last German offensive in the west had collapsed and he had returned to the Reich capital in January to direct the defence against the Russian onslaught in the east. Hitler had long planned to strike at the exposed northern flank of the Soviet invaders from Pomerania, on the Baltic coast, but I had warned him in my Intelligence summaries that there were clear indications that the Russians intended to thwart this by acting first to cut off the Pomeranian forces from the Reich. Now, on 24 February, my prediction had been confirmed: Russian tank forces had knifed through our 'Pomeranian Line' almost without effort, and they were poised to advance on Danzig and the Baltic Sea. Hitler desperately ordered the Army Group Vistula, commanded by the SS chief Heinrich Himmler, to defend at all costs the road and rail link with Danzig – the very corridor of land over which he had ostensibly gone to war in 1939. I reported to Hitler the unvarnished facts about the Russian tank strength opposing Himmler – figures we had pieced together from prisoners of war and deserters over the previous weeks. Then I returned to my barrack headquarters in the woods at Zossen, to the south of

Berlin. I suggested to Hitler that we use amplified gramophone records of tank tracks, marching feet and other sounds suggesting the arrival of massive reinforcements, to persuade the Russians that between the river Oder and Berlin at least we had built up an impregnable line of defence. There was little else that we could offer. We had called up our last reserves, and in the final fighting for Berlin even youngsters would be put in uniform to man bazookas against the Russian tanks. Hitler adopted the 'sound effects' idea, issued the necessary orders on 5 March 1945, and ordered my dismissal as chief of eastern Intelligence a month later. There is nobody less popular than a prophet of misfortune whose predictions have been proved true in every detail.

Now I was in a plane bound for Washington. It had taken some time to persuade the Americans that they would be needing an eastern Intelligence service. After going into hiding in the Bavarian mountains for the first uneasy weeks after the final collapse, I had surrendered with four of my principal staff officers to the Americans on 22 May. Early that Tuesday morning, we had set out from our mountain hut, with our knapsacks on our backs for the mayor's office of the nearby town of Fischhausen, on Lake Schliersee, where the Americans had set up their town headquarters. I well recall my feelings – a grim amusement at the situation as I, a major-general who had played a not unimportant part in the war, had to turn myself over to a young American first lieutenant in the Counter-Intelligence Corps (CIC). But there was no going back now. The town commandant was understandably quite agitated when a general and four staff-officers suddenly reported to him; we were unable to enlighten him as to just what a 'catch' he had made, as he could speak no German and we no English.

He excitedly telephoned his superiors and they told him to send us one at a time to headquarters at Wörgl. I went first – loaded into a Military Police jeep and delivered to the CIC unit commander at Wörgl. He interrogated me in the presence of a

uniformed female secretary who took a written note of everything I said. I remember being somewhat disappointed that his
main questions were concerned less with my former role as
chief of the Army's eastern Intelligence branch than with the
situation in Germany under Adolf Hitler. Since the Hague
Rules entitled me to an aide, I asked for Major Hinrichs to be
fetched, but he never arrived.

I was sent on to Salzburg to Counter-Intelligence Corps headquarters, but the Military Police officers driving me evidently
could not locate the building and after driving me back and
forth for some time finally bundled me into an inn, in the tap-
room of which there was already another prisoner. The other
prisoner was soon sent for, and I was left alone, while a sentry
stood guard outside with a machine-pistol at the ready in case I
tried to get away. After three days had passed and nothing had
happened, I suggested to an American officer who happened to
come into the deserted inn that it was high time that I was taken
to the Corps' headquarters. It was heavy going to make myself
understood. When at last he realised what I was talking about,
he burst out, 'We forgot all about you!' and promised to look
into the matter at once. Some time later, the Military Police
returned, and ordered me to pack my bags. I sat in a jeep and
was driven off to Augsburg a hundred and fifty miles away,
where the US Seventh Army had its big interrogation centre.

This was a compound consisting of a large number of attractive small detached and semi-detached villas, divided into four
or six apartments of two or three rooms each – the ideal
accommodation for prisoners awaiting interrogation, since we
were unable to contact each other or compare notes. Until now
I had met only American officers, including the interrogators.
These, without exception, viewed the situation in the manner to
which they had been accustomed by their official propaganda.
Almost all of them believed the Soviet Union would eventually
develop out of its communist phase into a liberal state; Stalin
was always referred to as 'Uncle Joe'. Not one of my interlocu-

tors had shown the slightest recognition of the real expansionist aims of the Soviet government.

I was held for about three or four weeks at this disappointing Augsburg camp while my interrogating officer, who was evidently a German émigré, gradually satisfied himself that I was not a particularly valuable prisoner. He could not have been less interested in the Soviet threat; he was concerned only with domestic German affairs. Alternatively he would ask me about purely organisational matters and personalities. On these scores I said little. But wheels must have been whirring somewhere, for one day my door was flung open, a voice bellowed, 'Get packed, get packed!' and I was off again. Again I was not told where I was heading. I was loaded into a truck with various other officers, most of them complete strangers, and we drove off for many hours in the general direction of Stuttgart and Frankfurt.

When we reached Wiesbaden, I was told I was a Gestapo general and despite my indignant denials, I was thrown into Wiesbaden prison. Here the American personnel were uncharitable, to say the least; for a time I even feared there might be violence. Then one day as I was being marched down a corridor, I found myself suddenly face to face with my old chief, General Franz Halder, who had been sacked by Hitler as chief of staff in 1942; with his granite face, pince-nez spectacles and closecropped hair there could be no mistaking him. Overwhelmed by spontaneous joy at this unexpected reunion, we slapped each other on the back and congratulated each other; the Americans were sufficiently impressed by this display to moderate their attitude towards me from that moment. Halder belonged to that unfortunate group of civilians and officers – like Pastor Niemöller – whom the Americans had liberated from various concentration camps only to incarcerate again immediately. Most of them belonged to the conspiracy of 20 July 1944; among them I also caught sight of Hermann Pünder, the pre-1933 State-Secretary in the Reich Chancellery, of Nikolaus von Horthy, the former Regent of Hungary, and of Admiral Dönitz, whom Hitler had appointed as his successor.

Together with them I was housed at Villa Pagenstecher, part of the main Interrogation Centre run by the US Twelfth Army Group under its G-2, Major-General Edwin L. Sibert. So I had not been 'shelved' at Augsburg, as I had at first feared. At Wiesbaden there were a number of civilian and military prisoners whom the Americans evidently considered of particular importance for political or military reasons. On the first morning after my arrival there I was led downstairs into the garden where a Captain John Boker invited me to join him on a bench in the sunshine. He was smartly dressed, and cultivated in manner; he was perhaps thirty-five, and in his bearing and demeanour every inch an officer as we understood the term in Germany. (I later learned that he did in fact have some German blood in him, being a third-generation American of German ancestry.)

I know more about Boker now than I did then. During the previous few weeks he had handled the German Air Force Intelligence Group commanded by Lieutenant-Colonel Holters; they had surrendered to the US Third Army and had been sent to an interrogation centre where Boker had formed a small special unit to work with them. That was where Boker had gained his first unflattering impressions of the CIC, and of the Army's document-collection groups who were interested only in shipping material back to the United States, and had no instinct for exploiting the German personnel who had been working on the documents before. Boker had previously taught German Army organisation and tactics at Camp Ritchie, and before that he had been assigned to an interrogation centre outside Washington which I was to come to know better myself. One of Boker's friends from Camp Ritchie had told him that, if he could fill a quota of 'fifteen tons' of captured documents, he would be allowed to return with them to the United States. Under that kind of pressure, Boker was clearly going to have to act fast if we were not to be deprived of our most important documents. Captain Boker was the first American officer I met who had expert knowledge of Russia with no illusions about the way political events were turning. He had formed his own very clear ideas about the future.

In retrospect I can see that meeting him was one of the most crucial stages in the development of my plans. Our meetings retained their official character only for a relatively short time, for after overcoming our initial reserve we became close friends and have remained so to this day. We had a long talk that morning about the political and military situation. He asked detailed questions about my former work, which I answered only partially. After he left I spent the night thinking things over, deciding whether to lay my cards on the table. Buried in various secret locations in the Bavarian mountains I had the most important files and indices of my former Intelligence branch; I had an organisation in embryo which I was prepared to offer the Americans for Intelligence work against the Soviet Union. Was this the moment to reveal this to my captors? We skirted warily round each other in several further conversations while I put out such feelers as I could to him, gradually disclosing my own ideas about the future, and my ambitions and intentions. I assumed that he was keeping his superiors – Bedell Smith and Sibert – fully informed on our talks, and that he was instructed to lend me a sympathetic ear. At any rate with each day that passed he became increasingly more frank in his remarks.

I now know that Captain Boker was acting on his own responsibility when he listened to my plans for the reconstitution of my wartime group. There were too many hostile officers still – people with a blind hatred of the Germans, which was intelligible enough, but also US military officers who believed they could co-operate with the Russians. There were high-level directives in existence to the effect that any German documents relating to the Soviet Union, and any German officers and personnel who had been involved in 'eastern area activities' were to be turned over to the Russians forthwith. Boker feared, he later told me, that if he had reported my existence too early to Frankfurt and the Pentagon I might have been handed over to them. Then I would have been beyond salvation. Instead, he discussed it with the CO of his interrogation group, Colonel W. R. Philp – an officer of whom I still have the fondest memories. Boker had formed an unusually close relationship with this colonel, and Philp gave him carte-blanche to form his own independent section to deal with us, reporting only to him. (Boker and Philp suspected that there was a Russian infiltrator at their level in the interrogation organisation.)

Boker and I agreed that I should send for a small number of my former colleagues from the other prison camps, so that the Americans could judge for themselves what specialised knowledge we had. I signed a number of letters for him, and gave him the names of the seven officers I had picked so he could identify them from the prisoner-of-war lists and have them transferred to Wiesbaden; Boker secured Philp's permission to bring them in himself so as to avoid going through the regular channels which might have attracted attention to these prisoners. He himself collected Gerhard Wessel, who had succeeded me in April, and Major Hiemenz from the camp at Bad Aibling, and drove them to me in his open jeep; I had also listed Colonel Stephanus, Major Hinrichs and Major Füner (a Russo-German we dubbed 'Papuschka'). It took several days to collect them all. When he returned, Boker told me with a grin that at first he had spoken to each of my men without showing them the letter in which I had authorised them to co-operate with him. Without exception they had been completely unreceptive. He had then produced the letter. This had acted like an 'Open Sesame'. Boker made no secret of how much this had impressed him.

At about the same time Boker had our names removed from the prisoner-of-war lists that were in circulation. He was very properly concerned because the Russian liaison officers had access to these lists, and our joint effort could still end in tragedy. As my officers arrived at Wiesbaden, he had them housed without official registration in the Villa Pagenstecher, and no access was permitted to us except by Boker's unit. As for our hidden archives of wartime Intelligence documents, some had remained undiscovered in the fields where they lay buried. I sent out my men from Wiesbaden and these caches were retrieved. Others had been found already by American military units and Boker was able to locate them – though not without some difficulty, in view of the need for secrecy – in a document-collection warehouse near Frankfurt. His unit produced a blanket requisition from Frankfurt Army headquarters to have an entire section from the warehouse delivered to two of his officers; they drove over in a two-and-a-half-ton truck, and returned with a printing-press and a vast load of documents, only part of which belonged to my group. The printing-press, with it boxes of forged stamps and other paraphernalia had formed part of a *Russian* 'line-crosser' outfitting section: it had been used to forge German pay-books and other papers.

Thus the first step had been taken. A small number of my closest colleagues were once again at my disposal. My files and archives had been reassembled under one roof. We were in a position to negotiate. My own talks with Captain Boker returned repeatedly to the same point: the collapse of the east-west alliance could only be a matter of time; a conflict of interests between east and west was bound to occur and this would jeopardise the safety of Europe and of the United States. So how could we reach agreement as rapidly as possible on suitable terms for collaboration? Neither of us was in any doubt as to the problem which stood in our way.

Boker himself was fearful that my group might still be broken up for individual interrogation by different agencies and that our documents would be removed and sent direct to Washington; even if after some months we were reunited with them, he feared that our morale would have suffered so much that even the loyalty my officers displayed would not prove strong enough.

I had proposed to Boker that our Intelligence potential should be put to work for the United States independently of the US Army's G-2 military Intelligence, but in collaboration with it. Boker, however, knew only too well that there was no provision whatsoever for the utilisation of German personnel for what amounted to espionage against America's Russian allies; indeed, there was strong opposition to such a plan. On the other hand, the G-2 service did not conceal its ignorance of 'Uncle Joe' and his vast empire, so our offer must have been a sore temptation, as we could deduce from our talks with the G-2 officers. It would save them a massive effort of organisation and afford them access to information and expertise which it would take them years to collect under their own steam: Soviet military manuals, the complete order of battle of the Red Army, digests on Russian industrial and economic strength, not to mention an espionage network in existence behind the Iron Curtain.

But uppermost in the Western mind was still the image of the Soviet Union as a friend and ally in victory, a nation in whose benevolence and democratic intentions many people still believed. And had not the Americans fought this war to stamp out 'Prussian militarism'? How could American public opinion be expected to stand for their officers collaborating with former German officers and members of the German Intelligence service, in view of the hideous crimes committed by the Nazis – crimes which among other things had resulted in Eisenhower's policy of non-fraternisation? Ambassador William C. Bullitt, a close confidant of President Roosevelt, was to write in 1946 that Roosevelt had died in the knowledge that he had used Beelzebub to drive out the Devil and that it was now that the United States was facing its most real danger; but, I recall, Bullitt added that it would take about five years for this fact to sink in. Nor was he proved wrong in his prophecy. While the American attitude towards the Soviet Union was shaken by the entry of Russian troops into Persia at the end of 1945, it took the Korean War to open the public's eyes to reality.

Captain Boker decided to try to persuade Colonel Philp to bring General Sibert himself on to our side. Sibert's aide was a Colonel Sapieha who was already a realist as far as America's future relations with the Russians were concerned; but more important than this was the fact that Philp was a close personal friend of Sibert, and an artillery colonel. Boker came to me and asked us to prepare the best report we possibly could on Russian artillery, as a *pièce de résistance* to produce at the dinner party at which, for the first time, we were to be presented in person to the colonel. We also wrote a detailed report on the 'line-crossing' activity of Russian agents at the end of the war, which had been on such a scale that it was bound soon to be a major source of trouble for the Western Allies. Boker afterwards told me that Philp had been so impressed by the professional nature of our reports that he immediately took up the question of our future with General Sibert. There was no way round this discussion if Sibert was to be convinced of our integrity and our desire unselfishly to serve the west; but equally it meant that we were now exposed to the hostile glare of the other Allied agencies who only now learned of our presence in Wiesbaden.

For a long time our future hung in the balance. Given the political situation in August 1945, it was understandable that nothing could be decided at once. Perhaps it was not anyway a decision that could be taken by the American commanders in Europe. Boker told me years later that it soon became apparent that the Pentagon wanted to have all our documents sent over to Washington, but not us; there was no wish that we should continue working. He had, however, been able to persuade Sibert's headquarters that these documents should not be separated from the experts concerned, and that the latter must be persuaded to co-operate. Sibert, in fact, would have liked us to stay where we were and to keep the documents as well, but in this he was overruled by the Pentagon.

That was how I and a handful of my colleagues came to be sitting in General Bedell Smith's personal airplane, flying to Washington at a time when the Russians were still dealing with the other three powers in London over plans to prosecute war criminals. I left Wessel in Europe to act as *locum tenens* in my absence. The agreement we had struck remained in force – he was to undertake no active operations for the Americans without my written authority, but he was to try to maintain contact with any of our former colleagues who might prove useful in the future – Lieutenant-Colonel Hermann Baun, for example, who had controlled our active espionage operations in the Soviet Union. One reason for shifting us to America was clearly a desire to reduce the risk of an indiscretion in Europe: by now we had all been deleted from the American prisoner-of-war records – with the curious result that as late as 1949 the Counter-Intelligence Corps still had me on their wanted lists. On the other hand, our shift to Washington would enable the negotiations to be conducted in an atmosphere more conducive to calm discussion than the turmoil of war-torn Europe.

Our airplane came in low over the Potomac river and landed at Washington's National Airport after thirty-six hours of flying. It was parked at the very end of the field and surrounded by sentries. We were met by a US army captain who was to be responsible for us at first, and by a uniformed official of the Department of Agriculture who was looking for any contraband plants we might be trying to import into the United States, and who was totally uninterested in the possibility that we might be bringing anything of greater value for the west. To our disappointment Captain Boker, who had become a faithful friend as time had passed and who had accompanied us in the airplane, took leave of us at the airport, although he did tell me he would try to see me again next day. Kohler escorted us cordially to an arrival lounge, where we had to pass a medical examination, sitting on a bench – like a row of sparrows on a twig – with thermometers stuck into our mouths.

Something about this reception made me vaguely uneasy. We were led out of the airport building and loaded into a Black Maria, a closed van with no windows and just one, barely adequate, ventilation slot. I could see that my travelling companions were equally taken aback by this transport and all that it seemed to imply. As the Black Maria started its journey through the airport gates I tried to work out where we were heading by sensing the van's changes of direction and timing each stretch of road between. When it pulled up we were about fifteen miles south of Washington by my calculations – I guessed we were in Alexandria, Virginia, and this later turned out to be about right. We were at Fort Hunt interrogation camp, although it was not identified to us for security reasons, the American soldiers calling it only by its Post Office Box number 1142. The ugly building was surrounded by a barbed-wire fence, guarded by four watch-towers; we dubbed it 'Truman's Hotel'. In it there was an adequately furnished room for each of us – but with one feature that struck us all as odd: there was no doorknob inside the room, so the occupant could not get out if he wanted to.

This was virtually solitary confinement, and it lowered our morale with a vengeance. The strain on our nerves increased as nothing happened to interrupt the monotony of the next few days. I was hard put to keep up the spirits of my colleagues. Captain Kohler tried to gloss over our new predicament by suggesting that all this – the cell-like rooms, the barbed wire and watch-towers – was being done in the interests of our own security. There was a further disappointment the day after our arrival when Captain Boker came to see me. 'I'm sorry,' he said, 'but I won't be able to take care of you any more, General. After to-morrow Captain Waldman will be at your service.' (He did not seem too pleased about being taken off the case.) As he did not enlarge on this announcement (perhaps he was not permitted to) it only increased our uncertainty.

Captain Eric Waldman arrived the next day. We went for a long stroll and talked together, putting out cautious feelers and trying to find out more about each other. He seemed reliable and frank enough as a man. While he was reserved, no doubt in part because of the tragic fate of his family in occupied Europe, this by no means ruled out all prospect of his co-operating with us. We later became firm friends. For many years to come, he was to make a strong contribution to our success, and in many other ways he also helped the youthful Federal Republic in West Germany wherever he humanly could.

He made it clear that the present, somewhat harsh, arrangements were the result of 'certain special circumstances', and he asked us not to lose heart: he would set things right as time went on. We gathered that this was an interrogation camp established for the exploitation of particularly important prisoners of war. Those in charge of the camp were not pleased that we had been withdrawn from their charge as far as exploitation was concerned; for, every day Waldman collected us from outside our accommodation block and drove us off for detailed conversations with experts of the War Department's G-2 division working under General George V. Strong. This provoked the authorities into inflicting various petty irritations on us, like the strange style of accommodation, in the hope that we would retaliate by refusing to co-operate with 'the Americans'. Once the Pentagon had lost interest in us, we would be returned to the camp for interrogation, and our new masters could then take the credit for exploiting our brains and abilities.

When I learned this, I saw that there were squabbles between the various factions in America as bad as any that had hampered us in Nazi Germany. For the people in the line of fire – in this case us – it could be highly uncomfortable, but there was nothing for it but to grin and bear it. After some time Captain Waldman managed to get us different accommodation: we were given three little rustic cabins in the woods with no fence of any kind and with complete freedom to move around on parole within certain geographical limits. In these huts we lived in twos and threes, and the bounds were sufficiently generous for us to be able to move around in almost complete liberty in the free time that was given. My professional mistrust prompted me to comb the three huts a few days later for signs of any hidden microphones, as I did not want the Americans to profit from every word we spoke in private. As I had expected I found a microphone ingeniously concealed in each hut. Next day I complained to Captain Waldman. I assumed that these 'bugs' had found their way in with his knowledge, and I suggested to him that, for security reasons alone, it seemed unwise to use listening devices against us, since the other end was probably monitored by some NCO who might well be tempted to gossip outside about our real identity, and jeopardise the whole project. Waldman was furious about the microphones: 'It's incredible,' he exclaimed. 'I'm going to get to the bottom of who was responsible for it!' It turned out that the 'bugs' had indeed been installed without his knowledge, presumably by some rural who hoped to glean enough information to make things embarrassing for him.

I now know that after Boker had brought us across the Atlantic he reported to the Pentagon, where he had found a complete lack of understanding for the fact that he had re-established a working Intelligence organisation of potentially enormous scope. The Russian section of the Army's G-2 branch had taken over from him, and they confirmed at once that we were essential to the security of the United States. But, for policy reasons, it was out of the question to develop our organisation – the most that G-2 could do was to interrogate us in minute detail and exploit our documents. In the circumstances it was fortunate that Waldman was a good friend of Boker's and committed himself with the same enthusiasm to our preservation as a group, for the Pentagon made it very clear to Boker that unofficial visits to us at Fort Hunt would be frowned on. He retired from the Army a frustrated man, visiting us once more in our cells shortly before Christmas and bringing little tokens – mostly pocket knives his firm had manufactured. We later sent him a piece of card to which we had sewn a number of foreign coins as a token purchase price for the knives so that, as the superstition goes, 'our friendship would not be cut'. Like certain other things in the United States, the Pentagon had been organised on a somewhat grandiose scale. The work that was set us consisted of answering oral and written questionnaires on the Soviet Union's armed forces and of writing studies based on the material made available to us. We were repeatedly visited by other experts from the War Department, wanting to get an idea of our plans and capabilities. The director of one of these study groups was Colonel Lovell (who was unfortunately killed in action in the Korean war). Before the Second World War he had been military attaché in Berlin and he used to tell people how correctly he had been treated while awaiting repatriation to America after Pearl Harbour. He assured me he would do his utmost to see we were not handled one jot worse in America. I learned to appreciate him as an upright American soldier with whom it was possible to talk frankly about everything. Their expert on Russia was also a particularly capable man, with excellent judgment on all eastern affairs. As time passed we were handed more and more material for evaluation and analysis, and the results we turned in gradually convinced the Americans that we were capable of everything we claimed.

It was during this phase that I briefed those of my colleagues whom I had kept in the dark about my future ideas and intentions – namely of creating an eastern Intelligence service on German soil using the same management as before, but with American backing. I well remember the incredulous reactions some of them displayed. Only their good breeding and their trust in me stopped them from speaking their minds there and then. When conversation with our American hosts came round to these same proposals, even at the end of 1945, the reaction was still an evasive one: apparently they still baulked at the political hurdles that would have to be overcome. We were told we would have to wait until public hostility towards Germany had simmered down, and the split with the Soviet Union had become more acute; the public must get to grips with the Soviet problem first, because otherwise, in a democratically governed nation like the United States, there would be the most awkward outcome in both domestic and foreign politics.

As late as December 1945 the Americans would go no farther than offering to sanction counter-espionage work on a restricted scale by a unit directed by Hermann Baun. I agreed to this as the thin end of a wedge which would make it possible for us to enlarge the scope of our operations later on. At this time, Baun was being held by the CIC at a camp at Oberursel, a former Wehrmacht interrogation centre not far from Frankfurt. The CIC knew nothing of the over-all plans that were being laid at the Pentagon in connection with myself. One consequence of this was that Baun at first believed the CIC were granting him permission to start up operations on their own initiative as a result of the proposals *he* had made.

The Russians had only themselves to blame for the final adoption of my plan. The foreign ministers of the four powers had agreed in London that all foreign troops should be withdrawn from their stations in northern Persia by 2 March 1946, but during October 1945 the first indications reached Washington that the Russians were in fact sending in additional troops. Reading the leading articles in the *New York Times* and the *Washington Post*, we could see American public opinion inching round to outright hostility towards Moscow. The final blow was struck in February 1946, as Russian troops occupied northern Persia in violation of the London agreement. The dramatic volte-face in American public opinion took us by surprise, but it was explained to me in a phrase I still remember: 'The Americans don't like to be taken for suckers.' Now at last the people saw that the Soviet Union was a leopard which could never change its spots.

The attitude towards us also changed. All at once we were given greater co-operation. We were allowed to drive into the city of Washington, accompanied only by an American officer to interpret for us, for it was taking us longer to learn English than we had thought. From our pay as prisoners of war we were able to make small purchases, and we were shown around Washington to see the sights and to learn its history. Captain Waldman displayed a real concern for all our problems throughout this period. The months we spent together in Washington established a mutual confidence between us that was to pave the way to the final success of our joint effort. By the middle of 1946, all the preparations had been made.

On 1 July 1946 we embarked on a Liberty ship, a troop-transporter, for our return voyage to Europe. We berthed at Le Havre a week later. Captain Waldman had preceded us to Germany by one month, but he was to remain with us there for a long time to come as friend and counsellor. Cramped though the troop-transporter was, we soaked up the sea air and the sunshine, we enjoyed the good food and spent the evenings on deck watching the films put on for the prisoners of war and crew. For the other prisoners outside our group, there must have been an agony of doubt and uncertainty as to what lay ahead of them. But our own morale could not have been higher: we were coming home to Germany, and we were on the threshold of a great new task.

Part 1

Foreign armies east

1. Initiation

On 1 April 1942 I was appointed head of Branch 12 of the German Army's General Staff; this branch was known as Foreign Armies East (*Fremde Heere Ost*) and it was primarily concerned with gathering Intelligence on our Soviet enemies. It was the first time I had direct responsibility for any kind of Intelligence work. My appointment resulted from the chief of staff's desire to see a change in the leadership of the branch as he was dissatisfied with my predecessor. We were on the threshold of a major offensive in Russia, towards the Volga and the Caucasus; and part of General Halder's reason for selecting me may have been that I had been his personal staff-officer from the end of 1939 until early 1940, and that I had subsequently worked on the planning for the new Caucasus offensive in the operations branch up to the date of my new appointment. I was therefore familiar with our objectives and military dispositions and with our intermediate and long-term aims on the eastern front.

For the first twenty years of my career as an officer, however, I had had virtually no contact with Intelligence work. My interest in the possibilities it afforded had first been aroused in the years before the Munich crisis of 1938, in which I had served in the 10th branch of the General Staff, the fortifications branch under Colonel Hansen, in which we were concerned with the theory and planning of German lines of fortification; this made it necessary for us to investigate the plans of the other side. On one occasion I had to tour the frontier between Silesia and Czechoslovakia together with a Lieutenant-Colonel von Riesen, to reconnoitre the Czech fortification works (Riesen was an officer of Admiral Canaris's *Abwehr* organisation, attached to Military District VIII in Breslau, who travelled under the code-name 'Schneider'). We spent some days with the photographic units on the frontier, obtaining long-range shots of the Czech installations by means of a giant telephoto lens of about a thousand millimetres focal length; by this means we secured information on the thickness of the concrete used at the sites even at ranges of twenty miles and more. The journey first kindled my interest in this kind of work; and a decade later, when I became head of the 'Gehlen organisation' in occupied Germany, I adopted the code-name 'Dr Schneider' in memory of the lieutenant-colonel with whom I had once worked.

There is a saying in the world of Intelligence – 'One report is no report'; an item of information is useless unless it can be confirmed by another from an independent source. It was at this moment, before Munich, that our staff unexpectedly received a complete set of the Czech plans for their fortification-construction programme. The general opinion among my colleagues was that it was so unlikely that one man could have procured all this material that it must be a 'plant'. But I believed the source was a sound one, and air reconnaissance along the zone in question soon gave clear indications that the programme was beginning just as the plans showed. The source, as it later turned out, was a Sudeten German.

In the course of my work at the War Department building in Berlin's Bendlerstrasse I established contact with figures who were already legendary, and some who were later to become notorious as well. Among the former, I valued most highly my acquaintance with General Ludwig Beck, Halder's predecessor as chief of the Army's General Staff. Beck was constantly looking for new methods and tactics, emulating General von Seeckt in this respect (the latter had held that in an armed conflict Germany could have no hope of victory unless she could force her enemy into fluid and mobile warfare from the start). Beck was aware of the possibilities of technology in modern war. He immediately gave his support for a costly new assault gun when it was demonstrated to him, even though he could afford only one detachment to be equipped with such weapons in each division. He hated the Nazis, and went out of his way to avoid them; he had only one personal meeting with Adolf Hitler, and that lasted only a few minutes. (This is not so improbable as it might seem; despite the Intelligence position I later held, I myself was only to meet Hitler in about four conferences all told.)

My recollection of other leading Nazis is only fragmentary. Heinrich Himmler once invited me to lunch alone, sounded me out about my organisation, and discarded me. In June 1938, I had what turned out to be my one and only meeting with Hermann Göring. He had been ordered to inspect the army's fortification work along our western frontiers, and I was attached for the tour as a specialist to the staff of General Adam, the Commander-in-Chief in the west. The construction programme had originally been planned on a magnificent scale by the War Department for eventual completion by 1964 (an astonishing example of long-term planning) as a permanent barrier in the west; but by mid-1938, of course, little of this programme was visible in concrete form. Göring made no secret of his criticism. Adam was normally a sanguine and receptive general, but after two days of Göring's onslaught he walked out, leaving me – a 36-year-old army major – to represent the War Department's point of view. No sooner had I opened my mouth to answer Field-Marshal Göring's criticism than he interrupted me, referred to me as 'Young man', and silenced me. Afterwards I spoke to his deputy, General Milch (one of the more upright and capable personalities in the Luftwaffe) and asked him to make it clear that, as I was the only War Department officer present, I must be listened to. Milch must have spoken to Göring, because the latter gave me a proper hearing after that. I spoke afterwards to Halder (who was on the point of succeeding Beck) and told him I thought

Hitler's orders to Fritz Todt, the engineer, to take over the fortification work from us was an ominous development. But it was symptomatic of the Führer's deep-seated mistrust for the General Staff and of our specialised knowledge. He once said, 'If I want a project to run smoothly, I always give the experts a wide berth.'

From 10 November 1938 until the outbreak of war I was battery commander in the 18th artillery regiment. When the Polish campaign began in September 1939, I was posted as operations officer to the 213th infantry division, a *Landwehr* (reserve) division in which the average age of the 'troops' was 45 and one of the regimental commanders was no less than 67; I was one of the three active officers seconded to this division. Apart from some fighting around Modlin, in which we acquitted ourselves with dignity, the campaign ended with little excitement for us. During October 1939 the General Staff recalled me to the fortifications branch at headquarters in Zossen south of Berlin, and I stayed there – apart from tours of inspection along Germany's eastern and western frontiers – until the eve of the German attack on France and the Low Countries.

General Halder detailed me to act as von Brauchitsch's liaison officer with the Sixteenth Army, and during the second phase of the French campaign I acted as liaison officer first to General Hoth's armoured group and then to General Guderian, whose armoured corps played a crucial role in the final collapse in France. For the following three months I accompanied General Halder as his adjutant, while Hitler went through the motions of preparing to invade the British Isles.

From the very start I gained the clear impression that Hitler did not take operation 'Sea Lion' seriously, and this impression was strengthened from observations I was able to make as Halder's adjutant and after October 1940, when I headed Group East in the War Department's operations branch under Colonel Adolf Heusinger. There were certain clues in Halder's behaviour that led me to conclude that Hitler regarded the entire 'Sea Lion' plan as nothing more than a highly elaborate but very effective means of deceiving the Russians as to his real strategic intentions in the east – a decision Hitler had evidently reached some time before I was given Group East. Not even the Army Group commanders had been initiated into Hitler's real plans.

Unpopular though this view may now be, I must state that I am in no doubt that Hitler's decision to invade the Soviet Union was correct. Indeed it was inevitable. While Moscow had no firm plans to attack us before the Polish campaign of 1939 (in which Stalin aided Hitler) by the time we attacked Russia, in June 1941, the picture was very different. It was clear that Stalin had resolved to postpone his attack on his erstwhile ally only so long as was necessary to see us bleeding to death after our conflict with France and Britain. Then he would have grinned and attacked us, safe in the knowledge that the capitalist powers had meanwhile torn themselves to pieces too. He might have waited until 1943 or 1944, but I and my colleagues in Group East of the War Department were convinced that, sooner or later, he was going to attack. The advanced state of the Soviet Union's own preparations for an offensive war supports this conviction: for example, the echelonned, in-depth deployment of their divisions at the time of our attack indicated that they were putting together a powerful land force for an assault on us. We were able to draw similar conclusions from the structure of their industrial economy. But if Hitler was correct in taking the decision, he was undoubtedly wrong in the manner in which he conducted the Russian campaign.

In this connection, I might add that the Führer nurtured something like a love-hate relationship with Joseph Stalin. When he was in difficulties, Hitler sometimes asked himself out loud, 'What would Stalin do in a situation like this?' It was in emulation of Stalin's example that Hitler instituted the arrest of the *relatives* of certain of the conspirators of 20 July 1944. Both men were completely without scruples.

The military tragedy which eventually brought ruin and disgrace to our country, was that Adolf Hitler lacked the necessary training to appreciate the military factors and strategic possibilities correctly, but nonetheless remained convinced of his genius as a warlord until the very end. This was a belief in which he was supported by those of his subordinates who had emerged from the Party. It was rooted in the fact that the first military decisions which Hitler adopted against the considered advice of his officers – the occupation of the Rhineland, the assimilation of Austria, the two Czech crises – met with unqualified success; and the initial campaigns of the Second World War – in Poland, Norway and France – confirmed his predictions and apparently disproved the cavilling prognoses of General Halder.

Thus events served to strengthen Hitler's unjustified self-confidence, and to throw the General Staff into sharp relief as a pack of pessimists and defeatists. But Hitler's method was to base his far-reaching decisions on the assumption that his enemy would behave in the most illogical way possible. This was a gamble which was some day bound to fail. Instead of considering carefully each step he took, he began to play a dangerous game of poker and to shut his eyes to the fact that sooner or later he would be dealt a losing hand. Even in 1939 he did not deserve to win: our forces were nowhere near ready for war, and if the Western Allies had shown resolution in their political and military actions when war broke out, a short period of fighting would have been followed by the defeat of Germany, a defeat which seemed certain from the very outset. This claim may seem far-fetched, but in support I would mention that the entire stock of heavy artillery ammunition – apart from heavy field-howitzer ammunition – consisted of $8\frac{1}{2}$ train loads, and that significant production of this ammunition had not begun by the summer of 1939. At the end of the fighting in Belgium and northern France at the beginning of June 1940, there remained only enough ammunition for the light field-howitzers.

Our stock of heavy artillery ammunition, including this time that of the heavy field-howitzers, was virtually exhausted.

Major Hasso von Etzdorf, a diplomat who was attached to my branch as liaison officer to the Foreign Ministry, once characterised Hitler's unrealistic logical processes with a bitter parody of the title of one of Schopenhauer's studies, *The World Considered as Will and Idea*; Etzdorf described Hitler's world as 'the world of will without imagination'.

Among the conspirators of 20 July 1944 who later paid with their lives was Admiral Wilhelm Canaris, head of OKW's *Abwehr* Intelligence organisation. It was during my months of office as Halder's adjutant that I began to come into more frequent contact with the admiral, for he had to pass through my office to reach Halder's; but I soon learned that my presence was not desired – for reasons of privacy as much as of security – and I tactfully withdrew. When I then became head of Group East, working on the planning of Operation 'Barbarossa' – Hitler's attack on Russia – one of the proposals I made was for *Abwehr* units to be attached to the assault troops taking part in the attack. Canaris warmly endorsed this suggestion at a conference I attended in his offices late in 1940. Although I was only a major, he was always charming, receptive and genuine; and afterwards our relationship deepened into one of great mutual trust.

That Canaris's character is shrouded even now in mists of ill-repute is a fate he shares with many other figures of the Intelligence world both in Germany and abroad (Colonel Nicolai, the Kaiser's chief of Intelligence, for instance). Some authors, who obviously cannot have been truly acquainted with him, have criticised his character. Canaris is accused of procrastination, of lack of resolution and, repeatedly, of doubtful conduct. The 'disclosures' of certain treason cases have tended to damage his reputation. For my part I am convinced that none of these vague and all too superficial histories has done the admiral justice. The great respect for his memory, even now displayed by former *Abwehr* officers, shows that they recognised the regard he had for his staff, and considered him a man of exceptional character. In addition to his deep-seated religious feelings and his impeccable conduct as an officer, Canaris was blessed with broad intellectual interests far in excess of those normally expected in senior officers. He was endowed with traits not seen in officers since the first half of the nineteenth century – traits that had helped officers like Roon, von der Goltz and Count Yorck von Wartenburg, as well as Clausewitz and Moltke, to spectacular achievements in sciences other than the purely military. In addition, and unlike many an army or navy officer whose vision was bounded by the frontiers of Germany or the North and Baltic seas, Canaris knew how to think in global terms: this was how he was often able to predict the future course of world affairs with uncanny accuracy. Admittedly he did not always find the right audience – men who were as ready and willing to listen to his prophecies as were Fritsch, Brauch- itsch, Beck and Halder – but this was a fate he shared with more than one of his colleagues. It was hardly surprising that, when war broke out in 1939, he had taken a very pessi- mistic view of the outcome and that the mantle of a Cassandra had lain heavy on his shoulders.

Canaris was a convinced opponent of the Nazis. Like General Beck he suffered deeply from the internal conflict between the military oath he had sworn in God's name and his opposition to the regime. The fact that Germany was caught up in a life and death struggle, and that in the event of defeat, not just the Nazis, but all of Germany would suffer (whatever the Allied propaganda might claim about the Nazis being the only enemy) only intensified this inner torment. I recall a long private talk I had with Canaris in 1942, in which he discoursed at length on the concept of treason, and concluded that it could be justified, given the exceptional circumstances of the war Germany was now fighting. But Canaris added that the traitor must recognise that only one thing would guarantee justice to the conspirators – the plot must succeed. He said, too, the traitor must realise that meanwhile he and his relatives would be exposed to grave risk. Canaris acted accordingly, gathering into the *Abwehr* many people endangered by their political beliefs, rescuing them from the grasp of the Gestapo. He set the seal on his beliefs – after hideous torture, as we know from the survivors of Flossenbürg concentration camp – by execution on 9 April 1945.

Admiral Canaris absolutely rejected political assassination as a means; his religious convictions forbade him even to consider such methods.[1] I remember well the occasion when he indignantly told me that Hitler had assigned to him the job of assassinating Winston Churchill. He had turned the job down, he said (just as he did when ordered to eliminate the escaped French general, Giraud). I can state with certainty that *Abwehr II*, the sabotage branch headed by General Lahousen, was employed only in attacking vital military objectives in the enemy's rear. The Soviet KGB and its predecessors did not share these scruples: the organisation embraced all these functions, espionage, sabotage, and liquidation of unwanted individuals, within one agency.

Canaris's *Abwehr* organisation collected not only military but political Intelligence, and this was channelled through the OKW – to which his agency was subordinate – to the various authorities concerned, like the Foreign Ministry or the War Department. He himself had a number of political contacts at very high level abroad, and he used to pay frequent visits on them. Even during the war he maintained his excellent contacts in the Spanish and Portuguese governments. One consequence of this was that in 1940 he was sent to Madrid to persuade the Spanish to declare war on our side. He told me at the time that he thought the value of any Spanish declaration of war would be

[1] This is confirmed by an entry in General Erwin Lahousen's diary of 2 February 1943: Canaris refused to sanction a sabotage attack on Russian military headquarters, since he had 'expressly forbidden *Abwehr II* (i.e. sabotage) attacks directed against individuals on principle'. – *Translator's Note*

nil, a view General Halder shared; he believed it would bring Germany only fresh burdens rather than relief, and quite apart from that it would slam one more door between us and the rest of the world, which to an Intelligence chief was a matter of personal importance. He was very relieved at the failure of his mission.

The latter part of 1940 was taken up with work on the preparations for our invasion of Greece, planned for the spring of 1941, using Bulgarian territory as a jumping-off point. After the Führer Directive had been issued for that operation, we turned our greater attention to the coming Russian campaign: I myself was preoccupied with the logistical problems, the details of reserves and transport, and later with the objectives of the Army Groups.

Hitler launched his invasion of Russia on 21 June 1941. In its early weeks it was obvious that we had caught the Russians off balance, and there was jubilation at Hitler's headquarters as the front line advanced farther and farther into Soviet territory. Within our army's General Staff, a special branch had been set up under Colonel Eberhard Kinzel to control Intelligence on the Russian front and contiguous areas. Kinzel, however, found it difficult to get on with General Halder, as some of the entries in Halder's diaries indicate, and he had failed to adapt his Intelligence organisation to keep pace with the rapid movement that characterised the early months of the campaign. The outcome of Halder's dissatisfaction with Kinzel was that on 1 April 1942 I was appointed to succeed him as head of Foreign Armies East.

The general military situation in early April 1942 was that we had succeeded in stabilising our front line in the important sectors held by Army Groups Centre and North where the front had been dangerously weakened during the disastrous winter months. The setbacks there had led to considerable loss of ground and this had still to be made good; a great quantity of equipment had been lost in the retreats, but far worse was the effect of the winter crisis on the German soldier, who after two years of victorious advance had for the first time experienced a reverse if not an outright defeat. Even though the severe weather conditions – first the mud and then temperatures of minus fifty-six degrees – coupled with shortage of winter equipment and greatly reduced divisional strengths, were the real causes, there were bound to be dangerous psychological results.

But it was not only for psychological reasons that we had to regain the initiative and begin the offensive again as soon as possible. There was a real military threat: the Soviet counter-offensive which began in November 1941 showed that Stalin was not averse to switching strength from the Far East to relieve the pressure on his western front; moreover, the winter fighting had displayed the Russians' capacity for improvisation. Any respite we gave them now would disproportionately add to the fighting strength of the Russians, which had declined severely during the summer of 1941. The conflict would become in-definitely prolonged, and with it would grow the danger of war on two fronts. We could not expect the intervention of strong American forces to be delayed longer than 1943. Thus by the start of 1942 Hitler faced a situation similar to that confronting the Supreme Army Command during the Great War in the spring of 1917.

During my spell in the operations branch we had had the job of investigating where and with what units our new offensive ought to be mounted. In the course of doing so we concluded that despite every effort on its part, the Wehrmacht and its supporting armament industry would not be able to replace manpower and equipment losses fast enough to justify launching an offensive along the entire length of the eastern front from the Crimea in the south to Leningrad in the north. On the other hand, the divisions confronting Britain in the west would pro-bably get by in 1942 without needing reinforcements. We should therefore limit ourselves to smaller offensives – recapturing the ground lost during the winter, particularly in the Crimea and at Kharkov, and capturing Leningrad to neutralise the Baltic and strengthen our land-contact with the Finns.

We concluded that we ought to use any other divisions remaining to us to attack the Russians in places where they would have no option but to stand and fight. In the opinion of the chief of staff, General Halder, our main attack ought to be centred on Moscow: in addition to the psychological effect, the capture of Moscow would deprive the Soviet empire of its political nerve centre; while it would not make it wholly impossible for the Russians to continue the fight, it would certainly hamper them considerably. There were bitter arguments with Hitler on this issue, since he insisted on an offensive in the direction of Stalingrad – to eliminate the River Volga as a waterway – and the Caucasus. Hitler's argument was that the capture of the oilfields there would decide the war: without them Germany's fuel supplies would dry up within six months. This prediction was in fact to prove unfounded, for even without the Caucasian oilfields we were able to keep fighting for two and a half years more.

Even during the French campaign of 1940, Halder's relationship with Hitler had not been devoid of friction. During the summer of 1941 it had been placed under further strain by Hitler's obstinate demand for the main military effort to be shifted to the south. His decision did indeed result in the greatest encirclement action ever fought, the Battle of Kiev in August 1941, with its capture of nearly two million prisoners; but this modern Cannae remained a local victory upon which were to follow the winter catastrophe outside Moscow and the failure of the 1941 campaign, with all the consequences that inevitably flowed from them.

The controversy over the 1942 campaign exacerbated this conflict until it was unbearable for both Hitler and Halder and it led to a final parting of the ways on 24 September 1942. I recall one remark Halder made to me which vividly illustrates the atmosphere existing at the end between Hitler and his principal strategic adviser: 'I'll just keep contradicting Hitler until he gets rid of me. He won't listen to the voice of reason any more.' (Hitler always refused his senior officers' requests to be relieved of their commands.)

As the emphasis on Caucasian oil showed, Hitler's decisions were conditioned only by economic considerations – not the demands of war or the requirements of foreign policy, all of which spoke against sweeping operations into the depths of the Soviet hinterland. The insoluble problem of logistics once we had crossed the River Don to the south, where there was only a single railroad track and very poor highways, also argued against starting such an operation; but Hitler cast all these misgivings to the winds. This was why it was so vital to identify, confront and destroy the enemy at the very onset of the offensive, and why the General Staff branch entrusted to me in April 1942 had to be able to brief our Supreme Command as completely, precisely and rapidly as possible on the enemy situation and on the enemy's short- and long-term strategic and tactical intentions.

I was now head of the Intelligence agency (what is now called G-2) responsible for the entire eastern front. I moved into Colonel Kinzel's office at the headquarters of Foreign Armies East immediately. It was a large hut in the middle of the General Staff encampment on Lake Mauersee, south-west of Angerburg in East Prussia – a small compound made up of wooden and brick-built huts in the depth of the forest, invisible to any aircraft that might pass overhead, and only half an hour's shuttle-train journey away from Hitler's main headquarters, the 'Wolf's Lair', at Rastenburg. The huts were all well equipped, and kept at a comfortable temperature by a main heating plant for the whole compound; an ultra modern communications centre enabled us to contact Wehrmacht units anywhere in occupied Europe within seconds. My office was in the hut directly opposite General Halder's living and office quarters: its centre was filled with a big map table, and my own desk in an alcove at one end, illuminated by powerful lamps that I soon found brought anybody who came within range of them into perspiration.

In peacetime the branch's job had been to build up the most comprehensive picture it could of the defence and armaments potential of the eastern countries, in conjunction with other agencies both inside and outside the army's General Staff. Of particular value was any data we could gather on the so-called 'fighting quality' of each unit – the beginning of what we now refer to as a 'psycho-political appreciation' of the enemy. The information we had filed on the Soviet fighting man in this respect during peacetime was to be wholly confirmed during the first year of the Russian campaign. We had predicted that the Russian soldier would be tough and frugal and that his modest material needs would enable him to fight on long after the battle itself was lost. We anticipated too that indoctrination would affect the officer corps but not the bulk of the recruits, and this also was proved correct. We expected that when the Soviet defeats occurred, the desertion rate would increase, and here too we were not wrong.

We were not concerned solely with the Soviet Union. During the early war years we were required to provide digests on the armed forces and equipment of all the Scandinavian countries, and on Czechoslovakia and the Balkan countries as well. We reported regularly on their fortifications, their attitudes towards Germany and their internal political situation. In addition to compiling the Order of Battle reports on the regular armies confronting us, we had also to conduct Intelligence work against the growing partisan activity in Yugoslavia. During the early part of my tour of duty, the branch was ordered to include in its work the gathering of Intelligence on a powerful new enemy, the United States. I recall that the American secret rearmament plan, of which only eight copies existed, came to our attention as early as the spring of 1942 simply through our careful sifting of the American press. The US general Wedemeyer (who had attended our staff college in Berlin from 1936 to 1938 and was perhaps one of the most outstanding American strategists to be produced by the Second World War) told me in 1960 that nobody had ever established how this top secret document came into the hands of the press. In 1942 he was himself the principal General Staff officer in the US Army's operations branch. In the course of the investigation of this information leak, he suffered probably the most nerve-racking hours of his life, but he finally emerged from the investigation with his reputation intact. He told me that the investigation indicated that the source of the disclosure was somewhere in President Roosevelt's immediate entourage.

In the middle of June 1942, I was able to give Halder a bulky report we had compiled on the American strength and strategic intentions for the coming year, with photographs of US tanks and landing craft, details of the US Army's expansion plans, and an analysis of the tonnage of shipping available for the transport of American troops. We concluded that lack of shipping space would rule out any danger that the Allies could mount a full-scale Second Front that year. We quoted an *Abwehr* source in the British embassy in Lisbon which pointed (correctly) to the Allied intention meanwhile to intensify the bombing of Germany and to carry out minor landing operations on the French coast. A few days later, I was able to circulate a detailed report on the US Army in which I noted that a 'European Theatre of Operations' had been activated under Brigadier-General Eisenhower. Although the American Middle East command set up in June was apparently only of divisional strength, I emphasised: '*in the near future we must take into account the fact that American forces will appear, in moderate strength at first.*'

Our principal Intelligence target was, of course, the Soviet Union. In peacetime, in order to build up an exact picture of the Russian units, we had used every possible source of information

– the files of the *Abwehr*, the dispatches of our military attachés and the reports circulated by the Foreign Ministry all played a large part. Of course we had also exploited the available non-secret publications, even though these were subject to stringent press censorship; by careful analysis we could often extract valuable facts to extend our own knowledge from secret sources. Despite the difficulties imposed on him by the Soviet Union's extensive counter-espionage organisation and by Hitler's absolute embargo on any kind of espionage activity in the Soviet Union after his pact with Stalin was signed in 1939, my predecessor Colonel Kinzel had already succeeded in building up a relatively accurate picture of the Russian defences, Order of Battle and mobilisation measures, and of Moscow's strategic planning. It was on the basis of this information that our 'Barbarossa' campaign plan had been developed and adjusted to meet each changing circumstance. Kinzel had also instituted detailed surveys of Soviet manpower and industrial reserves, and I found these reports of particular value when I took over. As we became more deeply embroiled in the conflict with Russia, we had to extend our staff and task until we had thousands of files on the Soviet armed forces, NKVD units and agents, comparisons between German and Russian units of similar size, maps of communications, wireless links, poison-gas depots and principal lines of advance, and the most intricate card indices on high-ranking Soviet officers.

Seven days after I took over Foreign Armies East, I reported in detail to General Halder on the Russian rate of reinforcement and their aircraft movements over the previous month, and I then discussed with him the way I proposed to work in future. He told me with some emphasis that he expected not only a thorough estimate of the daily situation, but also a long-term appreciation of the enemy's strategic intentions and capabilities. This was an important innovation. In a note appended to a collection of these reports, I explained in December 1944:

At the beginning of the campaign against the Soviet Union, Foreign Armies East did not issue any written appreciation reports on the situation, as the enemy's command showed that it was totally dependent on the German operations and was incapable of any strategic initiative of its own. Apart from its verbal reporting, therefore, this branch was able to limit itself to issuing daily 'digests' (*Lageberichte*) until the beginning of the winter of 1941 and 1942.

When the Soviet command managed to regain the initiative on some sectors of the front at the beginning of the winter of 1941/1942, the branch began to issue daily 'reports on hostile trends' in which some attempt was made to make an appreciation of the enemy's probable intentions.

As the war progressed, however, it became necessary for the appreciations of enemy plans which had previously been discussed verbally each day with the Chief of the General Staff to be set down in writing.

From 11 April 1942 onwards, therefore, a 'Brief Appreciation Report on the Enemy Situation' was prepared each day and circulated to the authorities concerned (Chief of the General Staff, Chief of the Operations Branch, Intelligence officers at Army Group level, Luftwaffe operations staff).

In addition to these, we prepared 'Comprehensive Appreciation Reports on the Enemy Situation' at various intervals (usually four to eight weeks) so that as the war went on our command should have material on the actions to be expected of the enemy over long periods of time.

After a very short time as head of the branch, I realised that there was need for much improvement if Halder's wishes were to be met, and that a number of administrative and psychological problems would have to be overcome. The main psychological problem was the traditional lack of regard for military Intelligence and anything to do with it, and particularly for Intelligence procurement (according to Colonel Nicolai, the Kaiser's Intelligence officer, the service had an annual budget of only three hundred thousand Reichsmarks before the the First World War). In one of his capable studies, Field-Marshal Count von Schlieffen also commented on this disdain for Intelligence work – a failing of which I was originally not entirely innocent myself.

A sign of this was the small number of active officers employed in military Intelligence in peacetime. The army's organisational chart of January 1939 shows only seven officers in Branch 12 (Foreign Armies East); at Army Corps level there was the *Ic/AO* officer – the G-2 and Intelligence officer, usually a young army captain on a posting to the General Staff. The peacetime organisation made no provision for an expert on enemy Intelligence at divisional level; in wartime this position was usually occupied by a reserve officer. Of course the disdain for this work was wholly unjust, as the enemy Intelligence expert, especially in the higher echelons, had to think with two brains at once if he was to perform his assignment properly. It was not enough to know the precise military units and equipment opposing him; he had to be able to forecast the enemy's intentions, and this called for a subtle empathy with his mentality and a detailed knowledge of his command tactics. He then had to be able to put all the facts convincingly to his superiors, acting the role of *advocatus diaboli*, a role not without its difficulties for the staff Intelligence officer, who was usually junior in both age and rank to the *Ia* (operations officer) and chief of staff in his echelon.

Very soon after taking office I therefore proposed to General Halder that the *Ic* (or G-2 officer) should be given the same rank and seniority as the *Ia* (or principal staff officer); this request was granted, particularly in the higher levels like Army Groups and Armies. While the *Ia* continued to be the *primus inter pares* the military Intelligence officer at least now had the same rank. The result was inevitably an increase in the latter's influence.

The second deficiency in my view was the inadequate co-operation between Foreign Armies East and other important

Intelligence agencies, particularly Admiral Canaris's *Abwehr*. For example, the *Abwehr* repeatedly passed on to me information of considerable interest, but its evaluation by them left much to be desired.

This deficiency was not caused by any negligence or lack of interest. Hitherto in the wars the initiative had always been in German hands; each campaign had in turn resulted in rapid and overwhelming victories. It was therefore natural, as I indicated in my note of December 1944, for the organs of military Intelligence and tactical command to be primarily concerned with the events of the day and of the immediate future. There was little that the *Abwehr* could contribute to this kind of work, simply because of the time it took to communicate the results of its investigations. During this period of fast-moving operations we therefore largely relied on forward Intelligence and reconnaissance by the combat units themselves; this satisfied our needs, although in retrospect I am amazed at the accuracy of results obtained from such primitive material. The failure of the summer campaign of 1941 ended that phase. The enemy had gained the initiative, at least for the time being; and it was now that we were confronted for the first time by the need to make a long-range analysis of the enemy's capabilities and strategic intentions, if we were not to run up against unpleasant surprises.

It was in this situation that I made personal contact with Canaris, and persuaded him to extend the areas in which we could collaborate. We soon established a close personal relationship. He was formally head of the OKW's Foreign and Intelligence Office (*Amt Ausland/Abwehr*). The former section of this attended to the affairs of our attachés in friendly and neutral countries, while the latter was subdivided into three branches. The first controlled espionage, under Colonel Piekenbrock; the second sabotage operations, under Colonel Lahousen; and the third counter-espionage under Colonel von Bentivegni. The *Abwehr* had its own Intelligence network, operating as did the British service largely with freelance agents of proven reliability but not employed on a permanent basis. Canaris had no organisation for analysing the Intelligence data he received: the raw material was circulated to the recipients who seemed most likely to be interested, with the result that any piece of Intelligence depended on the sound judgment of its recipient if it was to have any effect. In the absence of any continuous and systematic process of analysis, the importance of some items might be grossly overrated while others were wholly ignored. It was the lessons I learned during my collaboration with Canaris's *Abwehr* system that impelled me, when I came to set up the Gehlen organisation after 1945, to establish an efficient section of analysts inside the organisation; and I did what I could to dispel the heresy that secret services should concern themselves solely with secret sources, and pay no attention to the 'open' material freely available from newspaper stands and book stores throughout the world.

Canaris, of course, was not without difficulties of his own by 1942. The destruction of many of his networks in foreign countries that became our enemies with the outbreak of war made his agency's work harder, but not impossible. In the United States the FBI had closed down virtually every German contact, but as I have said, the garrulous newspapers and magazines of that nation made it possible for him to bridge the gap until he could rebuild his networks. A further difficulty was that since 1933 the Nazi party in the shape of the so-called Foreign Organisation (*Auslandsorganisation*) and Himmler's SD (security service) had been attempting to establish rival networks in a manner that verged frequently on the dilettante.

More than anybody else, the Reich Main Security Office (RSHA) which Himmler had formally established by decree of 27 September 1939 – an office in which the Gestapo, criminal police and SD had already been unofficially combined since 1936 – had struggled to get control of espionage and counterespionage. Hitler had ordained in 1933 that the defence ministry alone was responsible for counter-espionage and counter-sabotage operations to protect the state, its national economy and armed forces; but by 1935 it was plain that Himmler and his trusty police chief Reinhard Heydrich were not inclined to heed Hitler's ordinance. Thus 1935 had seen the creation of 'Special Bureau Stein', for investigations into suspected treason cases on behalf of both the Gestapo and SD and the armed forces: it was built into the RSHA with the express aim of encroaching on the *Abwehr*'s preserves. The *Abwehr*'s response was to turn its scrutiny on to Stein himself, but he fled abroad and tried to work for the Poles and British (without enjoying much success). These inroads into his authority caused Canaris to come to terms with Dr Werner Best of the RSHA. Together they hammered out a basis for collaboration, summarised in the 'Ten Commandments' of 1936, which laid down guidelines for the co-operation of the *Abwehr* with the Gestapo and SD, and clearly set out their individual responsibilities.

Two years later the SD's carefully camouflaged foreign Intelligence service was refashioned into Branch VI of the RSHA and this was taken over by Walter Schellenberg, in June 1941. In May 1942, or about a month after I took up my position as head of Foreign Armies East, a new agreement was reached between the SD and the *Abwehr* allegedly based on a ten-point programme drafted by Schellenberg[1]; the negotiations were conducted by Canaris and Colonel von Bentivegni on the one side and the head of Branch IV of the RSHA, Heinrich Müller, on the other. It was only now that the SD's espionage activity abroad became legal, and Canaris had to concede that it might undertake military Intelligence work abroad as well. This concession was the beginning of the end for the *Abwehr*, and heralded the take-over two years later of the whole Intelligence service by Himmler's RSHA. Without doubt Walter Schellenberg was the driving force behind the SD's struggle for

[1] Deputy Head of Branch 6 of the RSHA 1939-42 and Head 1942-5.

ascendancy in espionage and sabotage operations. Canaris always warned me that Schellenberg was a dangerous adversary, but he was a man of clever and winning ways, and many people praised his knack for Intelligence work. I heard that he had got on well with Canaris's man during the years of co-operation between the *Abwehr* and the state police authorities; but all that changed when Schellenberg became head of Himmler's Intelligence service.

I saw my first task as establishing much closer contact between Canaris's *Abwehr* networks and the various military commands. In peacetime, apart from informal contacts within the defence ministry, the *Abwehr* had been linked to the military commands only at the Military District (*Wehrkreis*) level, in the person of the *Ic/AO* officer. With mobilization even this tenuous link went by the board, as he now had to act purely as the enemy Intelligence officer at the forward headquarters of the Army Corps concerned.

Canaris's organisation operated highly mobile forward Intelligence and reconnaissance units under three control stations (code-named 'Walli I', 'Walli II' and 'Walli III'), each with a different kind of mission. I requested him to place all his *Abwehr* units on the eastern front under my control, with the exception of the Branch II units (i.e. the sabotage commandos) with which I wished to have nothing to do. I told Canaris I would not interfere in any way with the running of the *Abwehr* units, or their upkeep, but that we must find some faster way of getting their data to the fighting commands. It was typical of his readiness to co-operate that he agreed to my request without a moment's hesitation.

My first step was to transfer the control station Walli I, from its site east of Warsaw to Nikolaiken, about twenty miles from the main field-headquarters of the Army (OKH) at Angerburg, so that the contact between the secret Intelligence units and my branch, Foreign Armies East, should be as close as possible;

Walli I, commanded by Major Hermann Baun, controlled the agents and special reconnaissance units operating along the whole eastern front. Baun himself was a brown-eyed, undersized Russian-born German who spoke accent-free German and Russian like a second mother tongue. He remained in control of my Intelligence procurement operations until the end of the war, and beyond. The new organisation provided for a rapid flow of Intelligence data from the front line to our branch along two parallel channels – the first following the military chain of G-2 officers at each command level, and the second the *Abwehr* chain. Canaris's agency, for its part, received copies of all the reports reaching Foreign Armies East. One final innovation was that, to speed up the communication of reports, I ordered that preparation of the daily Intelligence summary was to begin virtually simultaneously at every level; the result was that each G-2 was usually able to hand his commanding officer a complete Intelligence summary by evening.

An example will make this clearer. Hitler had directed that in the coming spring offensive, the break through into the Caucasus was to come first and foremost. On 10 April 1942, in my first brief appreciation report to General Halder, I stated that the Russians would probably also concentrate their main effort in the south, although it was still not clear whether they would adopt a defensive strategy, or try to stall us by a surprise counter-attack. A few days before von Manstein launched the German offensive on 8 May, Foreign Armies East received from the *Abwehr* the following signal:

WSEA 1530 30 April 42 23.30 hrs –

To Foreign Armies East, Section 1. –

Secret. *Abwehr* unit reports 13 April: member of Central Committee, Nossenko, has told editor of newspaper *Pravda* in conversation from Kuibyshev that in the last joint session of the Central Committee's Presidium with the High Command it was decided to snatch the operational initiative from the Germans before they could launch their offensive. It was decided to go over to the offensive with the Red Army first on the occasion of the Mayday festival.

3979/42 secret.

Baun, Major

It will be noticed that this report had taken a long time to reach us. I showed it to General Halder on 2 May. By that time there were other indications that the Russians were planning to spoil our attack, and indeed before we could launch the planned second phase of our Caucasus offensive, the Red Army launched a sudden and concentrated assault at Kharkov on 12 May. Thanks to the War Department's and the General Staff's determination not to lose the initiative, however, the following sixteen days saw an encirclement action at Kharkov which ended with two Russian Armies destroyed and the taking of 240,000 prisoners.

To accomplish everything General Halder expected of us, it proved necessary to expand the staff of my branch and change its structure. From about twenty-five officers attached to Foreign Armies East at the time I took over, it expanded to about fifty by the end of the war. As principal assistant (*Ia*, or operations officer) I took Lieutenant-Colonel Baron Alexis von Roenne. Roenne was a tall, fair-haired, bespectacled Balt, with the superior air of a schoolmaster addressing pupils on a matter which was far beyond their comprehension. He could be very sarcastic to those he considered his intellectual juniors, but he was a fanatical enemy of the Bolsheviks and spoke a fluent and cultivated Russian as well as passable French and English. I sub-divided the branch into three groups: Group I, was under Major Heinz Dano Herre,[1] an athletic, tall officer with fading

---

[1] Herre was born on 23 January 1909 at Metz, and had acted as chief of staff to a mountain corps in the Ukraine; he succeeded von Roenne as my *Ia* (operations officer) early in 1943 and then played a leading part in the activation of the Vlassov divisions. He rejoined my organisation on 10 January 1946 as my personal assistant, acting as Chief of the Evaluation Section from 1953 until 30 June 1958; he then took over as Chief of Operational Intelligence Procurement

blond hair, who, like von Roenne, was a highly-qualified Russian-speaking staff-officer; this group was responsible for the daily enemy Intelligence digest. Group II, under Major Kühlein, dealt with long-term appreciation of the enemy's position: it assembled from other agencies and analysed the facts necessary for an assessment of the enemy's capacities in manpower, in arms production – in short in every aspect of interest in war. The group owned a magnificent library of books and documents from all over the world and kept files of statistics which were brought constantly up to date; after the German defeat in 1945, this collection formed the starting point for my colleagues and myself when we came to establish the Gehlen organisation.

Group III, which was run by a Captain Petersen under the supervision of von Roenne, consisted of our experts on Russia. They were a remarkable group, shrouded in an air of conspiracy, and with a penchant for throwing drinking parties on the most tenuous of pretexts; they had an ill-deserved reputation for sloth, but in fact their accomplishments were many. Most of them were Baltic Germans or Germans who had been born in Russia; they knew the terrain and to them Russian was a second mother tongue. Among them were many outstanding Russian experts, for instance Wilfried Strik-Strikfeldt, a forty-five-year-old former Czarist officer born in Riga, who had fought against Germany in the Great War. The group was responsible for all translation work and the task of interpretation in, for example, the interrogation camps. Russian military manuals and documents were translated and circulated to our own field commands; on one occasion in July 1943 we captured a *Smersh* counter-espionage manual advising Russian units how to detect 'parachutists, radio operators, saboteurs and other German

from Colonel Lothar Metz (who succeeded Colonel Conrad von Kühlein in that position) until May 1964, when he was posted to our Washington Embassy as the Federal Intelligence Service's representative there. He resigned from the service on 1 February 1971, with the rank of brigadier-general.

espionage agents'. It was translated by Group III and we modified our tactics and forged documents accordingly. Altogether
the group was of particular importance, since there were
regrettably few experts on the Soviet Union in Germany, and
our leaders had to be kept well advised on everything connected
with the Russian enemy.

Within a few weeks the new system was already working well.
During the course of the day the Intelligence data and digests
arrived from all the Army Groups on the eastern front; the
dispatches from Major Baun's office, Walli I, were rushed over
from Nikolaiken by an NCO dispatch rider on a motorcycle
(Baun himself was rarely seen at Angerburg). These were
processed within my branch in the preparation of the evening
Intelligence digest. Many of the incoming reports had to be
checked back, and we had to issue follow-up orders to the
reporting units at the front. Out of these incoming reports we
gradually digested an over-all picture of the day's main events
and a basis for an assessment of the enemy's probable situation
and intentions, even before we received the appreciation reports
composed at Army Group level. By the time the G-2 reports
began to arrive from the Army Groups in the course of the
afternoon, the respective sub-group heads had already been able
to form views of their own which they compared with the new
material. In the evening, about an hour and a half before Halder
called his main situation conference, I summoned a branch
conference in my room attended by Major Herre, head of
Group I, and the heads of all his sub-groups. Herre reported to
me the latest news from the Army Groups, from aerial reconnaissance, from wireless monitoring (these reports were always
very bulky documents indeed) and from Walli I, and the details
were discussed with his sub-group heads; about a dozen officers
clustered round the map table in my room, as each sub-group
head reported on his own Army Group and outlined his views
on that Group's G-2 report. On the basis of this briefing, I then
decided on the general line to be adopted in the final over-all

daily intelligence digest to be issued by Foreign Armies East. Under considerable pressure this document was then produced, usually two or three pages long, and I took it with me when I went to the main conference called by General Halder as chief of staff each evening.

All the General Staff branches concerned with the strategic situation were represented at Halder's conference. The head of the operations branch usually opened the proceedings, followed by myself as head of Foreign Armies East, and then after the others had also reported Halder would decide on the orders and other measures to be issued. At about nine o'clock next morning, after the night's batch of incoming reports had been processed, there was a further situation conference in my own office, followed immediately by a ten o'clock situation conference called by Halder, similar to the evening one but shorter and based on the situation maps freshly printed during the night. He would then take this information with him to the main conference called by Hitler at midday at the 'Wolf's Lair', half an hour's train journey away.

Obviously, if our Intelligence digests were to be of any value to the field commanders, speed was of the essence. (If speed was necessary for offensive operations, it was even more vital when the enemy seized the initiative.) I believe that the new organisation and system I introduced met this vital requirement. From the daily digests, we also produced a comprehensive appreciation report on the enemy's situation at intervals of one or two months. This long-range digest then formed in its turn an important basis for comparison with the current *daily* digest: any marked divergence from the pattern established in the long-term digests acted as an early warning that the enemy was up to something. It was a warning system which would have been very difficult for the enemy to evade. Any palpable increase in the rate of sabotage incidents or in partisan activity, or a sudden concentration of espionage operations in certain areas acted as an immediate alarm signal to my branch: we reacted by issuing orders for an intensive Intelligence effort in the particular sectors of the eastern front concerned. Armed reconnaissance units crossed the lines and brought in Soviet prisoners, and our wireless monitoring units eavesdropped on the enemy's wireless traffic near the front lines. (In this respect, the radio communications of the Soviet military police always made rewarding listening.)

It can be seen that to achieve the results we did neither I nor my colleagues resorted to any kind of black magic. It was application, thoroughness, expert knowledge and speed that made our Intelligence digests so valuable. This did not mean that our reports were always in accord with Adolf Hitler's wishful thinking. I myself briefed him on only four occasions; the rest of the time it was the duty of the chief of staff – of Halder, and then of his successors Zeitzler and Guderian. I know well, however, how manfully my superiors battled with this man, trying to reverse decisions that were obviously wrong. But with a man of Hitler's obstinacy, decisions could often be altered only by the force of destiny. Again and again Hitler dismissed the warnings contained in our reports as 'defeatism', and hinted that we were trying to sabotage his plans. The chief of staff always did what he could to shield me from these outbursts, which might otherwise have resulted in my peremptory dismissal. My own few meetings with Hitler passed placidly enough, but Guderian frequently got the rough edge of his tongue. I well recall one occasion when Guderian went to Hitler's headquarters at the end of the unsuccessful Ardennes offensive in January 1945, a few days before the start of the Soviet invasion of Germany itself. When he returned he described vividly to me how the Führer had thrown my charts and situation report to the ground, and had recommended that I be sent to a lunatic asylum for writing such things.

2. Stalingrad and 'Citadel'

Over the first half of 1942 hung one vital question: how many new divisions could the Russians create from their reserves? My predecessor had assembled a file which indicated unmistakably that the flow of reinforcements to the front was drying up, and tried to establish whether this was because the Russians had no manpower reserves or because they were secretly creating fresh units somewhere to hold in reserve for the summer operations. There were many indications from the interrogation centres, and from wireless monitoring, that workers were being recruited from important factories like those of the aircraft industry to fight at the front, and in February 1942 a friendly Intelligence service had supplied us with the resolutions of the Presidium of the Supreme Soviet proclaiming something very like the Total War announced by Goebbels in Germany one year later.

Late in May 1942 I produced for General Halder my own conclusions on the Russian position, and by the following month we had collected enough information to permit us to make a reliable estimate of the size of the reserves. It was an interesting example of the use of both secret data and the readily accessible statistical information published by the Soviet Union itself. In the January 1939 population census, Russia had had a total population of 170 millions, but natural population growth and the annexation of large parts of Europe had by 1942 swollen this to 199 millions. In the course of our operations, we had overrun the most densely inhabited area with about one-third of the entire population of the Soviet Union, some 66 millions, of which up to one third had probably been evacuated or drafted into the Russian armed forces. We took into account the fact that the Russian nation was at that time a young one, with almost half the population below twenty (in Germany it was less than one-third) but this fact could be offset against the high mortality rate and the general ravages of war among the older age-groups. This meant that on the one hand a relatively high proportion of the Russian people was of military age, a proportion which would increase in the years that followed, but, on the other, that there could be less recourse to the older age-groups than was possible in Germany. The proportion of women in Russia was also unusually high, over 52 per cent, which provided a greater incentive to use female labour in industry. On this purely statistical basis, since experience showed that any given country could mobilise at most 10 per cent of its total population, the Russians could have about 17 million men under arms.

From our interrogation camps and the captured documents we knew that Russia had called up all able-bodied men from 18 to 45 years old (of the 35.4 million men, 28.4 million were able-bodied); there were also indications that in some places 46 and 47-year-old men were being recruited. Using our own experience in Germany as a basis for calculation, we could assume that 11 million men at most had been placed in 'reserved' draft categories in Russia, and probably only 9 or 10 million in view of the lost territories. By this method we also arrived at an estimate of about 17 million able-bodied men available to the Soviet armed forces.

From these 17 millions had to be subtracted the losses since war broke out. Our armies' reports and the estimates of our allies, assessed these at 430,000 dead or permanently disabled in the war with Finland from 1939 to 1940; and the losses since our own attack on Russia had brought the total to 7,530,000 dead, disabled, or taken prisoner, up to 1 May 1942. This would leave 9.5 million men in the Soviet armed forces. These were

On September 10, 1931, *Lieutenant* Reinhard Gehlen married Herta
von Seydlitz-Kurzbach

The staff of Foreign Armies East outside their headquarters at Zossen south of Berlin. In command was Gehlen (**x**). The present head of BDN, Gerhard Wessel (**xx**), was at the time Gehlen's deputy

Major Reinhard Gehlen during the French campaign of 1940 (as liaison officer to General von Brauchitsch), with his son Christoph

believed to be distributed as follows. Of 7,800,000 active troops, about 6 million were in the army, 1,500,000 in the air force and 300,000 in the navy. On paper, the Russians therefore had a manpower reserve of up to 1,700,000 able-bodied men, but for various reasons these could only be made available gradually to the combat units, and several thousand men must be tied down in supply, training and logistics.

There were theoretically ways in which Russia could, in an emergency, find the manpower to raise new divisions, and we would no doubt learn more as the year progressed. But we had to bear in mind that with Russia we were dealing not with a Central European country, but with half of Asia, a territory thirty-two times the size of Germany, or covering about one-sixth of the earth's surface, so we were entitled to assume it would not prove possible for Moscow to tap more than a fraction of these ultimate manpower resources. My predecessor had somewhat optimistically concluded in March that the Soviet reserves were 'virtually exhausted', and added:

Only a meagre reserve is available over and above the armed forces already existing, and in view of the prevailing conditions in Russia one must be sceptical as to whether this reserve can be built up to the theoretical estimate.

The Russians will never again be able to throw reserves into the scales as they did in the winter of 1941/1942.

In June 1942 I did not see any such prospect of the springs of Soviet manpower drying up, as the ruthlessness with which the enemy was prosecuting the war was such that we had to expect Moscow to reinforce the front line without regard for the effects on the national economy, on arms production, or on the supply of foodstuffs. Thanks to their talent for improvisation, and to the endemically rigorous qualities of the Soviet state, Moscow had succeeded in mobilising several million men in new divisions, they had put them into uniform, given them the rudiments of a training and conveyed them over great distances into the front line. For this reason we now found that, despite the disastrous Russian losses at Kiev, Vyaz'ma and Bryansk, there were as many Red divisions confronting us as there had been when we launched our attack, and the Red Army appeared to be maintaining its front-line strength of 4,500,000 attained in January 1942. As for the Soviet air force, we noticed that it had shifted its main focus to our own Army Group South, which indicated that the Russians were either planning a major offensive there themselves, or were anticipating a German offensive.

I concluded my June 1942 appreciation with these words:

It is clear that the enemy has suffered major losses in the defeats of these last twelve months. The fighting so far has shown the German soldier to be justified in feeling he is superior to the enemy, and we have seen that where an assault is launched in force, success is guaranteed. But the enemy's numerical superiority in manpower and equipment must not be underestimated. If we are to carry the impending operations in the East through to final victory, we shall have to make a supreme effort.[1]

Far more crucial to the Soviet position was its dwindling supply of vital raw materials. I endeavoured to make this plain in a paper delivered to our staff college late that summer.[2] With the loss of the Donets coal-bearing region, Russia was entering a major industrial and transportation crisis: by 1942, had war not broken out, total Russian coal output would have reached about 200 million tons a year, but now they could not obtain more than 80 million tons. The railroads had traditionally swallowed half the output, and the industrial regions along the central and northern reaches of the Volga, including Moscow, and of the Urals and Siberia took the rest. The coal output of

---

[1] This June 1942 paper is still in my possession.

By way of comparison with the Soviet armed forces the German figures were: army, 4,100,000; air force, 1,800,000; and navy, 430,000 which were engaged in the East, North Africa and western Europe.

[2] This paper 'The Economic Potential of the Soviet Union', dated 7 September 1942, is also among papers in my possession.

the remaining fields in the Urals, Karaganda and Kuznetsk would probably be adequate for the eastern industrial zones, but the coal supply for the remaining western industrial zones was far more difficult to ensure, as it had to be taken by rail over distances of more than 1,500 miles from Karaganda and Kuznetsk. Several steel mills in Kuibyshev had had to close down in March 1942; shipping on the Volga was without fuel, and the railroad system was beginning to show signs of strain. With the loss of the coking plants in the Donets region, coke output was down to about forty per cent of Russia's pre-war output, and this in turn was affecting iron and steel production: iron-ore production would reach only 13 million tons instead of the planned 40 million, pig-iron only 7 million instead of the planned 22 million, and steel only 8 million instead of 28 million.

Soviet arms production was also likely to suffer from the shortage of other raw materials. We knew that the output of manganese ores in the Urals and western Siberia was inadequate for the local steel industry, and that manganese was having to be transported north from Chiatura in the Caucasus; since the Caucasus was the objective of our summer offensive, its capture would have a severe effect on Soviet steel production. Furthermore, the second richest veins of tungsten and molybdenum in Europe (after those in Portugal) were also in the Caucasus. In 1941 there had been an output of 700 tons of tungsten concentrate and 450 tons of molybdenum concentrate, and these were also processed in the Caucasus – the smelting works were located at Sestafoni in Georgia. We calculated that the loss of ferrous alloy production at Sestafoni would reduce high-grade steel production for the arms industry by at least thirty per cent. As far as petroleum production was concerned, however, we did not expect the loss of the Caucasian oilfields to have much effect on Soviet fighting capacity until mid-1943, as there had been extensive stockpiling in Central Russia. Similarly Russia had devoted considerable effort to developing independent sources of natural and synthetic rubber; we had overrun her most important plantation areas for natural rubber, and two of the three original synthetic rubber factories had been evacuated, but four or five more were known to be opening up, and we believed the Soviet Union could meet all its war needs with a probable output of 80,000 tons a year.

Finally, we also had to take into account the increasing rate of deliveries of arms and materials from the United States. The transport of large quantities of war equipment like lorries, anti-tank and anti-aircraft guns, shells and bombs, together with tanks and aircraft had built up initially through Persia, but from November 1941 onwards the Allies had been making increasing use of the Arctic sea route to Murmansk. According to prisoners captured during attacks on the Allied convoys, the ships carried foodstuffs, tanks, aircraft, aero-engines, guns and ammunition. By July 1942 the Allies were estimated to have shipped no fewer than 2,800 tanks to the Soviet Union, and our Intelligence suggested that about thirty armoured brigades had put in an appearance on the eastern front equipped with British and American tanks. The Russian troops, however, were not very happy with the quality of these tanks, as they were inferior to the Soviet T-34 in every respect, and with their narrow tracks their cross-country performance in Russia was poor; moreover, their engines could not comfortably digest the low-grade fuels common in the USSR. The British and American aircraft had also been severely affected by oil-freezing in the sub-zero temperatures; the Russians considered their own makes far superior.

By this time, Hitler's major offensive towards the Caucasus was well under way. Voronezh had been captured, our armies had advanced along the River Don and the River Volga had just been reached south of Stalingrad. In my view we were justified in hoping that our forces would shortly overrun the oilfields of the Caucasus and consolidate our position on the Volga before winter set in, although we had to expect strong resistance. As early as 12 July the Russian high command had created a 'Stalingrad Front' under Marshal Timoshenko, and on the 15th I had briefed General Halder, the chief of staff, about the new Russian forces appearing in the eastern front, and about agents' reports that the enemy was making determined preparations for the defence of Stalingrad itself. On the following day Halder and Heusinger had discussed with me the probable scale of the coming battle, and how far time was in our favour.[1] As our armies, principally the Sixth Army under General Paulus, advanced farther and farther towards Stalingrad that summer, General Halder and I had cast anxious eyes on the lengthening left flank along the River Don. Halder repeatedly warned of the possibility that Moscow would launch a counter-attack on this flank, most probably across that part of the Don that extended between the Khoper tributary and the great bend at Kremenskaya, for this sector was held not by hardened German forces but by our Rumanian Allies.

Even if the coming operation was insufficient to destroy the Red Army or to bring about an early collapse, the physical occupation of the vital Caucasus region, and the blocking of the Volga as a Soviet waterway, would cause untold harm to the enemy's economy. Between us and the military goals of the coming year, there lay, however, yet another Russian winter, in which the enemy could rely on his superiority in winter combat, as he had the year before, to inflict such a drain of manpower and equipment on us that we would have to dismiss all thought of renewing the German offensive in 1943, particularly in view of our obligations in other theatres. I warned that we should be on the lookout for enemy formations specially trained for mobile warfare in winter, and that we should expect violent partisan activity in the rear of our armies. It was by no

---

[1] Halder notes in his diary that day, 'We shall have to prepare for and perhaps even commence this battle while we are still fighting the battle for Rostov north and south of the Don.'

means impossible, I stated in September 1942, that, given the sparseness of our own front-line troops, these Russians tactics might produce crises as serious as those of the previous winter.

In the event, using Intelligence methods which I will describe in some detail, by 9 November 1942, ten days before the beginning of the Soviet counter-attack, which was to lead eventually to the Stalingrad disaster, my branch had clearly predicted precisely where the blow would fall and which of our armies would be affected. The Stalingrad tragedy marked the turn of the tide in the eastern campaign; it heralded the final defeat of the Third Reich. Since the complete file of our branch's 'Brief Enemy Situation Reports' is available, it can be seen that our claim to have given good warning is more than substantiated.

Between 25 October and 9 November, the incoming reports yielded a persistent impression of a weak but steady flow of reinforcements to the front facing the Rumanian Third Army, although it was not until the latter part of this phase that the Soviet intentions became clear to us. We received reports very early on about the arrival of further troops at Serafimovich, a town on the Don about 100 miles north-west of Stalingrad: there was heavy transport and loading activity along the railroad line leading to it, and our reconnaissance aircraft could see the lights moving at night and extensive traffic crossing the River Don at Kletskaya, about twenty miles closer to Stalingrad (it was from Serafimovich and Kletskaya that the first Soviet counter-attacks were launched). On 29 October I took my latest report across to General Zeitzler, the new Army Chief of Staff; Zeitzler, a bustling, stocky, bald-headed dynamo of action had replaced the exhausted General Halder a month before. My report said, 'There is nowhere any sign of preparation for a major attack, but the entire area needs continued intensive observation.' Two days later I repeated this view, but added that there was an increased impression that there might be localised attacks on the Rumanian position at Serafimovich. To this I added on 2 November: 'In connection with the increasing troop movements west of Serafimovich, we must expect the continued reinforcement of the enemy confronting the Rumanian Third Army, and possibly even an attack on them. We must await further indications.'

At the same time, we observed the corresponding withdrawals of troops and equipment from neighbouring Russian formations – particularly the Sixty-Fifth and Twenty-First Armies – to build up the sectors from which the Soviet attack would begin. On 2 November I reported the first indications of this from wireless monitoring reports and on the following day I cited a number of specific instances where air reconnaissance had observed tanks and field artillery disappearing from locations just north of Stalingrad and reappearing a few days later near Serafimovich. 'There emerges an increasingly clear picture of preparations for an attack on the Rumanian Third Army, though they are still in their early stages,' I wrote on 3 November. 'We cannot yet be certain whether the object is an attack designed to lure our forces away from Stalingrad, or an operation with a much broader objective.' At that moment I was still inclined to favour the former possibility.

It was clear from the active reinforcement of Stalingrad itself and from the very heavy Soviet air raids on our positions there that the enemy had by no means given up the fight for the city. On the 4th, I mentioned for the first time that there were indications that the Russians were planning further major relief operations from Beketovka just south of Stalingrad. The reinforcement of the Soviet forces in Serafimovich, at the expense of their front line between the Volga and the Don continued over the next few days; our air reconnaissance detected between two and two-and-a half thousand vehicles moving north of Kletskaya, and we were able to identify the new divisions concerned. Finally, on 10 November, I warned, 'The appearance of the Soviet headquarters for the south-western front somewhere to the north-west of Serafimovich indicates that a major enemy attack operation is in sight.'

From one of the *Abwehr*'s offices controlling agents in Moscow, I had received the following signal a few days earlier:

An agent states: on 4 November Stalin presided over Council of War in Moscow, attended by twelve marshals and generals. Following basic principles were laid down at this council:

a] operations are to be executed cautiously to avoid heavy casualties;

b] loss of ground is unimportant;

c] it is vital to salvage industrial and public-utility installations in good time by evacuation, which explains orders issued for dispersal of refineries and machine-tool factories from Grozny and Makhachkala to New Baku, Orsk and Tashkent;

d] rely only on oneself, don't count on getting aid from allies;

e] take sharp measures to prevent desertion, either by better propaganda and rations or by firing-squads and tougher GPU[1] supervision and;

f] all the planned attack-operations are to be executed before 15 November if possible, insofar as weather permits. These are primarily from Grozny towards Mozdok; at Nizhni-Mamon and Verkhni-Mamon in the Don basin; and at Voronezh, at Rzhev south of Lake Ilmen and at Leningrad. The necessary troops are to be brought out of reserve and up to the front line.

Events over the next months showed that this report must have been genuine.

But what use are the best Intelligence reports if one's own forces are too weak to withstand the enemy, or if the warnings are not heeded? By 11 November it was clear to us that the flow of reinforcements to the Russian front at Serafimovich and Kletskaya was slackening off, and on the 12th I stated in my written report to General Zeitzler:

In front of Army Group [Don] the enemy's intention to

---

[1] *Gosudarstvennoye Politicheskoye Upravlenye*, the Soviet office of Political security, espionage and counter-espionage which succeeded the infamous *Cheka*.

attack, which we have long suspected, is gradually becoming more clearly defined: in addition to establishing two main groups of forces which we have detected opposite the two wings of the Rumanian Third Army – where the enemy can now be said to be ready to attack – there are growing indications that forces are being concentrated still farther west, primarily in the Kalach area (we have intercepted radio traffic between the Russian Sixty-Third Army and six or seven unidentified formations, rail traffic to Kalach is possibly transporting sections of the Fifth Tank Army, and we also have *Abwehr* reports of reinforcements arriving at Kalach) and possibly in front of the Hungarians as well.

I warned emphatically,

While it is not possible to make any over-all assessment of the enemy situation with the picture as uncertain as it is at present, we must expect an early attack on the Rumanian Third Army, with the interruption of our railroad to Stalingrad as its objective so as to put all German forces farther to the east at risk and compel our forces in Stalingrad to withdraw, which will thereby reopen the river Volga as a waterway.

That the railroad from Morozovsk to Stalingrad was the objective of the attack had been confirmed by a captured Russian officer. I added that it remained to be seen whether we should also expect a major Russian offensive across the Don against the Italian Eighth and the Hungarian Second Armies (possibly with Rostov as its goal) at intervals after the impending attack on the Rumanian Third Army, or whether the Russians would launch simultaneous, but somewhat more limited, operations against the Italians and Hungarians. While the Russian troops confronting the Rumanian Third Army continued to take up their assault positions (according to a deserter, three new tank brigades were being brought into the line opposite the Rumanian Sixth Army Corps), I reported on the 18th that a simultaneous Russian attack from Beketovka south of Stalingrad on the sector held by this corps could not be excluded.

At 5 the next morning, 19 November 1942, the Soviet offensive began, precisely where we had predicted: from the bridgeheads of Kletskaya and Serafimovich, under the over-all command of the Russian 'South-Western Front'. On the following morning a second offensive began from Beketovka, just south of Stalingrad. I reported that day:

> While it is so far not possible to investigate the tactical situation in detail, it appears probable that a major crisis is now upon us, particularly in consequence of the breach effected in the Rumanian 5th infantry division. We must expect these attacks to be pressed southwards, using for this purpose the forces held in reserve in the rear.

On the 22nd, the two arms of the Soviet pincer movement met at Kalach, encircling our Sixth Army in Stalingrad and a number of lesser formations – a quarter of a million of our finest troops, with a 100 tanks, 1,800 guns and over 10,000 motorised vehicles. The rest of the tragedy belongs to history.

I was understandably bitter about the outcome. A few days after the last shots were fired in Stalingrad, and the starving remnants of Paulus's gallant army had gone into captivity, I wrote a summary of the causes of and the lessons to be learned from the defeat:

> Any retrospective look at the events since mid-November must be overshadowed by the fact that all of them – with the exception of the first moves in the offensive against the Rumanian Third Army – have resulted from a sequence of basic command errors on our own side, as to whose extent and effect the *military* authorities were perfectly aware from the moment they were committed . . .
>
> Leaving aside the failure of our allies, the Russians can credit their great victories to the fact that they have applied standard German command principles: Zhukov as military commander enjoys complete freedom within the framework of the task assigned to him. In the meantime, we have borrowed from the Russians their earlier system of rigidly

laying down the law on virtually everything. German military leaders who can think and act independently are discouraged – indeed, both such qualities can lead to court-martial. Thus we have forfeited one of the fundamental requirements of a successful and versatile military command. We have become benumbed, and are incapable of strategic action; we have forgotten that warfare is an art, which calls not only for a real man and a man of character at that, but for brains and training – for training and still more training – in other words, for an expert General Staff embodying all the best qualities of the active officer in its individual members.

This introduction was clearly recognisable as criticism of Adolf Hitler's leadership; I continued by reviewing the military trends we had witnessed since November and emphasising that we had always correctly identified the enemy's intentions well in advance. Summarising the mid-November offensive on the Rumanian Third Army and our own Sixth Army, I continued:

After General Halder had repeatedly warned of the possibility that the enemy would launch an offensive across the Don between the River Khoper and the great bend, at the end of October and early in November we identified the first indications of the impending offensive. . . . On 21 November we underlined the enemy's intention of isolating the Sixth Army, and three days later the Sixth Army was indeed encircled.

For the sake of history it must be recorded here that from this time on . . . the General Staff was adamant that only the immediate withdrawal of the Sixth Army could save it from annihilation. It was as early as this that – at least in our Intelligence digest – we pointed out that only the virtually immediate withdrawal of Army Group A behind the Don (a bold decision, but one characteristic of German staff training) while retaining a bridgehead east of the Taman peninsula would leave us with any chance of using these forces to crush the Russian offensive across the middle reaches of the Don, and to retain the initiative for a fresh offensive to the south. At the time it was objected that ground conditions in winter would prohibit any such operations; but subsequent developments have scotched that objection with a vengeance. Ludendorff also managed to 'operate' in winter, in Poland.

The story had been the same with the Soviet offensives against the Italian Eighth Army on 16 December, which had finally sealed General Paulus's fate in Stalingrad and ensured the failure of the assault on the Hungarian Second Army four weeks later. Again we had given adequate warning. My February 1943 survey continued:

In our Intelligence digest of 9 December we pointed out that after the Russian offensive in the centre had come to a halt, they were transferring their main effort to the southern wing. The attack on the Italian Eighth Army followed on 16 December, followed by one on the Hungarian Second Army on 12 January 1943. On each occasion we witnessed the complete collapse of our allies soon after the Soviet attack began, despite the presence of a number of German units. By the time of the Italian collapse in mid-December at the latest it should have been clear that only a major decision would enable us to stabilise the front and regain the initiative, and that meant withdrawing the German and allied line where necessary; but the orders for the withdrawal of Army Group A were not issued until the end of December. We can still see the effect of this delay in the plight of Army Group Don, which could not withdraw until the sections of Army Group A diverted towards Rostov in the north had arrived. On 11 January, we warned of the new threat to the Hungarian Second Army, and on the 15th, three days after that offensive began, we warned of its implications on the situation of Army Groups A, Don and B. Despite the increasingly acute situation on the right wing of the Second Army, the proposed withdrawal was postponed, with the result that when the Russians began their attempt to destroy the right wing of the

Second Army on 24 January, it proved successful. The danger to the southern flank of Army Group Centre and thereby to the whole eastern front was clearly visible from our digest of 29 January.

Finally, I looked at the remaining events as far as they affected Army Groups Don and B up to 10 February 1943:

From 26 January onwards we warned of the increasing danger to Army Group Don from enemy forces approaching its long flank, heading through Star'obel'sk to Slavyansk. Again there was a delay in issuing the unquestionably necessary order for the withdrawal of Army Group Don – a move which could have begun any time after 31 January when the last sections of Army Group A withdrawing northwards reached Rostov. In fact the withdrawal did not begin until 9 February. The ten lost days will *possibly* have an effect on the maintenance of Army Group Don's fighting strength; and *definitely* will have an effect on the whole situation insofar as we will now not have enough strength assembled in time to stop the enemy.

Even if the Russian forces currently facing Army Group Centre should be transferred to the southern wing, there will still remain sufficient strength in the centre to develop local offensives there. We must therefore expect the Russians to transfer the main focus of their operations to an attack on the Second Army. Their aim will be to bring about the collapse of the front held by Army Group Centre, starting from the right wing, in conjunction with the present frontal attacks. If the enemy continues to conduct his operations with his present initiative, he will always be ahead of any counter-measures we may take.

With the Russians, as I was always at some pains to stress, we were dealing with strategic and political brains of high calibre and cunning. For example, early in February 1943 we learned that the Soviet agents we captured were under strict orders to play down Russian military capabilities when we interrogated them. And again, their military objectives were well calculated, as we learned from an *Abwehr* report we received from a recently dispatched agent who had established contact with a western Allied military mission in Moscow. From time to time, as I shall mention again, the Allies considered it in their own interests to pass on to us some of the information the Russians were giving them. In this case, the Soviet authorities had handed to the mission a statement of their military objectives, in reply to a *Wehrmacht* communiqué which had stressed that Moscow had attained none of the strategic objectives it had set for its offensives of the winter of 1942/1943. The Russian statement read,

The principal Russian strategic objective is not one of regaining lost territory or pushing the enemy back to the west; rather, the Russian war leadership intends to crush the German army's striking power. This aim can be realised only if Germany's war-making potential – and that means her military equipment – is destroyed. This is the objective of every Russian operation; for this reason it is of no consequence whatever to the Russian command how many 'hedgehog' defence-positions the Germans establish in the Soviet rear, or how many of her soldiers Germany sends to their doom.

While the deep Russian strikes may seem to be ambitious or fool-hardy operations, or may even seem to have been launched solely with the aim of cleaning up the war maps where possible, in reality the aim of these operations has always been to seize the main German supply dumps and destroy them. Conditions on the eastern front call for a completely different kind of warfare from that in the rest of Europe. While on the western front the German Army command can place its munitions dumps and other depots hundreds of miles behind the front and still keep its combat units rapidly supplied in an emergency by means of motor transport – thanks to the excellent and extensive highway networks – on the eastern front the supply dumps must be kept comparatively close to the fighting front. The frequent and sudden weather changes, with dense snowfalls or sudden thaw, could otherwise result in a unit being cut off from its supplies at a crucial moment when the enemy has launched a surprise attack on it.

This is why the Russian High Command has concentrated on the German Army's supply bases in the Caucasus, at Stalingrad and in the Don bend. The collapse of the German front on the Don, at Stalingrad and in the Caucasus is mainly a consequence of the successful thrust of the Russian spearheads into the heart of the German Army, which then suddenly found itself deprived of sufficient supplies for relatively long sectors of its front. The enormous quantities of German war equipment which have already been captured or destroyed by the Soviet forces are therefore the 'Russian strategic objective'. For the Russians, a small village in which a large munitions dump has been located is more important than any city, however magnificent the winter quarters it might seem to offer the German troops.

In countless publications Germany has repeatedly stressed that this war is primarily an industrial war. In logical progression from this, the Russians are fighting their war against German war industry on the eastern front. In the summer of 1943, we shall see that the Soviet military command has achieved a crucial victory by eliminating a significant part of the enemy's heavy and light arms and equipment.

It was no easy task to see through the increasingly sophisticated Russian tactics of deception. At first it was relatively easy to detect the truth; for instance by sending out reconnaissance aircraft to photograph the areas concerned. Soon, however, the enemy became more devious. They began faking dummy tank-tracks across muddy fields using rollers or other vehicles. They had learned a lot from their defeats of 1941. We discovered from

a captured Russian general that Stalin had established a committee under General Shaposhnikov, his former army chief of
staff, to investigate the causes of the Soviet military un-
preparedness. We, on the other hand, learned nothing from our
errors: rival decoding organisations were, for example, maintained by Göring's Luftwaffe, by the OKW, by the Foreign
Ministry and by the navy (a chaotic situation which I was able
to prevent in post-war Germany until my retirement).

Such decoded material as Foreign Armies East did receive
during the war was of great value, particularly for assessing the
true conditions behind the enemy lines: for example, the OKW
forwarded to me in 1942 a lengthy cable from the Yugoslav
ambassador in Kuibyshev (to which city the diplomatic corps
had been evacuated from Moscow) to his exiled Foreign Ministry
in London, reporting at length on the plight of Soviet agriculture. At about the same time we were reading the cables of
the American ambassador to the State Department in Washington, reporting on Soviet labour problems and arms production;
from decoded Turkish Intelligence cables we were extracting
information on Russian armoured brigades. (On other occasions
the Turkish Foreign Minister supplied us with information of
interest about Russia). The army's own radio monitoring units
would also pick up tactical signals from which we could identify
the movements of units behind the enemy lines, their supplies
of tanks and assault weapons, whether particular units were
preparing to attack or digging into well-prepared defensive
positions.

Another most important source of Intelligence was captured
prisoners and documents of the Soviet Army. I might mention
that even Soviet newspapers (and those of her western allies)
and the Soviet radio yielded worthwhile information from time
to time despite every effort at censorship. Even the letters the
Soviet soldiers received were rewarding reading; by a stroke of
luck Army Group South captured no fewer than eight thousand
sacks of Soviet forces' mail in the middle of June, and I ordered

a small army of interpreters to screen every single letter, paying particular attention to Soviet morale, region by region. On 7 July 1943 the first detailed analysis was shown to Zeitzler, and he showed it to Hitler. The letters showed that a food crisis was about to grip the Soviet population, that black-market trading was flourishing, and that the civilian population was suffering appalling hardships. The report cited some examples of the human tragedies reflected in the captured letters, and commented pointedly: 'The people who wrote these letters were no sub-humans!'

Accurate though our strategic predictions had been proved, I was still dissatisfied with our tactical Intelligence system. In December 1942, I called a conference of the Army Group and Army G-2 officers together with my own Group I, and outlined to them methods by which I proposed to speed up the inflow of Intelligence reports from the front, and its dissemination by my branch. At that time, the system of forwarding aerial reconnaissance reports was a constant source of worry, as they usually reached my branch undated, so late as to permit at best only a retrospective survey of events. The daily reconnaissance reports forwarded by the Army Group G-2's were of great importance, but did not always arrive in time for us to digest them before the Führer's conference, as Göring would not accept them as being 'official'. To speed up the system I introduced the practice of telephoning reports through, so that the verbal reports from the reconnaissance units reached the air Intelligence officers at army headquarters by 7 p.m. each day, and the night's report reached the War Department by 7 a.m. I insisted that these verbal reports be made regularly and on time, whether or not all the facts were known; an incomplete report was better than none. I insisted on the same procedure with the reports on the enemy's artillery strength, since when these reached the General Staff on time they provided a valuable parameter for assessing the enemy's strength, particularly by indications whether he was regrouping or creating new units. I also introduced a system of ten-day reports on the enemy's artillery situation, which were initially greeted with some scepticism, but were later widely accepted.

The Soviet winter offensive ended late in March 1943, with our victorious battle for Kharkov. Hitler now needed a major victory to turn the tide on the eastern front, and he picked the tempting Russian salient at Kursk, where he could both capture large quantities of Russian equipment and troops and shorten his own front by some 150 miles. On 15 April he issued his orders for the offensive, which was code-named 'Citadel': it was intended to place the initiative for the coming spring and summer campaigns firmly in German hands again. 'The victory at Kursk must act as a beacon to the world.' Hitler proposed to launch the attack late in May, as soon as his panzer divisions were refreshed. Over the weeks that followed, his armoured divisions gathered in the Orel bend, waiting for the attack to begin, but now Hitler repeatedly postponed the date, first for one reason, then another, while the Russians, who were fully aware of our intentions, took the appropriate dispositions and prepared a daunting system of defences extending some 150 miles back from the front line. With each week that passed, our prospects of success lessened; whereas initially the War Department and my own branch had been confident of victory at Kursk, by late June we were certain of defeat.

My own branch reported in compelling detail on the Soviet defensive preparations. From a reliable agent we received on 17 April the information that Stalin was summoning his sector and army commanders to Moscow six days later to discuss the 'indications of a German offensive'; another reliable agent reported on the 27th that an incomplete rifle division, a tank brigade, two tank battalions and two field-artillery regiments had arrived at Valuyki from Saratow (Valuyki was opposite the starting point for the southern pincer arm of 'Citadel') and that every day tanks, engines and tank guns were leaving the factories at Kazan and Gorki, bound for the sector of the front between Kupyansk, Kursk and Orel (i.e. the 'Citadel' area). On 28 April an untried agent reported that the Russians expected their enemy would soon mount a major offensive in the area between Kharkov and Kursk. From these and similar *Abwehr* reports there was no doubt that the Soviet high command had learned of our intentions and were taking the necessary counter-measures.

By the time 'Citadel' was finally launched on 5 July, it was clear that we had lost the advantages of both strategic and tactical surprise. I had taken every opportunity, as the files of Foreign Armies East show, to warn the German command against this major offensive. Since Hitler refused to be dissuaded, on 3 July I wrote an emphatic warning of the likely outcome, under the title 'Appreciation of the Enemy's Moves if Operation "Citadel" is Carried Out'.

Once Operation 'Citadel' begins the enemy can either restrict his counter-measures to the Citadel operational area, so as to block our attack – if necessary by bringing up reserves from neighbouring areas – remaining generally on the defensive apart from minor counter-attacks; or he will launch the offensives he has already prepared against Army Group South and Army Group Centre. . . . In view of their own degree of readiness to attack, and with regard to the situation in the Mediterranean[1] the latter course appears the more probable. We therefore have to expect that, probably soon after our offensive begins, the Russians will mount strong diversionary counter-attacks. . . .

This suggests that the German offensive will bring about the following probable development in the enemy situation, which broadly conforms to our appreciation of the Russian intentions so far:

[1] Where the Allied invasion was expected any day, and eventually occurred on 10 July, five days after Citadel.

a] *In the area of the German offensive:*

The powerful enemy forces assembling at Kursk, Valuyki, Voronezh and Yelets will probably be split up by the German offensive so that the bulk of them end up east of our attacking spearheads, and the rest, west of Kursk. Our attacking forces will therefore probably be exposed to particularly strong flank attacks from the east – from north-east of Bolgrad and west of Livny.

b] *In the area of Army Group South:*

We must expect the Russians to launch the offensives they have prepared against the southern wing and centre of this Army Group's front, soon after the German offensive begins. We expect both an encirclement action against the Sixth Army and the First Panzer Army, in the direction of the Donets basin, and a thrust by strong enemy forces from Kupyansk towards Kharkov, striking at the deep flank of the German attacking armies.

c] *In the area of Army Group Centre:*

The enemy will probably seek to relieve the pressure on his own forces, by attacking our Second Panzer Army with strategic reserves believed to be held in the region bounded by Tula, Kaluga, Sukhinichi and Plavsk. We must be prepared for early and powerful attacks on the eastern and north-eastern front of the Second Panzer Army, heading for Orel with the object of breaking through in the rear of the German attacking armies.

I added that if, unexpectedly, the Russians should concentrate their counter-measures on the 'Citadel' area and the front line in the immediate vicinity, we would have to expect them to move considerable reinforcements to Kursk from other areas; but this we considered most improbable, for we were certain that the Russians would try to thwart us by promptly launching spoiling attacks elsewhere.

On 4 July, the very eve of 'Citadel', I repeated my opposition in even more emphatic terms:

From the point of view of the general war situation, there is not one ground that could justify launching Operation 'Citadel' at the present juncture. The prerequisites for victory in the offensive were twofold – numerical superiority and the advantage of surprise. At the time originally planned for the launching of the offensive, both conditions were met. But now, from what we see of the enemy situation, neither is met. For weeks the Russians have been waiting for our attack, in the very sector that we have picked for the offensive, and with their customary energy they have done everything in their power to halt our offensive as soon as it begins. Thus there is little likelihood that the German offensive will achieve a strategic breakthrough.

Taking into account the total reserves available to the Russians, we are not even entitled to assume that 'Citadel' will cost them so dear that they will later be incapable of carrying out their general plan at the time they choose. On the German side, the reserves which will become so desperately necessary as the war situation develops (particularly in the Mediterranean!) will be tied down and thrown away uselessly. I consider the operation that has been planned a particularly grave error, for which we shall suffer later on.

The German offensive began next morning, with about two thousand tanks and eighteen hundred aircraft starting the pincer movement towards Kursk; the going was heavy, the rate of advance was slow and the Russians doggedly defended every inch of the ground. We later captured an enemy document listing correctly all but one of the divisions we had marshalled for the offensive. On 10 July, the British and American forces invaded Sicily, and on the 12th the move Foreign Armies East had anticipated occurred: the Russians launched a counter-offensive towards Orel, with a simultaneous counter-attack by strong forces at the southern end of the Kursk salient. On the following day, with some 17,000 Soviet troops killed and 3,300 of our own, Hitler ordered 'Citadel' to be stopped. That day I

congratulated my staff on the bitter fulfilment of our prophecies:
The Head,
Foreign Armies East   *Headquarters, 13 July 1943*

The course of the fighting on the eastern front these last few days has once again confirmed precisely every detail of the enemy-Intelligence picture we produced. . . . The chief of staff expressed particular commendation for this a few days ago.

I know this excellent result is the result of the hard work and magnificent co-operation of all this branch's staff and experts and of the support it enjoyed from the other agencies like Air Intelligence, the controller of signals reconnaissance, and Walli I.

I wish to express my thanks to all the staff and my hope that they will continue to do their utmost for the job assigned to us with the same effort and enthusiasm.

GEHLEN

Operation 'Citadel' was the last German attempt at a strategic offensive in the Russian campaign. With its failure the tide of the war in Russia finally turned against us. The German Army was forced on to the defensive and never regained the initiative. Foreign Armies East continued to do its duty, to reconnoitre the enemy's positions and strength and to obtain the necessary facts for the command decisions; we produced Intelligence digests, and showed which enemy moves we considered most probable. But the more our predictions were confirmed by subsequent events, the less Hitler as Supreme Commander was inclined to heed our reports.

By this time I had come to the conclusion that the Russians had an excellently informed source working for them in the German supreme command. Canaris and I repeatedly observed quite independently of one another that the enemy was receiving rapid and detailed information on incidents and top-level decision-making on the German side. Admiral Canaris came to my headquarters at Anderburg one day and told me in the course of a lengthy conversation whom he suspected to be the traitor, though I believe that he knew more than he was prepared to tell me. It was a personality about whom I had had my own doubts for some time. The secret was carefully preserved by the Russians, both then and afterwards, and I fully believed it only years after the war myself, when I came into possession of certain information as head of the Gehlen Organisation in West Germany.

What Canaris told me concerned the fateful role in which Hitler's closest confidant Martin Bormann was cast in the final years of the war and in the post-war epoch too. Bormann, who had been Hitler's personal secretary since early 1943 and chief of the Nazi party organisation ever since Rudolf Hess's flight to Scotland in May 1941, was working for the enemy as Moscow's most prominent informant and adviser from the very moment the campaign against Russia started. There is no foundation whatever for the allegations which have been made from time to time to the effect that Bormann is alive and well, living in the impenetrable jungle between Paraguay and Argentina, surrounded by heavily armed bodyguards. He crossed to the Russians in May 1945 and was taken back to the Soviet Union.

At the time, I believe, Canaris lacked proof. Our suspicions were largely confirmed when we found out that Bormann and his group were operating an unsupervised wireless transmitter network, and using it to send coded messages to Moscow. When the OKW monitors reported this, Canaris demanded an investigation, but word came back that Hitler himself had emphatically forbidden any intervention: he had been informed in advance by Bormann of these *Funkspiele*, or fake wireless messages, he said, and he had approved them. This was the sum total of our knowledge at the time the war ended. Canaris and I both realised it was out of the question to put watchdogs on Bormann, next to Hitler the most powerful man in the Nazi hierarchy, and neither of us was in any position to denounce the

Reichsleiter with any prospect of success. The disdain Hitler had shown for my own Intelligence summaries however right they had later proven, was one deterrent, and the increasingly exposed position of Canaris and the *Abwehr* was another. The smallest slip would have put an end to our investigations and probably to us as well. Canaris described to me his grounds for suspecting Bormann, and told me what he assumed to be the reasons for his treachery; he would not exclude the possibility that Bormann was being blackmailed, but he was inclined to see the real motive in the *Reichsleiter*'s immense and insatiable ambition. Bormann was driven by the ambition to succeed Hitler when the day came. We now know of course how cunningly he succeeded in bringing first Göring and then Goebbels into discredit with Hitler, for they were his great rivals.

It was not until after 1946, when I headed my own Intelligence organisation, that I had an opportunity of looking into Bormann's mysterious escape from Hitler's Berlin bunker and his subsequent disappearance. Some time later I received conclusive proof of Bormann's post-war movements. During the 1950s I was passed two separate reports from behind the Iron Curtain to the effect that Bormann had been a Soviet agent and had lived after the war in the Soviet Union under perfect cover as an adviser to the Moscow government. He has died in the meantime. The nature of these sources enjoins me from going into further detail.

3. Wooing the Russians

I still believe that we could have achieved our 1941 campaign objectives had it not been for the pernicious interventions of Adolf Hitler. The consequences of military victory would have been a matter for conjecture, since Hitler's ambition was the acquiring of *Lebensraum*, and this implied the total destruction of the Russian state, while we in the General Staff had come round to envisaging a more moderate and realistic political solution, in which a Russia would continue to exist. We had realised that this vast country, rich in manpower and raw-material resources, could in the final analysis only be conquered with the help of the Russian peoples themselves. This is how, even after the setbacks of the winter campaign of 1941/1942, we could still have succeeded had the war been intelligently directed. We could have won the Russians round, through their instinct for national self-preservation – quite apart from their pent-up hatred of communism in general and of the Stalinist system in particular. But Hitler refused to believe this whenever the possibility was put to him.

It is in Hitler's failure to exploit the psychological potential of the Russian peoples, most of whom had shown the greatest warmth of feeling towards us in the opening phases of the campaign, that we can see the very real mistake he made. We can see it again in the brutal way he imposed as satraps Koch, Sauckel and Kube on the conquered Russian provinces and converted their frustrated ambitions into blind hatred of the Germans. These mistakes counted more heavily against us than many a strategic blunder, because Hitler had stirred up moral feelings – feelings whose potency Karl von Clausewitz himself had recognised in his study of the French revolutionary wars.

Unlike the wars of earlier times, modern wars are basically wars between peoples. The wars of the eighteenth century were fought between the armed forces of each country; modern wars are fought by the people as such, who must bear the necessary sacrifice and devote themselves, body and soul, to that cause. Hitler and Stalin always emphasised the ideological aspect, and even Eisenhower titled his memoirs '*Crusade in Europe*', in deference to the convictions of many British and Americans. I do not believe the near future will see any change in the roles of war and ideology, nor do I believe politics (and hence wars) can ever be divested of their ideological character; however ugly the prospect may be, there always will be wars in the years to come. The teachings of Mao, of Ché Guevara and of Giap tell us so, as does a study of the work on '*Military Strategy*' by Marshal of the Soviet Union, Sokolovski, which reflects the official attitude of the Soviet Union towards war and politics.

It is this very extension of war to every facet of human activity that obliges us to see its essentially political character. It is the political goal that shapes war from one moment to the next; on the other hand it is the soldier's duty to ensure that he will not be presented with insoluble tasks by his political leaders (as happened in Russia in June 1941). The political leaders, on the contrary, should do what they can to ease the soldier's task by bringing both political and psychological weapons into play. This was the victory that we, the General Staff, aspired to with the help of Russian officers and men recruited from amongst the prisoners in our hands; and this was what we were denied by our political leaders. In retrospect we can only agree that it is a matter for regret that Hitler did not follow Clausewitz's teachings more closely and act accordingly.

Clausewitz stated that war is only a continuation of State policy by other means: 'War . . . is an act of violence intended to compel our opponent to fulfil our will.' 'The War of a Community,' he concludes, 'always starts from a political condition and is called forth by a political motive. It is therefore a political act.'[1] Since war has its root in a political object, then naturally this must remain the first and highest consideration in its conduct. But the political object must still 'accommodate itself to the nature of the means'. Policy, therefore, is 'interwoven with the whole action of War, and must exercise a continuous influence upon it'.

If we take this argument farther, we can see that in the summer of 1941 the destruction of the Soviet forces was the objective whose attainment would have created the necessary conditions for the realisation of Hitler's political end. Without question, this objective had not been attained; on the contrary, severe crises had been mastered only with the greatest difficulty and with the loss of virtually irreplaceable manpower and equipment. Hitler wanted to regain the initiative at all costs in 1942, but he chose his military objectives – Leningrad and the Caucasus – on a basis of economic rather than political necessity. This could still have been justified in Clausewitzian terms had the offensives permanently been able to weaken the enemy or had the capture of these focal points been able to create an improved climate for a negotiated peace. But that was far from Hitler's mind.

As early as the spring of 1938, General Ludwig Beck, Halder's predecessor as chief of staff, had pointed out in a study for Hitler that his policies must inevitably lead to world war involving the USA and that equally inevitably Germany was bound to emerge as the loser in the conflict. During the planning of the Russian campaign the Commander-in-Chief of the Army, Field-Marshal von Brauchitsch, and his chief of staff also expressed to Hitler their concern about launching a campaign with limitless objectives deep into Russia, because of the sheer logistical problems such an operation would pose. Hitler,

[1] General Karl von Clausewitz, *On War*, vol. I, Book I, para. 2. (Translated by Colonel J. J. Graham, London, 1956.)

however, was apparently convinced he could smash all Russian resistance within a few weeks, and certainly before winter set in. He refused to involve himself in any discussion of the detailed objections raised by his advisers. Even the impossibility of replacing personnel except at a rate which would at most have sufficed to make up the losses in a blitzkrieg type of war, seemed unimportant in Hitler's view. General Halder's criticisms, which were shared by the commanders of the three Army Groups, were confirmed only too rapidly by the events in Russia. Despite colossal initial victories, the German Wehrmacht was unable to inflict a decisive defeat on the Red Army during the first one or two months, and the enemy was able to continue his resistance, hurling more and more fresh divisions into the fight. After Moscow recognised that the Japanese were not going to attack Russia in the Far East, a number of Siberian divisions also appeared at key positions along the eastern front.

The General Staff had planned to direct its main effort against Moscow, as the centre of Russian communications and political life; but as a result of Hitler's whims the campaign was diverted in support of Army Groups North and South, and while this intervention, which deflected southwards sections of the main spearheads attacking Moscow, admittedly led to the great encirclement action at Kiev which yielded some more than a million Russian prisoners, it contributed little to the main objective of the Russian campaign. Our spearheads managed to reach the outskirts of Moscow, but lacked the strategic and tactical reserves to carry the operation through to final victory.

Hitler left nobody in doubt as to the political target he had set himself. He wanted once and for all to liquidate the Bolshevik menace and – as he had already indicated in *Mein Kampf* – to win in the east *Lebensraum* he needed for his people. Obviously, in his public proclamations he laid greater emphasis on the former argument, and with equal fervour German propaganda proclaimed the liberation of Russia from communism as the purpose of the war.

As I wrote earlier, the military command were from the outset sceptical about the prospects of totally smashing the Soviet *state* with the limited military means at our disposal, even if we were convinced of the superiority of our own soldier material and leadership. The inadequacy of the means was all too obvious to us. On the other hand, Hitler's pre-war policies had always proved right, and the General Staff's military doubts, based on a cautious appraisal of the situation, had always proved wrong: whether over the occupation of the Rhineland, the annexation of Austria, the incorporation of the Sudeten territories, Munich, the invasion of the rest of Czechoslovakia or the passive reaction of the Western Powers during the Polish campaign. He therefore prohibited the generals – sometimes in very offensive language – from voicing political objections. Never had the primacy of politics (and wrong politics, at that) been demonstrated more forcefully than during the Third Reich. The military leaders had to bow to Hitler's edicts in 1941; now, at last, events had proved us right.

The political objectives of the campaign, indistinctly formulated as they were, became less and less credible once the achievement of the military objective, the complete subjugation of the Soviet forces, had failed. First the autumn rains and then the winter laid their unimaginable burdens on our troops, already exhausted by four months of fighting. The casualties among officers and men and the losses of equipment had long passed a level at which they could be sustained.

It was therefore natural that, initially independently of one another and without co-ordination, the various branches and sections of the General Staff should have begun to cast about for ways of continuing the Soviet campaign with any prospects of success, and, even more, for a way to end it. All the discussions came to the same conclusion: a political line must be adopted which would awaken positive expectations for the future amongst the Russian peoples and enable us to recruit them in the fight against Stalin and his system. Soldiers have always been accused in the past of regarding war too much as a purely military affair, an affair of guns and bullets, but here quite the reverse was true. In 1938 Hitler complained: 'Instead of having to put brakes on my generals, I find I am having to whip them to go to war!' By early 1942, it was clear that the soldiers were increasingly in favour of depriving the war of its exclusively brute-force character and giving the political element full rein by formulating appropriate war aims. As time passed Reichsminister Alfred Rosenberg, who headed the Ministry for Occupied Eastern Territories, showed that he shared our views. But Hitler showed no inclination to contemplate any political solution: incapable of weighing the available means against the end *he* had set and the military objectives this implied, he opted exclusively for force and, in so doing, led the German people to their ruin. It was at this time that the propaganda slogan 'Führer command – suffer us to obey' was modified by public rumour to a bitter parody, 'Führer command – if we obey we suffer.'

That there was a possibility of gaining the collaboration of the Russians was clear to our troops because the Russian people had suffered grievously under the terrors of Stalinism before 1939. I need only recall the purge of the kulaks, the economic chaos, the purges in the Red Army, the decimation of the Party's cadre and the repression of the national minorities. The persecution of the Russian Christians had also left behind permanent and bitter scars on the deeply religious Russian peoples, as we discovered again and again. When Strik-Strikfeldt interrogated the recently captured son of Stalin, the prisoner told him: 'The one thing my father dreads is the emergence of a nationalist régime opposed to him. But that is a step you will never take." The interrogator asked why, and Stalin's son replied, 'Because we know you have not set out to liberate our country, but to conquer it.'

Our troops were welcomed by the Russians everywhere they

arrived, whether in the northern or central regions of Russia, in the Ukraine, in Bessarabia or elsewhere; they were greeted as liberators and garlanded with flowers. Entire Red Army formations of up to regimental and even divisional strength laid down their arms; the numbers of deserters in the first months, quite apart from the millions of prisoners of war, exceeded our wildest expectations. Colonel Herre used to recount how as acting chief of staff of a mountain corps he had watched the reactions of the Ukrainian townsfolk to the Germans as 'liberators' from Soviet oppression. Herre on one occasion had sent for the senior town citizen, and asked if he could supply a score of able-bodied Russians for guard duties in the motor pool. Within an hour over fifty Russians had mustered in the school which was his headquarters. As Herre's corps had advanced it had adopted this method in every town.

In the three Baltic republics of Lithuania, Latvia and Estonia – which had only been occupied by the Russians in 1940 – memories of their own national independence were still fresh. Lithuanians, Latvians and Estonians had therefore immediately offered help to the German liberating armies in the hope of thereby restoring their countries' independence. Ukrainians, Caucasians and Turkish minorities believed that, in addition to being liberated from Stalin's yoke, they would see their own nationalist aspirations fulfilled – even if these did not always go so far as many of their former leaders, now living in exile, would have liked. The re-establishment of elementary and basic human rights like the dignity of man, liberty, justice and sanctity of property, after twenty years of arbitrary injustice and terror united every inhabitant of the Soviet empire (insofar as he was not directly working for the Moscow system) in a common readiness to support the Germans. What could be more natural then for us to exploit this readiness?

By extending an honest offer to the Russian peoples and following it up in the appropriate way it would have been possible to unleash a War of Liberation which would almost certainly have ended in a rapid and satisfactory conclusion of the Russian campaign. Our military commanders in the field had already made a start in this direction, more from a healthy instinct of self-preservation than from any political motives. As we could not replace all our losses rapidly and increasing demands were being made on our manpower, our commanders recruited Russians, Ukrainians and other nationalities, as auxiliaries for various types of duty: voluntarily they acted as drivers, ammunition carriers, cooks, interpreters and the like. The number of such auxiliaries could never be exactly determined, since the individual commanders would frequently avoid reporting precisely how many they had; by mid-1943 there were about 320,000, of which a large number were actually fighting alongside our troops; the Eighteenth Army alone had 47,000 volunteers.

In addition to these somewhat makeshift measures, there were other signs of a Russian initiative which we could put to useful political effect. For example, in the German-occupied city of Smolensk, about half-way to Moscow, a committee of Russians had come together and offered to take steps to set up a Russian nationalist government and to recruit a Russian army of liberation about a million strong to fight against Stalin. Recognising that the enemy situation called for a clear over-all political line, Field-Marshal von Bock and other commanders gave initial support to the Smolensk Committee's proposals; but they were turned down by Hitler, as were the similar suggestions put forward by the Lithuanians, Latvians and Estonians. Army Group Centre also argued in favour of replacing its personnel deficiencies by recruiting 200,000 Russian auxiliaries over the following few months; von Brauchitsch described this proposal as being one of decisive importance, but it was never put into effect as both he and von Bock were relieved of their commands for other reasons in December 1941.

I recall having a number of discussions with Halder and other leading General Staff officers in the winter of 1941/1942 out

Gehlen (with cap) talking with
Klaus von Stauffenberg (right) who
was executed after the plot to kill
Hitler on 20 July 1944 had failed
(see p. 112)

Gehlen in the summer of 1943
standing near a Junker 52

General Vlasov reviewing Russian troops in German uniform at Munsingen

Martin Bormann

of which emerged a definite request for an urgent decision on the formulation of clear *political* war aims coupled with a radical alteration in our occupation policies. Those of us directly involved in these discussions anticipated that the worsening military situation must force Hitler to modify his views and that in consequence there would be a change in the current occupation policies. With Halder's approval therefore we took every step necessary to speed up such a decision. Those of us who were most concerned in this controversy were the heads of the operations branch (Heusinger), of Foreign Armies East (myself), the Quartermaster-General (Wagnes) and several others.

This group's first action was to regularise the position of all the auxiliary and volunteer units and to regulate their victualling, pay and position vis-à-vis the German troops. An order was drafted permitting our divisions on the eastern front to recruit and feed about three thousand to four thousand native auxiliaries each. We soon established that, while our German personnel losses could never be made good entirely in quantity or quality, the fighting fitness of the divisions in the front line would remain sufficient to continue the battle, assuming there were a number of changes in our political and military strategy. By the beginning of 1942, however, Hitler had still not agreed to modify his political objectives along the lines I have described. Far from it, for by the spring he had decided on his vast offensive towards the Volga and the oilfields of the Caucasus. If this campaign were to continue, our long supply lines to the front – which had been under constant threat since the winter from partisan warfare – would have inevitably to be extended almost ad infinitum. If the Russians were to make a stand and hold us, we should lose even more men and material; but if the enemy were to withdraw, taking all his forces and equipment with him, we should have to pacify and secure enormous areas. Yet since the existing Russian population in the areas we occupied continued to outnumber us, this task could be performed only if we could gain their friendship and recruit from amongst them.

In the early summer of 1942 the Russian Lieutenant-General Andrei Andreyevich Vlasov had fallen into our hands on the eastern front near Volkhov. Vlasov was one of the Soviet army commanders who had successfully defended Moscow against the German onslaught, commanding the Twentieth Army under Zhukov's over-all leadership. Soviet propaganda had made his name and face famous throughout the Red Army, which made what was to follow all the more painful for the leaders in Moscow.

We soon learned that it was Vlasov's dream to lead a Russian National Army of Liberation into the Soviet Union. While still a prisoner-of-war, he put his name to a proclamation released as a leaflet over the Russian lines, appealing to the officers and men of the Red Army. Tens of thousands of them answered the call and surrendered to German units within a few days. All this confirmed what the Soviet experts of Foreign Armies East had reported and suggested to the chief of staff. The success of the Vlasov proclamation was not without its impact on other senior officers who had at first been somewhat reserved about this line of approach. Thus the conviction grew that General Vlasov, who certainly never went out of his way to flatter the Germans and never left any doubt that he was collaborating with us only for the sake of Russian national independence might be the very man to fight for and build a new and different Russia with German aid. I later met him myself: he gave the impression of being forthright and reliable, his voice was firm and clear, and his language betrayed a fine intellect. Above all his military ability was testified to by his experience in the battles for Kiev and Moscow.

Hitler, however, lacked all sense of reality. He was neither able nor willing to deviate from his political and military intentions for the future conduct of the Russian campaign. Neither

Halder nor Zeitzler was able to change his views. Hitler saw Vlasov at most as a useful propaganda tool to weaken the Soviet armed forces; promises might be given to him and to deserters who came over to join him, but on no account should these promises be kept.

The German officers who negotiated with Vlasov faithfully reported Hitler's attitude to him, but persisted in their invitation to him to make common cause in fighting both Stalin and the ignorance of the Nazi leaders, as the quickest route to peace and the ultimate liberation of the Russian peoples. After much hesitation, and despite overwhelming doubts, Vlasov agreed; from this alliance between German and Russian officers there emerged the phenomenon of what was to become known as the 'Vlasov Movement'. In a sense, the movement was only one tragic stone in the mosaic of the war: it is a matter for conjecture whether, if it had flourished, it could have saved Germany from ultimate total defeat, once the United States was ready to intervene in strength. Its history serves to illustrate the difficulties confronting us at every level of the military machine, when we tried to accomplish something vital to our cause in the face of an arbitrary dictator immune even to the most powerful argument. The history of the Vlasov Movement also shows that even under a dictatorship there is no guarantee that all the arms of government will work in harmony: they usurp each other's functions in a manner which is at least tolerated, and probably even encouraged by the dictator. In such a case all efforts are made in vain.

Vlasov had been transferred to the High Command (OKW) in Berlin in October 1942 and shortly thereafter released from prisoner-of-war camp. He had been given the opportunity of collecting a staff of fellow workers. Hitler had placed no restrictions on this OKW propaganda effort, since one of the slogans under which the Russian campaign had been launched was 'the liberation of the Russian peoples'. The German field commands and the Russians themselves had at first believed in this slogan until, early in 1943, they found out how wide was the gulf between propaganda and reality. For the time being Vlasov and his staff were able to appeal to the Russian population on both sides of the front line. We received the clearest indications that even the Soviet Marshal, Konstantin Rokossovsky, was only awaiting the right moment to come out openly against the Stalin régime. It looked like a tremendous step in the right direction.

When we approached the Foreign Ministry with our view that the war could be won only if the Russian people actively threw in their lot with us, our former ambassador in Moscow, Count von der Schulenburg, and his Counsellor Gustav Hilger took up the cause and championed our proposals. They encountered either complete lack of sympathy or a paralytic terror of undertaking anything without the permission of, let alone diametrically opposed to the orders of, Ribbentrop and Hitler. Parallel to this, both Colonel von Altenstadt (of the Quartermaster-General's branch) and I drew up studies urging the necessity of psychological and political warfare in the east. We called for new methods of dealing with the partisan plague. The studies were highly praised, widely discussed and entirely without effect: on the contrary, Hitler personally issued orders for the ruthless liquidation of all partisans, regardless of whether they were willing to surrender or desert to us or not, and these orders resulted in a further escalation of the partisan conflict, and a renewed embitterment of the population towards everything that was German. Strik-Strikfeldt delivered a lecture on 'The Russian Character': in the light of Hitler's views it must have appeared almost revolutionary, but I had it duplicated and distributed to every division on the eastern front and to the prison camps as well. The document called for an understanding of the Russian mentality, and its general tenor was that the Russian must be won over for our cause; if we could not win him, we should have to rule by brute force. If we were to win him, we must set an example in word and deed. This was of course all aimed primarily at the eyes and ears of our German troops.

In the autumn of 1942 Colonel Stieff and Major Count von Stauffenberg of our Organisation Branch approved the organisation of a 'Russian Propaganda Section'. Thus there was officially born the 'Russian Leadership Centre' at Dabendorf, a prison camp south of Berlin. This was ostensibly still a purely propaganda exercise. Here Russian officers and propaganda workers were trained, a skeleton officer corps was established and Russian newspapers were printed. Here, in conjunction with the OKW's military propaganda unit and Foreign Armies East, the political and military objectives for a Russian liberation movement were worked out. At the suggestion of the head of the Operations Branch, a suggestion absolutely in line with my own ideas, an official post of 'General in Command of Volunteer Units' was created. The first incumbent was General Heinz Hellmich, who had been in Russian captivity during the First World War.

As a result of the work of these various officers, of Vlasov's own work and of the initiative of our front-line commanders in the east, by early 1943 we had between 130,000 and 150,000 'eastern troops', organised into 176 battalions and 38 independent companies. At that time, as a result of a policy decision higher up, there was no amalgamation of these into larger formations.

As early as August 1942 von Roenne and Colonel von Tresckow (chief of staff of Army Group Centre) had decided to resuscitate the Smolensk Committee. But when Hitler heard of it he forbade the plan, and the committee was permitted to exist as a fictional body only. Vlasov's staff and the OKW's military propaganda section drew up a proclamation for the Smolensk Committee, and this was signed by Vlasov and General Vasily Malyshkin at the end of October 1942, ready to be broadcast in millions of leaflets both sides of the Russian lines as the Stalingrad battle approached its terrible climax. The proclamation mouldered for many months in a drawer in Rosenberg's ministry, and does not appear to have been brought to Rosenberg's attention until the disaster of Stalingrad was over. Not until 12 February 1943 did he authorise its distribution, and that same evening Captain von Grote put the printing of the millions of leaflets in hand. This lack of action wrecked the General Staff's plan to test the effect of coupling military and political initiatives in the Caucasus campaign.

Under the pressure of military events we did finally succeed in forcing a conference at Rosenberg's ministry in December 1942 to discuss the whole problem. The Wehrmacht was represented in strength at the conference, and spoke out in unmistakable terms for completely new political objectives in Russia. Most of their representatives seemed to believe that Rosenberg, a Baltic German, was himself the father of Hitler's Russian policies. Rosenberg was clearly impressed by what he heard at the conference and promised to support these proposals with Hitler, although he was still unwilling to abandon his own ideas for splitting up the Soviet Union into separate national entities like the Ukraine. Rosenberg's subsequent discussion with Hitler was a complete failure, as Hitler brushed aside all his reasoning and arguments with a few conclusive words.

In the end Colonel Martin, head of the OKW military propaganda section, persuaded Goebbels to give General Vlasov a hearing so as to discuss with him a new manifesto composed for the Russian peoples. Goebbels had already recognised that the menacing trend in the war demanded nothing short of a volte-face in the Third Reich's previous attitude towards Russia. It was characteristic of the petty jealousies prevalent at the top that Rosenberg now flatly forbade Goebbels to interfere in his affairs; and by the time Vlasov finally saw Goebbels it was already 1945, and much too late.

In the spring of 1943, General Vlasov visited the eastern front, at the suggestion of Foreign Armies East. At the end of February he paid a two-week visit to units of Army Group Centre, and in April he spent some days with Army Group North. He made speeches to the Russian battalions and to the local Russian population, and was received everywhere with open arms. After many grim experiences the Russians now saw in him the only token of a future freedom, the guarantee of a better future. They no longer had the trust in the Germans that they had showed a year before. Keitel however found Vlasov's 'brazen' conduct in delivering speeches outlining Russian nationalistic policies quite intolerable: on 18 April he ordered Vlasov's return to prison camp and threatened that, if he repeated his conduct, he would be turned over to the Gestapo. We managed to save Vlasov from this fate but it was all we could do to salvage the beginnings we had made with our 'Russian Liberation Movement'.

We had managed to convince General Zeitzler that our ideas were right and he approved a major propaganda operation designed to step up the Russian desertion rate at the same time as we launched our next big offensive, 'Citadel'. We code-named the operation 'Silver Lining', and trained fifteen hundred officers and propaganda workers specially for it at the Daben-dorf training camp. A key element of the operation was that the deserters had to be 'welcomed' where possible by Russian reception teams. A special leaflet was designed with a facsimile of my signature instructing all our troops to treat deserters particularly well and find out if they wished to join the 'Russian Liberation Army'. 'Citadel' was planned to commence at dawn on 6 May, so on the evening of 3 May we issued the code word 'Silver Lining': the eighteen million leaflets were to be released over Russian lines as the offensive began. There was a last moment panic when we learned that 'Silver Lining' was a long existing Luftwaffe code word for commencing poison gas war-fare, but this caused no real problems. In the event 'Citadel' was postponed for two months, and our 'Silver Lining' opera-tion, which began without the accompanying military offensive on the night of 6 May, went off at half cock. It resulted in hundreds of deserters, but not the many thousands we had confidently expected.

When Hitler learned that the Russian nationalist policies propagated by Vlasov were threatening to get a firm foothold amongst the Russian auxiliaries aiding the German cause, he called a conference with Keitel and Zeitzler on 8 June 1943 at the Berghof in Berchtesgaden and destroyed all our hopes: 'One thing has to be prevented', said Hitler. 'Nobody on our side must get any wrong ideas. We have to draw a clear distinction between the propaganda we broadcast to the other side, and what we really propose to do.'

Hitler persisted in his stubborn opposition to the plan for a real army of Russian troops under Vlasov's command, and he categorically prohibited any firm promises being made to them about the future of Russia after the German victory he even now expected. He permitted the phantom propaganda army, using Vlasov's name, to march on for propaganda reasons, and we could tell how much anxiety this caused Moscow, for we rounded up many Soviet agents parachuted behind our lines with explicit orders to infiltrate that army at all costs and to bring Vlasov dead or alive back into communist hands. Moscow produced several anti-Vlasov leaflets, but faced with the impossibility of releasing them in their millions from the air without giving Vlasov still wider publicity in the Soviet forces, they chose instead to distribute them by hand through squads of agents in key areas.

In the end success was denied to Vlasov. We had sensed from the autumn of 1943 onwards that the Russian liberation movement was at an end. Hitler decided to disarm all the foreign units and turn them over to the labour service, alleging that the desertion rate was too high. Colonel Herre, who had been appointed chief of staff to the General of Volunteer Units countered this order by proving within a very few days that the accusations levelled at his volunteers were untrue. The desertion rate was in no way greater than in any German unit, he pointed out, and he stated that there was nothing giving cause for alarm that could have justified Hitler's order. Any dissolution of the foreign units would be bound to have catastrophic consequences for the German eastern front in view of the military and logistics problems. Even Keitel showed he had doubts in this respect. In mid-October the decision was modified so that the foreign units were instead transferred to the western front, and Hitler waived the order that they were to be disarmed by force.

This affair proved once again Hitler's inability to understand warfare as Clausewitz did. Through this order, the General Staff lost its sole means of introducing psychological warfare into the conflict on the eastern front. The transfer of the foreign units to the western front from the end of 1943 onwards was further proof of the hollowness of Hitler's Ostpolitik. In any case, since he had not managed to persuade our Allies – the Italians, Rumanians and Hungarians – to defend their fatherland on the Don and the Volga, how could he expect the Caucasians to fight any better if they were assigned to the Atlantic Wall! They rightly interpreted this as a lack of confidence in their reliability and as proof that the Germans lacked the will to co-operate with them.

From early 1944 onwards we had other worries on our minds. Himmler and his SD began to take an interest in the Vlasov Movement: he sensed in these units a rival to the non-German divisions of the Waffen SS, the so-called volunteer divisions; above all, he saw them as an obstacle to his plans to settle and administer a Slav colonial empire in the future. All this meant that Foreign Armies East, the OKW's military propaganda section and finally the *Abwehr* were increasingly forced to intervene to prevent the SS from interfering. A veritable 'war' broke out on several fronts, all of it ultimately at the expense of our effort in the east.

Himmler's attitude unexpectedly changed in August 1944.

Unabashed by the fact that he was the brain behind the 'sub-human' theories of the Third Reich, and that the year before he had referred to General Vlasov as 'a traitor' and 'a Russian swine', the rapidly deteriorating war situation now forced Himmler to adopt the very line that I and my staff had long been preaching, and against which the SD had fought tooth and nail. Despite all Rosenberg's protests Himmler sanctioned the creation of a 'Committee for the Liberation of the Russian Peoples' with General Vlasov at its head. He promised the general ten divisions at first, under his direct command; the figure was later reduced to three. Himmler also undertook to raise the status of Russian prisoners and the eastern workers within the Reich to the same level as those of other nationalities.

But this was all happening far too late. Born of opportunism and despair, the Vlasov army was doomed to failure from the start. On 10 February 1945, the first and only two Russian infantry divisions, numbers 600 and 650, were formally handed over to Lieutenant-General Vlasov by General Köstring, who had succeeded Hellmich as General of the Volunteer Units, at a ceremony attended by SS officials and Party representatives, and by Colonel Herre on my behalf. The Russian flag was hoisted next to our own, and these divisions' arduous path into their fatherland began. Vlasov's attempts to salvage them from the ruins of the Reich and to transfer them to the western Allies were thwarted by the Allies themselves, since the Yalta agreement bound all belligerents to surrender Allied prisoners to their countries of origin. Thus he and his followers found themselves treading the bitter road into imprisonment and eventually on to the gallows of their own country.

When I survey the tragedy of the Vlasov Movement now, after an interval of twenty-five years or more, I am bound to admit that given Hitler's manic ideas the movement was doomed to failure from the start. All the effort Germans and Russians alike had invested in the movement had been in vain; for countless Russians and their friends it meant being branded as 'traitors'. The lesson I learned was that the psycho-political element cannot be suppressed in modern warfare. If it is not taken into account, or if the nature of modern war is misunderstood, then however great the means that are provided by a country for its armed forces, they will be wasted, and all sacrifice will be in vain. While Clausewitz could write of war as 'a continuation of politics by other means', Lenin followed this dictum with a rider of his own: 'Peace is only a continuation of war by other means.'

Politicians are not the only ones whom this concerns, but officers as well. They should not take an interest in political implications only when armed conflict has actually broken out, but during the years of peace that precede the conflict.

4. Defeat and surrender

Hitler had always declined to bother himself seriously with unpleasant facts and figures, and this tendency increased after the unsuccessful attempt on his life in 1944. Any kind of contradiction threw him completely off balance and he refused to tolerate it from the more humble ranks, among which I – even as the brigadier-general I became in December 1944 – was included. Even officers of a naturally contentious disposition like Halder and Guderian found it difficult to put controversial opinions to him without being instantly interrupted. Hitler was interested only in hearing what fitted in with his own train of thought. If I had regularly accompanied the chief of staff and head of the operations branch into Hitler's war conferences, my dismissal would probably have taken place much earlier than it did.

As it was, Zeitzler or Heusinger took my Intelligence digests with them into the conference room and incorporated my findings into their own remarks, except for those few occasions when Hitler ordered my attendance in person. On these occasions I always stated my opinions forthrightly and unambiguously, while at the same time trying to speak in a language that Hitler's peculiar mind would understand. On the first two occasions Hitler had listened with interest. But the more the war situation turned sour on him, the less he was inclined to heed the sober facts and judgments of his Intelligence service. In military and strategic affairs he lacked the necessary sharp eye to perceive how far his ambitions were realistic. He was incapable of assessing the dimensions of major operations in time and space, and weighing them against the means at his disposal.

The wartime Chief of the Imperial General Staff, Lord Alanbrooke, refers frequently in his diaries to comparable arguments he had with Winston Churchill – but with an important difference: whereas Churchill was another enthusiastic amateur strategist, and extremely stubborn in arguing his ideas, unlike Hitler, he was ultimately open to persuasion; and he rewarded his colleagues for their persistence with his friendship and enduring loyalty. When someone argued consistently with Hitler that his plans were wrong – and when, worse still, he was proved right by events – Hitler soon found ways of getting rid of him. Admiral Canaris was a case in point. When an *Abwehr* agent defected to the British from Turkey early in 1944, thereby compromising 'Cicero', one of the *Abwehr's* most famous agents in Ankara, Walter Schellenberg cleverly fed the details to Hitler by using Himmler's liaison officer at the Führer's headquarters. Hitler seized this as a pretext to strip the despised admiral of his espionage organisation (he had had Canaris under suspicion for some time). On 12 February 1944 he ordered:

1] A uniform German Intelligence service is to be set up;

2] I put the Reichsführer SS [Himmler] in charge of this German Intelligence service; and

3] Insofar as this affects the military Intelligence and counter-espionage service, the Reichsführer SS and the chief of the OKW are to take the necessary steps after due consultation.

For the time being Colonel Georg Hansen was assigned to head the *Abwehr's* Intelligence arm, and from 1 June all *Abwehr* functions were transferred to the RSHA under Himmler and Schellenberg. Fortunately, thanks to Keitel's intervention as chief of the OKW, we were able to retain all front-line Intelligence work on the eastern front within the purely military aegis – in other words it remained in my control. We appointed Colonel

Buntrock, head of our front-line Intelligence section, to liaise with the RSHA. He was an expert on military Intelligence and I had complete faith in him. In his new capacity, Buntrock was directly subordinated to Keitel. Schellenberg, however, was dissatisfied with our success in retaining these units and tried very hard to get complete control of all G-2 work and of our front-line Intelligence organisation controlled by Major Baun. The senselessness of such an attempt – which was overtaken by the end of hostilities – should have been obvious to him. The G-2 officers and the reconnaissance units reporting to them were part of the military command structure. Had the Schellenberg proposals been put into effect they would have spelt the end of any kind of organised military command, as they would have destroyed one of the essential elements for the making of command decisions – the rapid, immediate and conscientious provision of Intelligence on the enemy. I have always maintained that the active Intelligence-procuring agencies need a firm guiding hand, while, conversely, the correct assessment of the military situation can only be based on a steady flow of Intelligence. In other words, it is often necessary for Intelligence procurement to be directed to particular assignments; and it is equally necessary to avoid jumping to conclusions supported by inadequate Intelligence. At the time, I could hardly have suspected that this mutual interplay of the procurement and analysis of Intelligence would decide the pattern of Germany's Intelligence service after her defeat.

By the spring of 1944 the military situation on the eastern front was so gloomy that I felt it safe to supply our long-term Intelligence digests only in sealed envelopes to other leading members of the General Staff and to Major Baun. I had to ask them not to show the reports to anybody else and to return the documents to me, 'in view of the way the enemy position is viewed therein'.

By 28 March we had assembled enough *Abwehr* material to report that the Soviet offensive would be conducted without respite on every sector of the eastern front, and that the Russian command had been given the following objectives: they were to occupy Estonia, Latvia and Lithuania; they were to advance through Rumania to Hungary, Bulgaria and Yugoslavia, and they were to occupy what had once been Poland. We knew all the details of Marshal Zhukov's military plans, and of his anxiety lest the Germans launch a counter-offensive from Galicia; and we knew in detail of the orders issued to Marshal Koniev and General Malinovski. In my summary issued two days later, on 30 March 1944, I opened with the words:

The present situation on the eastern front is overshadowed by the anticipated general enemy offensive against our Army Groups A and South. As it proceeds, a more menacing situation than ever before emerges on the eastern front, and in the not too distant future this may result in far-reaching political, military and economic repercussions on the rest of the war in Europe.

I recommended that the only prospect of regaining the initiative lay in bold command decisions taken without regard to the loss of ground they might involve. I predicted that the Russians would try, by occupying the Balkan countries, Poland and the Baltic states, to place themselves by the end of 1944 on the very frontiers of the Reich.

Hitler refused to sanction the necessary strategic withdrawals. He hung on to the Crimea until early May, when he was forced to order his troops to abandon their positions. By early June the Soviet armies had advanced to the frontiers of Poland and all the indications were that they planned a major offensive against Army Group Centre, commanded by Field-Marshal Busch, defending Poland and East Prussia. On 13 June I warned that the enemy had started building up their strength in the areas facing the Army Group. 'Particular attention should be paid to the areas south-east and east of Bobruysk, on both sides of Chausy, along the highway north-east of Orsha and on both sides of Vitebsk.' These were the precise sectors of the front that were to be breached a few days later; the only information we could not ascertain with certainty was the date. I suggested, 'According to various items of information at present there are increasing indications that the offensive will begin between 15 and 20 June.' But I added that Russian security was so good that we had never yet managed to predict the actual date and hour of an attack beforehand.

The Soviet offensive began early on 22 June, supported by four thousand aircraft. Within a few days the German front line had caved in and within a month the Soviet armies were on the very frontiers of East Prussia. As I had also predicted on 13 June, a second phase of the Soviet offensive began a few days after the first, with a general attack on Lemberg.

A few days after the Soviet offensive began, on 1 July 1944, I was stricken by severe blood poisoning and hospitalised at the field-hospital at Angerburg. After a short sojourn there, I was transferred to hospital in Breslau. It was this that probably resulted in my being 'overlooked' by the Gestapo when their witch hunt after the unsuccessful Bomb Plot against Hitler began. I played no active part in the conspiracy, but it would be false to deny that I knew one was afoot. Some months before my colleague General Heusinger had hinted to me about the elements of the conspiracy, in enough detail for me to gather what he was talking about. I regarded my own small task as being to ensure that the G-2 organisation was staffed only with officers upon whom we could count in such an emergency, and I asked Colonel Kleikamp of the personnel branch to make sure that I alone decided who was appointed to G-2 posts in the near future.

I was also aware of the opposition within the army to Hitler. In the winter of 1941/1942 I had a visit from von Tresckow (later General) who was at the time operations officer of Army Group Centre and whom I knew well from staff college. Comparing notes on the military situation we had both reached the conclusion that the campaign (and that meant the war as well) was bound to end in defeat, not because it could not be militarily or politically won, but because of continued interference by Hitler. Considering how this seemingly inevitable trend could be checked, we saw only one solution: Hitler would have to go. At the time we had broken off this dangerous line of discussion, somewhat dismayed at our own presumption: we had after all sworn oaths of allegiance to Hitler, and we had grown up in the old Prussian officers' tradition. After Heusinger hinted to me that wheels were now moving, I discussed the actual tactics with my old regimental comrade General Hellmuth Stieff, who was by now head of the General Staff's organisation branch: I tried to warn him of the importance of keeping the circle of accomplices as small as possible, and of the need to prepare the *coup d'état* with extreme care if it was to succeed. Another of the conspirators, Colonel von Freytag-Loringhoven, called on me at the hospital at Angerburg about three days before 20 July, to warn me that the plot was now under way.

As events later showed, the Germans – and here one is probably entitled to generalise – do not make the best plotters. I believe it was Lenin, sitting in his sealed railway truck in which the Germans transported him from Swiss exile back to Russia in 1917, who fumed: 'If the Germans want to start a revolution, they buy a platform ticket first!' My friends paid for the failure of the conspiracy with their lives: Freytag-Loringhoven committed suicide; Stauffenberg was shot and Stieff was hanged. Colonel von Roenne, who had transferred from my branch to take command of Foreign Armies West, was hanged in October for the part he had played. Fortunately Colonel Wessel, my chief assistant, smashed open my filing cabinet at Angerburg and destroyed all the incriminating documents he found in them, particularly my correspondence with General Halder (who like Heusinger was incarcerated for many months in a concentration camp after the failure of the plot).

The ethics of the plot have subsequently exercised many

minds and resulted in much moralising by both the participants and the bystanders. My own view is clear, I have always adhered to the principle that in a regular democratic country such as West Germany became, treason will always be treason. It can be morally justified only by some particular national emergency, the only circumstance imaginable to me. Together with those of my friends who took the ultimate risk, I would accept that Hitler's pernicious leadership provided such an emergency. Given the rigidness of the Allied demand for unconditional surrender, it is difficult to see how the *putsch* could have succeeded in absolute terms. The plotters were certainly aware of this: a few weeks earlier, Colonel Hansen – who had originally headed the South-East section of Foreign Armies East for the first few months of my office, and trusted me implicitly – had come to see me at our headquarters in Angerburg about a very delicate affair. He confided to me that he (as Piekenbrock's successor in charge of *Abwehr* espionage) had arranged to meet an 'emissary of Churchill' on a lonely road somewhere in southern France, and was going to put to him the all-important question of whether the British government would be prepared to negotiate an armistice with a new German government if Hitler were overthrown. Hansen returned some days later, having met the emissary as planned; I had never seen him looking so dejected in his life. The emissary had stated that the British position was that there could be no exception to the doctrine of unconditional surrender, and he was not empowered to talk about anything else. Hansen was executed with the rest of the plotters.

For many years I and my colleagues had trained ourselves to see things through the enemy's eyes – to think as he would think, and calculate his intentions. Right from the start we had sensed the growing Russian confidence in final victory, and now we could only agree that this confidence was justified. Early in October 1944 I told my more intimate colleagues that I considered the war lost and that we must begin thinking of the future: we had to plan for the approaching catastrophe and turn minds to the question of what must be done when the final collapse became imminent. These thoughts and discussions occupied us for many months, during which the burden of everyday work still had to be done. I was aided to an increasing extent by my deputy and successor (both in April 1945 and in May 1968) Lieutenant-Colonel Gerhard Wessel.

These dangerous internal conferences were made possible by the solidarity of my staff, which had withstood many a crisis before, and we were screened from hostile and curious fellow-officers by the fact that we could rely on each other entirely. While the older General Staff officers were generally hostile towards the régime and its ideology, this was not the case with the rising generation of officers, and particularly with the recently appointed 'National Socialist Leadership Officer' – Hitler's emulation of the Soviet commissar principle – which each unit and section now had to have. I had selected Major von Kalkreuth to act as our 'commissar', and when he protested to me that he could not reconcile this with his Christian ethics, I replied that that was precisely why I had chosen him. It had not escaped my attention that the war was taking its toll of many young officers' personal sets of values, and that the political indoctrination was resulting in either boundless national socialism or an equally unbridled fatalism. I recall that one of our female staff was a particularly fervent Nazi, until we gave her official clearance to listen to and monitor the British radio broadcasts; by the end of 1944 she had lost all her enthusiasm for Hitler.

Guderian had done what he could to build up our military strength on the eastern front but in the late summer of 1944, Hitler announced to his senior advisers his plans for a major offensive in the Ardennes, and large segments of Guderian's carefully built-up defences were dismantled to provide the forces Hitler needed in the west. The Ardennes offensive began on

16 December, while the Russians patiently waited for the start of their own onslaught. Guderian and I could see it coming, and, using our well-tried Intelligence methods, we knew exactly where and in what strength the Russian blow would fall. Particularly valuable were the maps my branch prepared, showing the lines of communication between the Soviet agents on our side of the front line and their controllers in Russian territory.[1] Guderian took these reports to Hitler's western headquarters, 'Eagle's Nest', at Ziegenberg on 24 December; but Hitler not only rejected his demand for massive reinforcement of the eastern front at the expense of this futile offensive in the west, but even dismissed our Intelligence picture of the Soviet build-up as 'pure bluff'. On the 31st Guderian again warned Hitler in person that the eastern front was in danger of collapsing like a house of cards; Hitler indicated that he felt the eastern front was strong enough to cope with any Russian offensive. On 8 January 1945, I handed General Guderian a further appreciation of the situation drawn up by my branch: I recommended that we should evacuate East Prussia, if the rest of the eastern front – and that meant Berlin – was to be held: 'The loss of East Prussia will hurt less than total defeat.' I believed that the Soviet offensive would commence on about 12 January.

On 12 January 1945 the Soviet invasion began with an offensive by Marshal Koniev's First Ukrainian Front, followed by the Third White Russian Front on the 13th and the First and Second White Russian Front under Marshal Zhukov and Marshal Rokossovsky respectively the next day. Within a few days the whole eastern front from the upper Vistula to East Prussia was in flames. The most horrifying reports of Russian atrocities began to reach us. Early in December a Ukrainian deserter had reported to one of my front-line units that in a Red Army briefing session at Warsaw he and his comrades had been told: 'On Stalin's orders robbing and looting is strictly

---

[1] Contrary to the version given in other accounts, I did not accompany Guderian to Ziegenberg on any occasion.

forbidden in the occupied Polish territory, and you are to adopt a friendly attitude towards the Polish population; but Soviet troops are permitted to do what they want on German soil.' My own family, and the families of many of my colleagues, were now in the path of this cruel Russian colossus.

Hitler had strictly forbidden any officers to evacuate their families to the west, but I could not stand by and leave mine to their fate. Besides, it was vital for my future mission to know that they were safe in the west. It was a simple matter for an Intelligence organisation to forge the necessary movement papers, with the faked signature of the gauleiter of Silesia. General Vlasov's troops helped them to load what they could on to some lorries, and on 21 January my wife left Liegnitz in Silesia in a motor car driven by Major Baun, with our four children – the youngest under three – packed in the back; a small lorry followed with their servant and some cases (which were later robbed at Oberstdorf). They drove to Reichenbach in Silesia, where the Vlasov units were billeted on an estate, and then continued on the following day westwards to Dresden where Baun's wife ran a small hotel. The city was already filling with refugees, so they left again for Turingia where I had some relatives living at Rossbach, near Naumburg; it was fortunate that they did not stay in Dresden, for a few nights later the city was devastated by an Allied saturation raid in which over a hundred thousand civilians died, including the luckless wife of Major Baun. Baun himself had collected the files and archives of Foreign Armies East and drove several lorry-loads of them to Naumburg, where they were stacked in the empty wine cellars of the vineyards. There I thought that both my family and the files would be safe from Russian hands.

Apart from these natural worries about our families, we were unconcerned about what fate held in store for us. This was hardly surprising, for we had managed by good Intelligence work to obtain shortly after the Teheran and Yalta conferences full details of the Allied plans for destroying and partitioning

Germany. We did not cherish much hope that the enemy coalition would fall asunder immediately after the war (as was widely believed in the front line); but equally we could not accept that this was the end for Germany. It was this stoicism that enabled me to apply my mind to the problems of the post-war period and to what my duty to Germany then should be. Obviously, once our Intelligence network had been broken up it would be difficult, if not impossible, to reconstruct an efficient secret service for many years; moreover, the longer the reconstruction took, the easier it would be for a communist enemy to penetrate the new service. It might have seemed a pointless and illogical exercise to many in early 1945, but to me it was clear that if a new German Intelligence service was going to emerge after the war, there had to be as little interruption as possible. It was obvious to me that the future German government would need such a service. It would be possible provided only that we could resume our work immediately the war ended, using my existing Intelligence staff and my leading colleagues as a nucleus.

Considerations of foreign policy also argued in favour of salvaging our Intelligence organisation as far as possible: for though the face of communism had changed in outward appearance, its aims remained the same. Stalin had mobilised the energy of the Russian people by appealing to their patriotic instincts and by encouraging an imitation Soviet nationalism. Hitler's senseless Ostpolitik and his attitude towards the Russians had been grist to the Soviet dictator's mill; all our experience taught us that Stalin was not going to abandon his aims now but would pursue his expansionist plans still farther. His goal would continue to be the world revolution that was going to 'bring the blessings of Socialism to all Mankind'. I and my staff anticipated that the need to defend the west would sooner or later force the west to make common cause with us against communism. Just when that would be, of course, we had no idea. We could not even hazard a guess.

We were strengthened in this conviction by a political appreciation drafted by Churchill, which reached us by devious means in February 1945. Perhaps I should indicate here that it is the duty of every sophisticated Intelligence service to keep open a channel of communication with the enemy's Intelligence service; perhaps it may sound strange that while I felt able to keep such channels active during the Third Reich – although it might have cost me my neck – I was unable to do so during the latter years of my work in the Federal Intelligence Service. Such contacts can often be of great advantage. It was through such a channel that the British M.I.6 supplied us with a copy of Churchill's political Intelligence appreciation of February 1945. When it landed on my desk at Zossen I saw that Churchill's analysis viewed our position in the east far too favourably but that it was entirely accurate in its picture of Soviet potential and intentions. The document indicated that the British did not share the optimism of their American allies on 'Uncle Joe's' democratic qualities; and it revealed that they had few illusions about the future development of Poland and the Balkan countries (including Hungary) into Soviet satellites. I now believe that the purpose of M.I.6 in supplying this document to us was that we might enable them to warn the British Cabinet how exaggerated was the British estimate of our ability to withstand the Russian onslaught in the east. I informed General Guderian of the existence of this explosive document, and with his approval filed it with no further action. It was destroyed at the end of the war.

On 15 February the first sections of my branch, Foreign Armies East, transferred by railroad from Zossen to Reichenhall in Bavaria. Ten days later I signed a further long-term summary of the enemy's intentions, in which I examined the probable main directions of the coming Soviet offensives and the implication to be drawn from Marshal Zhukov's appointment to the supreme command of the forces operating against us. 'While hitherto the Soviet strategic command has been guided almost exclusively by military considerations,' I pointed out, 'it is now coming increasingly under the influence of political considerations. In this connection we can clearly discern their endeavour to seize positions of strength regardless of any agreements reached at the Teheran or Yalta conferences, so as to confront their allies with a *fait accompli* as far as possible.' I considered the object of the coming Soviet operations to be the destruction of our armies in the east and the rapid occupation of the industrial area around Leipzig and Halle. All the Intelligence we received indicated that the main thrust was to be expected from the sector between Görlitz and Schwedt, although there was still no indication as to when the Russians would resume their westwards drive. While we were awaiting that moment, I turned over in my mind the various ways in which the Russians could be checked, and one unorthodox idea occurred to me: on 3 March 1945 I sent to Guderian a note on the possibility of using huge forest fires as a weapon of war.

Between 1866 and 1939 there had been a number of forest fires in that area – our files contained all the information I needed. My proposal was to find ways and means of setting fire to the 400 miles of forest front, particularly in the area between Görlitz and Guben. Pine forests were ideal, especially after a long period of drought; this, and a minimum wind force of four, might be expected late in April or in August, while the combination of pine forest and appropriate weather conditions was not likely to be found in southern or northern Germany, and therefore the Russians could not retaliate in kind. I explained that once a major forest fire really got going it was impossible to stop even with enormous fire-fighting effort and proposed, 'To achieve our object of annihilating the enemy's equipment and personnel, the fires must be started in such a way that the enemy has no chance of escape [a ring of fire].' My branch calculated that fires like these could be started with relatively modest means – some 360 sorties by FW.190 fighter-bombers releasing incendiaries along a hundred-mile line. I asked for an order from the Führer to prepare for such an operation, but that was the last I ever heard of it.

Another opportunity to stem the Soviet invasion occurred when we examined air-reconnaissance reports which showed that only four railroad bridges crossing the River Vistula from east to west were still intact. On 24 March I advised Göring's operations staff: 'Luftwaffe attack on Vistula bridges at Cracow, Deblin, Warsaw and Thorn is urgently needed. Enemy supplies for Neisse and Oder fronts dependent on the bridges at Warsaw and Thorn.' On the 26th, General Koller, the Luftwaffe's chief of staff, put this proposal to Hitler, but only reluctantly, for the special aircraft that would be needed had all along been earmarked for a strategic air attack on the entire western Soviet electricity supply. Hitler decided, 'In that case I would prefer to dispense for the time being with the attack on the Vistula bridges, they can be done later.' In desperation I called the attention of the SS, who controlled the sabotage units operating behind Russian lines, to the four bridges. 'Their total or even partial destruction would bring very real relief to our troops,' I cabled them. The reply reached me next day: 'Planning *re* one of the bridges listed is in hand. Execution of operation depends on fuel allocation, aircraft allocation, and various personnel matters.' 'I see,' I wrote on this reply, '*that means we can't expect any action for the next six months!*' The Vistula bridges were still intact when the great final Soviet offensive on Berlin started a few days later.

There could be no doubt as to what faced Germany. From one of our Intelligence units we obtained a report on a leaflet handed to every Red Army soldier and containing Stalin's Order No. 5 instructing that the German people were to be annihilated, all German factories and property were to be destroyed, and the 'German beast stamped out in its kennels'. On the western front, a copy of the Allied plans for post-war Germany, a brown-covered inch-thick folder with the code-name 'Eclipse', fell into our hands: from it we saw to our amazement the partition that was proposed for Germany after the war, with Berlin a Four-Power enclave in the heart of a Russian-controlled zone. Thuringia, where I had believed our precious Foreign Armies East archives were safe from the Russian invasion, was clearly assigned to the Soviet Union.

In what was to prove my final Intelligence digest, early in April, I indicated that the impending loss of Königsberg, capital of East Prussia, would release fresh Russian strength against us, and that the same was true of Vienna. Massive troop reinforcements were pouring into the area between Küstrin and Frankfurt on Oder for the final assault on Berlin. The digest was put before Hitler by Guderian's successor, the Infantry General Krebs. Hitler dismissed it as 'absolutely idiotic' and defeatist, and on 9 April I was relieved of my position as head of Foreign Armies East. Lieutenant-Colonel Wessel became my acting successor.

Meantime, I had ordered my family and the files of Foreign Armies East to be evacuated from Thuringia. They were loaded aboard two lorries, and the documents were brought out of their hiding place in the wine-cellars at Naumburg and loaded up too. Near Leuna the two lorries ran into an air raid, but fortunately they escaped damage; later that night near Hof they were halted by an SS unit and forced into a nearby SS barracks for their load and papers to be examined. Under the circumstances this exposed them all to a danger hardly less acute than the one they had so recently escaped in the air raid on Leuna; but the two skilful drivers – including Lieutenant Baun, the son of our front-line Intelligence section's chief – were on their toes and soon found a second gate unlocked at the rear of the barracks. Through this they drove out the two lorries and all escaped. My family found temporary accommodation in an industrialist's country house at Cham, a provincial capital near the Czech border, in the Bavarian forest. The lorry-loads of secret files and documents continued southwards in safety to

Berchtesgaden and nearby Reichenhall, where part of Foreign Armies East was waiting for them.

It was at this country house, Gutmanning, that my wife and I celebrated her 41st birthday, with a modest party appropriate to the grim circumstances. I invited all my former colleagues, officers and men and a number of the female staff. It was at about this time, in the first few days of April, that I went with Wessel to pay a private visit on Lieutenant-Colonel Baun, controller of the Walli I organisation at Bad Elster, some sixty miles north of Cham. In the Kurthotel there, I briefed Baun on my plans for the future. My view was that there would be a place for Germany in a Europe rearmed for defence against communism. Therefore we must set our sights on the western powers, and give ourselves two objectives: to help defend the west against communist expansion, and to recover and reunify Germany's lost territories. (The latter of the two objectives would, of course, find little acclaim from the victorious nations.) I felt that the interest of the western world in its own defence must inevitably lead its leaders to recognise that without Germany all Europe would be lost. This was why we could realistically expect all the western powers to show an interest in exploiting our Intelligence service for espionage work in the east. Given the total defeat that was now approaching, it was probably Utopian to entertain any notion of rebuilding the service immediately after the war ended, as the Allies would destroy every organisation sponsored by the Third Reich. But the attempt was still worth while, so that some day a future German government could take the organisation over, using our present staff as the expert nucleus.

Of course, many questions arose. We could not know when a post-war German government would be set up. It was doubtful in April 1945 whether we could succeed in establishing a working relationship with one of the three western powers that would prove acceptable to a later German government. We could not work purely as mercenaries for a former enemy, if we were not to burden the future Intelligence service with the psychological stigma of having been a Quisling organisation. I therefore tried to establish a degree of formal legality for our plans. In the last weeks of the war I outlined the plans to General August Winter,[1] deputy chief of the OKW's operations staff, and secured his blessing for them (since he was the only OKW authority I was able to reach). After the war I chanced to meet Grand-Admiral Dönitz in prison camp at Wiesbaden. Dönitz was formally Hitler's successor as head of state. He also approved my plans.

During the Bad Elster stage in our planning, the question naturally arose which partner would be best for us amongst the three western powers. I discussed it at some length with my principal assistant, Lieutenant-Colonel Wessel. Through Lieutenant-Colonel Baun, using the channel to which I have referred earlier, we made an offer of our future services to the British secret service; Baun received no acknowledgment, but from events in the Bavarian mountains some weeks later we gathered that it had been received by the British. Taking everything into consideration it seemed more expedient to me that we make our approach to the American military forces. I suspected that once the shooting stopped the Americans would probably recover a sense of objectivity towards us more rapidly than their European Allies. Subsequent history confirmed me on this point.

Baun, a first class Intelligence officer who not only knew how to give his contacts worthwhile assignments and proper leadership, but looked after them properly as well, worked mainly with Russian volunteers, and he was able to maintain contacts

---

[1] Winter confirms this in a memorandum in the Gehlen organisation's files dated 18 July 1952. In the conversation of Königsee near Berchtesgaden I told him that one result of Unconditional Surrender would be that our priceless files on the Soviet Union might either fall into Russian hands or be destroyed or vanish into low-level Allied agencies which would not appreciate their value; Winter noted that I proposed withdrawing with these files and my top associates into the mountains until the hue and cry died down, before offering our services to the west, as in this way we would be serving our Fatherland as best we could: 'For my part I wholeheartedly approved of General Gehlen's proposals.'

in the heart of Moscow until the very end. He agreed at once to make the necessary preparations as far as his networks were concerned, and I told him what I wanted. His adjutant took part in these discussions, but we took no one else into our confidence. From early April 1945, his headquarters, Walli *I,* was in the Allgäu – a province which was overrun by the Americans at the end of the month and later occupied by the French. Baun and his staff thereupon moved in plain clothes to a pre-arranged rendezvous, while most of his Intelligence workers went to ground and waited to hear details of their future employment. He secured his files in the same way as we had done with those of Foreign Armies East, putting the most important files on micro-film, and burying or hiding them in various locations.

During the last few weeks of the war events came thick and fast, making our preparations for post-war no easier. On 12 April, my colleagues insisted on holding a small farewell party for me, to mark my departure from Foreign Armies East; three years had passed since I had taken the branch over and started to build it up. It was a gloomy celebration, for nobody knew what now lay ahead. That our prognosis on the coming great conflict between east and west was shared by Moscow was shown by Intelligence reports now reaching us. In mid-April we learned that a group of Soviet agents had been parachuted behind our lines near Berlin on the night of the 7th with instructions to prepare for the entry of Russian troops into Berlin on or about the 20th. They also had the assignment of reconnoitring British and American preparations for attacking the Russians, and they were particularly instructed: if Berlin was captured by the British and Americans, to destroy all their papers and on no account to identify themselves as agents. The implications were obvious, and they spoke even more loudly from the statements of a Russian prisoner captured south-west of Küstrin on the eve of the final onslaught on Berlin by Marshals Koniev and Zhukov on 16 April:

Big offensive will begin on 16 April at latest. Artillery bombardment first, three or four hundred rounds per gun. Attack with one hundred tanks per regiment. Prisoner speaks of new assault tanks with 180-millimetre gun and of new 180-millimetre heavy mortars. Object of the offensive is to beat the Americans to the capture of Berlin. Russian officers anticipate clashes and offensive engagements with Americans; they will have to drench the Americans 'by accident' with an artillery bombardment, so that they get a taste of the Red Army's lash. Troops have been ordered to put their uniforms in order and wash and shave every day, to give a cultivated impression.

It was a depressing situation, but at least my former staff and I were resolved that, whatever fate might hold in store for us, we would try to remain together and work in harmony as we had always done in the past. In mid-April I began my own preparations: I scouted round for suitable hideouts in the Bavarian mountains, and supervised the microfilming and burying of the branch's files. The whole branch reassembled at Reichenhall in full working order with the exception of a small group under Major Scheibe which had been detached to the northern command staff of the OKW in Holstein, near the Danish border.

In view of my dismissal, there was one minor snag to be overcome. I had earlier expressed to the director of army personnel, General Burgdorff, a desire to command a combat division, and he now assumed that that was still my ambition. I asked him to post me instead to the generals' reserve, 'to enable me to train my successor', Colonel Wessel. I also claimed that Heinrich Himmler had a special job for me; since Burgdorff was a pious Nazi, my claim sufficed and he released me to the generals' reserve in the War Department. To give substance to my claim I telephoned Schellenberg and asked him if Himmler would be interested in a detailed study of the rise and fall of the Polish underground resistance, to see if we could learn anything from the Polish experience that might be of use to us in the ordeal we might well be about to face. Schellenberg phoned me back not long afterwards to confirm that this was a subject which would particularly interest Himmler. Over the next eight days I completed a bulky study based on our documents about the Polish resistance. I concluded that there was no point whatever in Germany's adopting similar underground methods if we were defeated or reached an armistice with our enemies. Major Hiemenz agreed to drive to northern Germany with the document to deliver it to Schellenberg; I drove with him as far as Cham, so that I could once more see my wife and children. Then I returned to Reichenhall; in the event, I was not to see my family again until July 1946, and much would have happened before then.

On 28 April 1945 our Odyssey began. We had buried our documents in scattered locations near the Wendelstein mountain in Algäu province, and at Hunsrück. Since we correctly assumed that we could not prevent some of the hiding places from being found, we tried to duplicate the caches as far as possible so that we would have at least one set of everything at our disposal, when we came to set up shop again. We had arranged to split up into three groups, which were to hide in the Alps as long as was necessary for the hue and cry accompanying the end of the war to die down – perhaps three weeks. These groups would then report to the nearest American unit and go into captivity. Since the Americans would probably try to capitalise on our expert Intelligence workers, each group was instructed to refuse any kind of co-operation until they had been shown written orders to that effect signed by me.

I had detailed one of our reserve-officers, Chief Forester Weck, to find and prepare three hideouts in the Alps – mountain huts which would be hard to find but easy to reach with provisions, and well supplied with water. The huts were to be so situated that we would have a good view of all roads of approach but could escape unobserved if danger threatened. Weck did his work well, finding one hut near Fritz-am-Sand, not far from the village of Reit im Winkel on the Austrian border; the second hut was Wild Moss Lodge, on the Wild Kaiser slopes, and the third was Elend[1] Lodge near Lake Spitzing.

I packed my belongings and left for the easternmost of our assembly points, the hut at Fritz-am-Sand, but hardly had I arrived when I learned that Himmler had issued orders for the liquidation of General Heusinger and myself. I decided prudence was the better part of valour, and moved instead to the western-most hideout, the Elend Lodge, as too many people had learned of my intention of going to ground at the other. While I was on my way I picked up a radio message from Baun, who had settled with his Intelligence procurement section in the Algäu. He asked me to rendezvous briefly with him at Hindelang, to give him further instructions. Instead of my usual Horch automobile, I took an elderly DKW. My old staff officer from the Polish campaign, Captain G., accompanied me as we set out for the rendezvous on the other side of the mountains. As we drove up the mountain pass we ran into retreating sections of one of our divisions which had been in combat, heavily out-numbered by American forces as they tried to defend the mountain passes. It was fortunate that I had chosen the smaller car, for, short though this stretch of highway was, it took time and effort to fight our way through the traffic jams. It was dawn before we reached the southern foothills of the mountains, and there our way was barred by the combat troops, who told us that all the mountain highways were blocked, either by fighting or by demolished bridges. So we had to turn back without having managed to establish contact with Baun's group.

It was on the return journey that I asked to be set down somewhere below the Elend Lodge, not far from the so-called Zipfelwirts, an Inn right on the Austrian frontier. I left the road and climbed upwards through a valley to one side. The climb was tougher than I had expected: there was deep snow, and I made heavy going of it. Weck had warned me more than

[1] *Elend* is a corruption of the old-German *Ödland:* 'barren ground'.

once that there were scattered SS units around the Elend Lodge, who had at one stage wanted to take over the hut themselves. That was why I considered it better to use this side valley for my approach. I must admit that had I known at the beginning how arduous it was to climb in snow without path or road, I would not have embarked on it. The climb took me many hours, or so it seemed, and as I climbed my thoughts circled endlessly around the events of the past few weeks, and the uncertainty that lay ahead. My sober and sceptical intellect told me, as I toiled upwards, that our enterprise could hardly be more Utopian; but my resolve remained unshaken by this inward scepticism. I was finally redeemed by the sight of open snow ahead, as the forest came to an end; a gently sloping snowscape unfolded ahead of me, in the middle of which nestled a large, low-roofed wooden hut, with broad eaves, a tall brick chimney and a veranda. This was the Elend Lodge. A wisp of smoke curling up out of the chimney informed me that it was occupied, and as I approached I found my comrades waiting for me – six officers and three of our female assistants.

It was important to our plan that we should not be captured too soon. We had to bear in mind that, despite the Americans' reluctance to climb into the mountains, they might still institute a search for us. On the other hand we did not expect any search during the hours of darkness, so as dawn broke each day one section of our group would climb higher into the mountains, while the three girls and the two younger officers who could not manage the difficult climb because of their injuries stayed below and kept guard on the lodge. We usually climbed to the Auer ridge, and set up camp about a mile south-east of the Red Wall, in a terrain that was partially open and windswept, and partially tree-covered. We passed the days studying the country-side and rejoicing in the first signs of green, shooting up gradually through the snows. Had we not been burdened with uncertainty about the future, had this not been May 1945, this mountain sojourn would have been an idyllic respite. I myself had known this country since 1921, when I had been at infantry school and learned to ski among these slopes.

As dusk fell each evening, we would set off down the mountain slopes again. Before we reached the Elend Lodge we would check to make sure our comrades had hung out a table cloth on the washing-line, as the signal that all was clear. A few days after the capitulation, three civilians appeared at the lodge during our absence, looking for me by name; we suspected that they were German-speaking members of the British secret service, a suspicion that was later confirmed. No doubt this was a result of the signal we had sent to London via Baun some weeks before. Somewhat less peaceful was the visit paid by a small American infantry unit, who carried out a textbook raid on the lodge, raking it with machine-gun fire before storming it and searching it from top to bottom. They subjected the fortunately uninjured occupants to a thorough interrogation, and took the three female staff and the two young officers with them down into the village where they were put through a further grilling. They then asked their captives where they would like to be discharged to, and all asked to be permitted to stay at the Elend Lodge for the time being. When we returned that evening from our mountain encampment we found the table cloth on the line, and our five loyal comrades waiting for us; proudly they showed us their discharge papers from American captivity, bearing the provisional address, Elend Lodge. It was an unexpected stroke of good fortune, for it enabled us to keep at bay other people interested in requisitioning the hut for themselves.

Chief Forester Weck acted as liaison between us and the other groups. He had exchanged his Wehrmacht uniform for that of a forester and was able to move about freely in consequence. Somewhat later in May, with the thawing of the snow and the warmer nights, we had to abandon our practice of leaving the hut each morning and returning in the evening, since the danger of being raided by night was now just as strong as by day. We set up a permanent camp of carefully camouflaged tents in a fir-tree glade south of the Auer ridge, and here we passed another week of fine weather. These days of living in the arms of nature were truly enchanting. We had grown accustomed to the peace, and our ears were attuned to nature's every sound.

Meantime Weck had not been inactive either. From the forestry office he obtained the key to a secluded and almost inaccessible hut near the Maroldschneid ridge (it was so well hidden that despite the clearest directions it took us a long time to find it). The hut was at the crest of a steep rockface, densely surrounded by forest on three sides, but with a magnificent view across the mountains. We enjoyed to the full every minute of these last days of freedom. The chamois which we encountered all about us were a particular delight, and they gradually lost all fear of us.

By now it was the end of the third week in May, and high time for us to put our plan into action, to go down into the valley and report to the nearest American unit. The parents of one of us, Major Schoeller, lived at Fischhausen, on Lake Schliersee. He suggested we spend the Whitsun holiday there, and report next day to the Americans. We decided to make our way down from our hideout along the northern face of the Maroldschneid ridge, cross the Ruchen Heads, the Red Wall, and the Taubenstein slopes to the east of Lake Spitzing, and then follow the highway down to Fischhausen. We would keep off the actual road, walking about half way up the slope west of it, through Neuhaus. It was important to stay as high up the slopes as we could, so as not to fall into the hands of any of the numerous patrols moving about lower down. We were determined not to be taken prisoner: we wanted to surrender on our own initiative to the Americans. It was all part of the plan.

Under other circumstances our mountain trek would have been a wonderful experience, but for us this was still almost war. The evening before we had stripped off our badges of rank and abandoned our red-striped trousers – symbol of the General Staff. Now we were heading like countless other stragglers in a generally westward direction. The view from the Taubenstein mountain, which all five of us – the two injured officers had been left behind – reached together, was superb; then we split up and set off again at ten-minute intervals. Near the Lower Schönfeld Alp there was a French mountain unit; we could see them through our binoculars. We had no choice but to cross this valley if we were not to spend the night on the bare mountain. The French unit was lying there at ease, its mules grazing and the soldiers scattered amongst the dozen or so houses. As I approached the houses, a window opened and a curious French mountain infantryman looked out. I walked steadily on, greeted him with a 'Bonjour, m'sieur!' and went past him; he returned my salutation and closed the window, evidently satisfied.

Soon afterwards we passed the northern end of Lake Spitzing, not far from the mountain railroad station; here too we had to take care, for the road was frequently used by American jeeps and military police patrols. By evening we were safe in the house of Major Schoeller's parents at Fischhausen. Three days later we would be in the hands of the American Intelligence Service; and three months later in an American DC-3, flying the Atlantic to Washington.

Part 2

The partnership

5. Gentlemen's agreement

A week after we sailed from the United States, our liberty ship berthed at Le Havre in north-western France. It was July 1946. In Nürnberg the war crimes trial was coming to an end; Europe was swept by hunger and devastation, and the Cold War was just beginning between east and west. Captain Eric Waldman, who had arrived at USFET's G-2 section from Washington in June, was waiting for us on the dockside, and got my small group off the boat even before the American soldiers were able to disembark. We were driven in a number of cars to Orly airfield, outside Paris. I myself went in a US Army reconnaissance car alone with Waldman, who briefed me about everything that had happened at USFET's G-2 which would be of consequence for our combined Intelligence project. From Orly we were flown to Frankfurt in a special plane.

Our new home was to be at Oberursel, which had become famous as a Luftwaffe interrogation centre during the war. The chief of USFET's G-2, Brigadier-General Edwin L. Sibert, was now using the compound for the same purpose. For the time being we were regarded as a study group, and three houses in the compound were placed at our disposal; they served as both office and living quarters. The American liaison team, consisting of Captain Waldman and a new arrival, Lieutenant-Colonel John R. Deane, was housed separately in a fourth building, the so-called 'Blue House'. A few days later we also saw Captain John Boker, who had returned to a staff post at USFET.

A formality came first: we were discharged from prisoner-of-war status so that we could move around at will, bound only by the need to return to our place of employment. The first few days were taken up by conferences with the two American officers on the question of how best to organise our work and how the American and German aims could best be reconciled. The American Colonel William Russell Philp, who was now in command of Oberursel, would supervise the work and furnish logistic support.

The cluster of houses in which we worked was surrounded by barbed wire; but this time it really was for our protection, to keep out unwanted visitors. The American zone was overrun by Russians, probing everywhere for a variety of reasons; General Eisenhower had adopted a lenient attitude towards them, hoping (in vain) for some kind of reciprocity. An added advantage of the barbed wire was that it made our section look like part of the main Oberursel prison camp, in which there was the most motley collection of largely political prisoners. It was excellent camouflage and did not depress us in the least. I was able to see my wife and children again after a year's separation, and so could my staff see theirs.

Soon after our arrival, General Sibert called to see us. He was now the military Intelligence chief of staff on the staff of the commander of US forces in the European theatre (i.e. G-2, USFET) and one of the few senior Americans to have seen the coming east-west conflict from the outset.[1] He was also a man of great moral courage. He had been the target of a lot of ill-informed criticism for having failed to detect Hitler's preparations for the Battle of the Bulge in December 1944. I have always held that no logic could have indicated that a sane military leader would commit thirty-five divisions in the manner Hitler did that winter. Now that Sibert agreed to take my organisation under his wing, he said to us in effect, 'If anything goes wrong, God help the lot of you!' Sibert and I went over every aspect of the new

[1] Sibert was later a major-general and chief of staff to General Mark Clark in the Korean war.

organisation; he fully understood why I felt bound to impose certain conditions on our co-operating with the Americans.

As far as the political ambitions of the communist bloc were concerned, Americans and Germans were now sitting in the same boat, and we had to think in terms of a common defence effort. This, if nothing else, justified us as former enemies working together; it was for the diplomats and politicians to attend to the rest. There was no escaping the future as we saw it. The events of the last twenty-five years have confirmed that we were right. I had gone over much the same ground in my first talks with Captain Boker at Wiesbaden and with the authorities in Washington and yet again in the negotiations with the American liaison team here at Oberursel, so my remarks can not have been much of a novelty for General Sibert, though I expressed them now in greater detail.

My later discussion with General Sibert in Oberursel ended with a 'gentlemen's agreement' which for a variety of reasons we never set down in black and white. Such was the trust that had been built up between the two sides during this year of intensive personal contact that neither had the slightest hesitation in founding the entire operation on a verbal agreement and a handshake. This unconditional trust was crucial to our success in the years that followed.

I remember the terms of the agreement well:

1] that a clandestine German Intelligence organisation was to be set up using the existing structure to continue gathering information in the east just as it had been doing before. The basis for this was our common interest in a defence against communism;

2] that this German organisation was to work not 'for' or 'under' the Americans, but 'jointly with the Americans';

3] that the organisation would operate under exclusively German leadership, which would receive its directives and assignments from the Americans until such time as a new German government was established in Germany;

4] that the organisation was to be financed by the Americans with funds[1] which were *not* to be borne from the occupation costs, and that in return the organisation would supply all its Intelligence reports to the Americans;

5] that as soon as a sovereign German government was established, that government should decide whether the organisation ought to continue to function or not, but that until such time the care and control (later referred to as 'the trusteeship') of the organisation should remain in American hands; and

6] that should the organisation at any time find itself in a position where American and German interests diverged, it was accepted that the organisation would consider the interests of Germany first.

The last of the six points may raise some eyebrows, since it might seem that the American representatives had gone overboard in making concessions to us. But this point, more than any other, demonstrates Sibert's great vision. He recognised that for many years to come the interests of the United States and West Germany must run parallel.

This was the key to our success – right from the start we had concluded an agreement strong enough to stand all the difficulties that were to beset it in the years that followed. I admire Sibert as a general who took the bold step of requisitioning the Intelligence experts of a former enemy for his own country, in a situation that was fraught with political pitfalls. It was very much to the credit of everybody concerned on the American side that they were able to find the right psychological basis and the climate of mutual trust for the launching of this unique venture.

The political risk to which Sibert was exposed was very great. Anti-German feeling ran high, and he had created our organisation without any authority from Washington and without the

[1] I later learned from Sibert that the small sum of money involved came out of the general funds for support of G-2 activities in USFET.

knowledge of the War Department. I understand that he informed his opposite number in the British zone, Major-General Sir Kenneth Strong, of our existence, but he asked him not to inquire too closely into the matter for fear that the press might discover our activities. This Sir Kenneth undertook to do.

6. The Gehlen organisation

Those of my former officers who had stayed behind in Europe had not been idle in the months before my return from the United States. Shortly after my flight to Washington, Lieutenant-Colonel Wessel had established contact with Hermann Baun. Baun had been through much the same as we had: he had surrendered to the Americans, as we had arranged; he had been shipped back and forth across Germany, finally he had ended up not far from Wiesbaden in the CIC interrogation centre at Oberursel.

The régime there was strict, as the centre also housed a number of suspected war criminals. It was controlled by USFET's G-2 branch. Baun bore with this situation as did his colleagues, displaying a characteristically grim humour, and eventually he told the CIC he was willing to work for them as we had arranged. I had already described in the prologue to these memoirs how during my talks in Washington at the end of 1945 I had agreed to Baun and our other former colleagues left in Germany resuming active operations on a trial basis. Two considerations had been uppermost in my mind at the time. First, we had to convince the justifiably sceptical Americans that, quite apart from our document files (which the natural process of obsolescence would render valueless in time) we could offer them other topical and worthwhile Intelligence. Secondly, the passage of time would make it harder with every week that passed to recruit the nucleus of workers we needed. Once they had been discharged from captivity and swallowed up into civilian life, we would probably never manage to find these experts again.

Wessel learned from the Americans that I had agreed to a resumption of operations; Baun was put in the picture by the CIC at Oberursel. Unfortunately neither Wessel nor I knew at the time that Baun had not been told the whole story by the CIC, as its members had been kept in the dark as to my existence and the plans evolved in Washington. They remained in this state of ignorance until 1949. We later found out that Baun had put his own plans for a practical Intelligence operation to the Americans, ideas which were not dissimilar to the layout of Admiral Canaris's *Abwehr* between 1933 and 1941. What he wanted was an Intelligence procurement agency under his leadership which would work as and where he saw fit, handing over its information to an independent second agency for analysis and evaluation. This was in flat contradiction to the plans that had been approved in Washington, and I certainly would not have supported him, if only because it would have made it easy for the Americans to play off one agency against the other. Greatly though I valued Baun's experience there would have been no guarantee that the Americans would have been passed only such information as I would personally have taken responsibility for. My own experience of certain *Abwehr* reports during the war made me uneasy in this respect. The existence of two parallel organisations would also have proved an unnecessary complication when the time came for a new German government to take us over, quite apart from the fact that it was this very biaxial structure that had yielded such a large and damaging crop of command errors during the war.

Nor did the Baun plan resemble the way in which the American authorities in Europe envisaged our work. They showed a marked preference for dealing with me after my stay in Washington was over. While Washington had, after protracted negotiations, given its general agreement to our starting work, the actual terms of this joint operation remained a matter for General Sibert: his was the neck that would get the chop if the experiment proved a failure, or if there was a political scandal. That was another reason why he and his colleagues preferred to work with one German who would take responsibility for the whole operation, and who was, moreover, the senior ranking officer of the former Foreign Armies East staff concerned. Yet another factor was that to the Americans Baun seemed a complex personality. He had been born in Odessa and had spent the formative years of his childhood there before his family returned to Germany. He had grown up bilingual, and had absorbed the Russian mentality. As with so many other foreign-born Germans who had spent years in Russia there was something of the Russian soul in him, that emotional and immeasurable element that distinguishes the Russians from the rest of the world. But equally Russian was his lively imagination, which did not always help him to pass sober judgment on hard facts. This, and his years under Canaris and the *Abwehr* put a natural barrier between himself and the Americans who had to deal with him, and inevitably roused at times certain misgivings in them which were not entirely justified.

It was largely because the CIC had not been able to put Baun fully in the picture that when we came to discuss our detailed plans in August 1946 Baun was reluctant to subordinate himself wholeheartedly to me, even though by then the outline of our future joint effort with the American Army had been broadly mapped out. I was planning to put Baun in charge of my espionage section, and Wessel in charge of the analysis section. Had the proper degree of frankness been displayed to Baun by the Americans it would doubtless have spared us much later unpleasantness. Of course the possibility can not be ruled out that the Americans may have considered it in their interests initially to keep two irons in the fire. There were certainly some officers in USFET's G-2 branch who were less enthusiastic about identifying themselves with the joint operation than Colonel

Philp, Captain Boker and Captain Waldman. The fact that we did not secure a formal agreement with the American secret service (by then the CIA) until much later, shows just how unstable the situation was, despite the goodwill shown by both sides.

The difficulties facing Wessel and Baun early in 1946 when they had first started their attempts to rebuild an Intelligence organisation, were largely the result of the post-war chaos in Europe. But the remarkable feature was that not one of those whom they approached to act in one capacity or another was ever to let them down. Although virtually every German refugee from the east had lost everything he possessed, again and again over the years we found among these homeless fugitives people who were willing to risk everything for us even if meantime they had found some kind of new employment. It made no difference what their personal politics were. There were allegations that it was this very loss of livelihood and property that made working for us attractive, and that the organisation we were building up consisted of nothing more than a lot of adventurers joined together to learn a new and murky trade. This kind of accusation was repeatedly levelled at us by communist propaganda from the Soviet zone until about 1954, and in some cases it was even picked up by the mass media of the west.

The truth was that we had nothing of value in the ordinary sense that we could offer our workers in return. Our very existence was a closely kept secret; essential if we were to remain successful and guard against infiltration by the enemy. So our fellow-workers' return to normal life as regular citizens was blighted from the start: for security reasons they could not mention their work to their relatives; they had no government protection, because the German state as such had ceased to exist, and the protection the occupation authorities could afford them was less than marginal. The jurisdiction of the United States authorities was restricted to their own zone, even after

the economic fusion of this with the British zone and the formation of the Bizone late in 1946. On top of this, initially only
USFET's G-2 knew of our existence, a state of affairs we
wanted to last as long as possible; so for a long time our
operatives were at the mercy of the ultra-suspicious organs of
other American security agencies, and particularly the ever-
watchful CIC and the Military Police. The pay was meagre –
my own salary being only about twelve hundred marks a month
in 1952.

Before the West German currency reform of June 1948 our
working capital was in the form of US dollars, at first sight well
worth having but in fact presenting innumerable difficulties for
us. For example, we were not allowed to cash dollars at any
bank, to avoid having to answer awkward questions about where
they came from; so we had to try and change them with the
assistance of our American friends. Otherwise we could not have
obtained the German currency to keep the organisation on its
feet.

In short, it took a lot of idealism after six years of war, captivity, expulsion and the many other personal privations from
which no German had been spared, for any man to agree to
work for us.

The first trial Intelligence procurement operations started early
in April 1946. The results met with the approval of the Americans. We were not able to awaken all of our network of agents
who had become dormant in the Soviet Union with the end of
the war, and in fact they were to play a smaller part in our
rebirth than has been suggested in some publications. Baun
made a start in that direction, but I felt it was better to concentrate on recruiting fresh agents while we could, as we could not
be sure which of the old ones had been turned round by the
Russians. Those that we could trust were 'woken up' by pre-
arranged signals, but in the disorder existing in post-war
Europe it was comparatively easy for our people to be sent deep
into the Soviet Union to establish personal contact. Of far

greater value were the files and indices we had maintained on the Russian military units.

Meanwhile, after the July 1946 conference with General Sibert had resulted in the 'gentlemen's agreement' referred to above, espionage operations proper had begun. Our first requirement was the creation of a small but efficient brain for the organisation, followed by a somewhat larger but capable operations staff to control the espionage work, and a reliable analytical section. This vital spadework took up much of our time, eager though we all were to get started, since we lacked many of the things we needed. We had little space to work in, no technical equipment like wireless transmitters and receivers, and we urgently needed a larger staff. But we had lost contact with many of those who had been working on Intelligence during the war. We also had to recruit enough clerical staff for our purposes. But beginning again from scratch like this did have its big advantages: it is far harder to take over a large existing organisation and to try to convert and modernise it than to create one from nothing, benefiting from all the experience gained in the past. Wessel and I wanted only one thing – to form a nucleus for *one* future German Intelligence service that would profit from all we had learned during the war and pre-war years.

Where there is a multiplicity of national Intelligence services there can only be rivalry, overlapping and security risks – for they offer the enemy's Intelligence organs ideal opportunities for penetrating them from within. I therefore planned to spend the years that followed until a new German government came into being in creating one uniform Intelligence service capable of carrying out every kind of espionage work against the enemy. It would unite under one agency diplomatic Intelligence, economic Intelligence, military Intelligence and counter-espionage. Clearly such an agency could only be a civilian body, in view of the sheer size of the task if nothing else. For this reason we tried to recruit high-grade civilian staff in addition to the former army officers at our disposal; for example we took on former members of the foreign service, former civil servants and the like, provided that they had had a clean slate in the Third Reich and had done nothing reprehensible since then.

The speed with which we could set up the new organisation was bound to depend on the funds and equipment placed at our disposal. To the Americans we were still something of an experiment; so improvisation characterised the first trial runs of the 'Gehlen organisation' as we soon came to be known to our friends. But we still had to show worthwhile Intelligence results if we were to convince the Americans that there was a future in us. Only less important than getting Baun an efficient operations staff for his work on the Intelligence procurement side, to speed up this in-flow of reports, we had to find him accommodation near our organisation's headquarters. We finally found room for him at an inn at Schmitten, fifteen minutes by car from Oberursel. Our headquarters stayed in the 'Blue House' cluster of buildings at Oberursel itself. We initially accommodated our analytical section there too, but later on we removed it to Kranzberg castle where there was room for it to expand.

We soon established good relations with the American liaison team – Colonel Deane and Captain Waldman. The former was an outstanding active service officer who had distinguished himself in combat but had had little to do with Intelligence work for some time. His main job was to throw the weight of his personality and rank into the scales on our behalf. It was Waldman who bore most of the brunt of the co-operation with us. I have already emphasised how much we owed to him. Even when his superiors showed little sympathy he committed himself wholeheartedly to our cause, putting up without a murmur with the personal disadvantages in which this involved him. A number of minor difficulties resulted from the colonel's lack of experience in Intelligence affairs. When, for example, I tried to bring home to him the need for us to obtain false identity cards his first retort was an astonished: 'That's against the law!' It took some effort on my part to bring home to him that it was not a true violation of the law and that the use of false identity cards is common practice in Intelligence circles. After I had succeeded in convincing him of certain other peculiarities of our trade, this trusty officer swung round to our side and gave us his full support. That is why I have always followed the later career of the colonel, who is now an influential general in the United States, with a particular sense of gratitude.

More serious were the difficulties that arose during this period with Hermann Baun, whose concept of the organisation was very different from my own. He tended to regard the job from the purely Intelligence procurement angle, and overlooked the political need to limit ourselves strictly to what we were capable of besides what was desirable. He attempted to carry out his own plans rather than mine, and this disinclination to accept that I was in charge led to increasing friction. In April 1947 I therefore found it necessary to replace him as chief of Intelligence procurement, but since he had otherwise served me well I put him in charge of another responsible job. I did not 'elbow him out' as was subsequently claimed in various publications. His successor was Colonel Hans Dillberg,[1] a loyal staff officer with great vision, particularly on the administrative side. He had picked up a lot of experience in Intelligence procurement during the pre-war period, and had later worked extensively in military Intelligence as well. Under his expert management, our networks expanded and the information they handled swelled to a considerable volume.

It is difficult to describe the exceptional problems confronting us in 1947 and 1948. What is now the Federal Republic of West Germany was at that time occupied territory, partitioned into three zones, with all passenger and goods transport under strict Allied surveillance. Even on our own side of the demarcation lines we had to operate under a cloak of conspiracy which

[1] Dillberg was the code-name used by this officer at headquarters; it was not his real name.

would scarcely have been possible without American aid. It was no rare occurrence for one of our workers to be seen acting suspiciously near the zonal border and to be arrested by the CIC or the British security forces. We then had to secure his release from arrest with the help of the American liaison team but without disclosing his real job – no easy undertaking. Our officials setting out from Bavaria to our regional office (*Aussenstelle*) in the American enclave at Bremerhaven in northern Germany had to fill their cars with spare petrol canisters, for if they ran out of petrol on the way they could expect no mercy from the British or French occupation authorities. Railroad connections were bad, telephone lines were indistinct and overloaded and anyway tapped by the Allies. The economic situation was catastrophic. But our organisation was gradually expanding and its mouths had to be fed. The fact that our operational bases were distributed across the length and breadth of western Germany and had to be given realistic 'fronts' as camouflage did not make things easier. Our workers were not able to give the authorities any information on their circumstances if they had to report to them in connection with personal matters. Nor was it possible to register them under any kind of state insurance scheme, as officially there was no employer, a problem that persisted long after we had been transferred to the West German government.

Every piece of our equipment, from typewriters to wireless transmitters, had to be supplied by the US Army. Here too there was a great danger of our being exposed with all the undesirable consequences that would follow, and we often had to put up with long delays. The problems facing us in establishing links by courier, post and telephone across the Iron Curtain were equally formidable. That we succeeded in solving all these problems seems a miracle even now.

We restricted our investigations at first to purely military questions. This was inevitable, as we had rebuilt our organisation on the existing foundations of the forward reconnaissance units (*Frontaufklärungseinheiten*) which we had used on the eastern front. It soon became clear, however, that parallel to the growing estrangement between the former Allies, the Americans' interest in purely political problems increased. By the end of 1946 we were already keeping an eye on political trends behind the Iron Curtain. From that it was a logical progression to embrace espionage on communist economic affairs and arms technology as well. In this latter field, which the orthodox American services had begun to watch only comparatively recently, we were able to communicate to them particularly important results.

In the autumn of 1947 we unfortunately lost both General Sibert and the American Colonel Deane; the latter was replaced by Colonel 'L', who failed to see eye to eye with us and un-wittingly jeopardised the whole joint operation. He was a good soldier – even as a full colonel he still regularly practised para-chute jumps – but he regarded his position as one of authority over us, an attitude totally at variance with the agreement I had concluded with Sibert. He knew only one military relationship: he gave the orders and we had to obey them; it was a creed he had practised his entire military life. He was not the best of partners for myself as head of an organisation which had by then already expanded to a considerable size, employing several thousand men. I am sure he did his best to work in harmony with us, but the differences of opinion multiplied and they began to affect our work.

One achievement must be chalked up to this colonel, during the few months before I secured his removal. By now we were bursting our accommodation at the seams. He managed to secure for the organisation a small housing estate at Pullach, a village some five miles south of Munich. At the time it housed the Anglo-American Civil Censorship Division, but he had them moved out; the Gehlen organisation settled into this compound in December 1947. The twenty-two houses in the compound had

originally been built as the 'Rudolf Hess' estate, and designed
for use as a reserve headquarters for the War Department, in a
tree-shaded setting on the banks of the little Isar river. Although
it has been considerably expanded, the site still serves as the
headquarters of the Federal Intelligence service (BND) in
Germany. The American liaison team moved into the biggest
building, Martin Bormann's former offices, in Heilmann-
strasse (the road running through the compound, which was
now blocked off at each end); I moved into a small ground-floor
office in one of the houses opposite. The camouflage drab
painted on the roofs and walls was gradually removed, the
buildings renovated, and the gardens put in order.

The move to Pullach brought enormous relief to our cramped
headquarters staff. For security reasons we all brought our
families to live within the Pullach compound as well. (My own
wife and children had been permitted to join me at Oberursel in
July 1946 after my return from Washington.) The presence of
our families made it necessary in turn for the headquarters to
become self-sufficient: we had our own school, our own kinder-
garten and all the other things necessary for us to restrict to a
minimum our contact with the outside world. The local village
believed that the compound housed German civilian internees.
The Americans were not enthusiastic about the arrival of our
families inside the compound, but the presence of wives who
were not tied down by small children – and these women
included several with academic degrees – resulted in an immediate and worthwhile addition to our labour force. The
discipline of the German families within the compound, living
in overcrowded conditions, was particularly commendable; in
retrospect the decision was undoubtedly a proper one, because
our staff were thus spared the added burden of living apart from
their families, on top of all the other deprivations that belonging
to my organisation involved. Of course everybody was allowed
complete freedom of movement and was permitted to leave the
compound whenever he liked, but nobody was allowed to make

any kind of contact within a certain radius, or to do any shopping in the neighbourhood. To destroy such temptation at its root we opened our own food stores, and this did grand service over the years and even now serves the tenants of BND accommodation within the compound.

The move took place at a time of crisis – a crisis of confidence within the organisation. It had been caused by the fact that we had not always been able to meet the demands made on us for better accommodation and the provision of equipment appropriate to the job, including motor transport, wireless and other technical equipment. The US Army's provision of office equipment and the necessary funds for our continued existence also left much to be desired. An official budget had been negotiated between us and the American authorities, but again and again it proved inadequate. On all these matters there were lengthy and tedious negotiations, and for the most part I had to conduct these in person. It is difficult to give in writing an impression of the myriads of trivial questions which had to be dealt with like this – matters that I frequently had to push through almost in unarmed combat. I see from my records that in 1948 alone I had to submit to the Americans no less than four long lists of urgent and explicit requests.

Our field workers could of course see little or nothing of this constant fight on their behalf, so I could well understand the reasons for their grumbling. The US Army liaison team did what they could to satisfy our demands, but the army suffered from bureaucracy and insisted on our following the proper 'service channels', and since those channels led from Pullach to Frankfurt and from Frankfurt to Washington and all the way back again, the process was long and time-consuming.

The disputes with Colonel 'L' finally culminated in my flatly refusing to obey a certain order he issued to me in March 1948, since it would have cost the organisation its hard-fought independence. I told him bluntly that the management of the organisation was my affair and mine only, as had been laid down in the 'gentlemen's agreement' with Sibert, and that I would therefore accept no 'orders' which directly interfered with the internal affairs of my organisation. I *might* be prepared to accept recommendations, I added, provided they would serve the mutual interests of Germany and the United States. At this he withdrew his 'order'.

This episode finally obliged me, despite my respect for this soldierly and distinguished officer, to ask for his replacement by someone better versed in our affairs. The negotiations were not particularly easy, since the American authorities were at first inclined to put their prestige into the scales on the colonel's behalf; but they finally came round to my view and in August 1948 he was recalled. He was replaced in December of the same year by Colonel Philp. The change occurred at a particularly fortunate time, for the following eight months were to see my organisation labouring under great strains. These resulted primarily from the currency reform in West Germany, but there appear to have been certain domestic American difficulties as well. Philp reconciled the two positions and kept the collaboration going; illustrating vividly by his example, how much can depend on one trustworthy and reliable personality if different nations are to co-operate in Intelligence work.

The proof that the Americans set great store by our work was that they came to us with more and more missions to fulfil.This meant we had to recruit more and more staff, which in turn brought us a number of administrative difficulties. My own view was that if an organisation like ours was to start producing results virtually from the first day, we would have to make do with a bare minimum of red tape. Lack of funds forced this on us too: what money we had was there to produce results, not to finance a large superstructure. There is always a risk that a body of this kind will tend to follow Parkinson's Law and finally become an end in itself. This was a tendency which I was determined to combat from the start.

In any case, even by 1948 there could be no certainty that the organisation was a permanent fixture. That was why I had to keep the number of permanent employees as small as possible. Another reason was that the security problem would be tougher if we expanded – the smaller the superstructure the easier it would be to keep it under surveillance and the greater would be our chance of rapidly detecting 'leaks'.

In Intelligence the most delicate leadership problems are always those posed by the procurement sector. There is little to be gained here from the old and well-tried military tradition of rigidly obeying orders, even if the orders are limited to the out-lining of an assignment. The agents, the last links in the chain, and at the extreme periphery of the organisation, are dependent on themselves alone; often they alone can judge whether and in what manner an assignment can be accomplished. The same goes for the intermediate links as well, people who are often called upon to take snap decisions involving a high degree of responsibility and initiative. In general assignments have to be issued in the shape of broad directives, and success depends on mutual trust, the ability of one link in the chain to rely on the next to act in the appropriate manner. In addition to political insight, a talent for organisation and an ability to improvise, the head of the procurement section must also possess a strong element of psychological intuition and an ability to control his men firmly while still giving them enough rein.

One seldom finds among one's colleagues people coming anywhere near this ideal image; the proper solution is therefore to try for a constant upward flow of officers and for regular personnel changes at intervals of two to six years. Dillberg was the first of my senior colleagues to whom I applied this maxim; I replaced him as chief of the procurement section after about a year. Credit was due to him for having injected great impetus into the job; but there are times, particularly in the early years of an organisation, when too much impetus can be positively harmful. This is particularly true where security is concerned. It can be a hindrance during the vital period of running-in that any new machine must undergo.

This was the time of the first Berlin crisis, and I had to find a successor to Dillberg who was cautious and who would conduct the business of Intelligence-gathering with due deliberation. My choice fell on one of the older generation of former *Abwehr* officers, Herr Schack,[1] whose Intelligence experience went back to well before the war. He was just my type of man, exceptionally thorough and deliberate, the kind who reached decisions (whether on security affairs or on matters of command) only after he had inspected every possible angle in his mind's eye. Even so I recognised that Schack could not fill the post for ever, as the prevailing political winds alone could dictate whether we were to be active or to show prudence. I left Schack in control of procurement for a relatively long time; he did good work, and this deserves to be underlined, because he was already comparatively old when he took on the office.

Strange though it may seem, this was a period when we feared the Allied fiscal authorities more than the long arm of Soviet counter-espionage agencies. The June 1948 German currency reform brought particularly severe monetary problems in its train. During the reign of the Reichsmark, our budget had been solidly based on the allocation of dollars, a currency of real value on which we could depend. Though the disappearance of the dollar and the post-war bartering of cigarettes and other commodities was a blessing for the national economy, it was a disaster for the Gehlen organisation. Forthwith our allowance was paid to us in the new Deutschmarks: our over-all American allowance was cut back, and coupled with the artificial rate of exchange which we were given of one dollar to three marks (the official rate was one dollar to 4.20 marks) we suddenly received seventy per cent *less* than before. To add insult to injury, the

[1] 'Schack' was his code-name only.

Deutschmark was for a long time regarded with a certain hesitancy by the public, and its value sagged markedly. The outcome was that for months our organisation did not have enough funds to make ends meet. Our most urgent commitments could only be met if the Americans increased their subsidy by at least fifty or even a hundred per cent. Even this would have left a serious gap to be plugged. It was a bitter experience after so many years of work.

It is necessary for the reader to bear constantly in mind that we were not some kind of official government agency backed by the resources of the state or one of the occupying powers. We were an independent organisation financed by such funds as the US Army could spare for us. The need for efficient camouflage alone forced us to lead something of an underground existence; in the midst of this financial crisis, we had to do what we could to keep our heads above water. To raise the funds we needed to continue, I set up a special section for raising funds: with the 125,000 dollars that remained to us, we purchased as much cocoa as we could from American stocks, and sold it around Munich – particularly in the notorious Möhlstrasse black-market area – at a profit so large that we more than tripled our original outlay. If our operatives were caught, their special American passes provided of course for their immediate release. The American authorities connived wholeheartedly in this, as they had no option. But the general shortage of funds was so crippling that other field units frequently had to discontinue important sources which they had built up while agent leaders were forced to take new commitments upon themselves, underwriting the costs themselves in the dim hope that everything would somehow turn out all right in the end. Of course it was hard to make them understand how it was that the wealthy United States was suddenly unable to part with more money for us; but the negotiations on this were taking time, because the domestic currency reform in Germany had taken the American authorities we worked with as much by surprise as it did us, and no kind of advance planning had been possible.

On the other hand, the German public's willingness to help was very great in 1948. We received much financial assistance at Pullach from wealthy industrialists, partly in the form of loans and partly in the form of valuable goods, and in due course I established under General Horst von Mellenthin[1] a 'Special Connections' section whose responsibility it was to maintain touch with government and industry. (Unfortunately, West German industry was reluctant to go beyond purely financial assistance: when we suggested to certain firms with major contracts behind the Iron Curtain that they employ key members of our organisation to provide them with a legitimate cover, without exception almost all refused.) Above all it was the individual *people* who came forward – people who owned little or nothing themselves, but were fired by a great and idealistic desire to help. I was often deeply moved by the positive disposition towards us that we encountered everywhere at that time – a period which is characterised to-day as one in which only material considerations were of any consequence. It was the little things that showed how closely the public identified themselves with our cause. The villages were as one man in my support when I moved with my family to my present house near Starnberg, after they gradually learned who I really was. They regularly misdirected strangers who inquired the way to my secluded villa; when one car driver asked a local chemist, within minutes the chemist had telephoned to warn me of the stranger. When we did our shopping in the town of Starnberg, I was cordially addressed as 'Herr Gehlen' by the shopkeepers– but only if there were no strangers in the shop.

Only one thing could eventually rescue us from this chronic financial crisis – the rapid transfer of the Gehlen organisation

---

[1] Mellenthin had headed the War Department's attaché branch during the war, and had later commanded an Army Corps; in the late fifties he became my deputy at Pullach, as predecessor to Worgitzky.

from US Army control to the special co-ordinating agency the US government had set up in 1947, the Central Intelligence Agency. We confidently expected the CIA to have a much broader horizon in consequence of its global assignment to collect and collate political, economic and military Intelligence. It would surely recognise the possibilities inherent in close German-American collaboration over Intelligence work, and it would have a realistic idea of how much this kind of operation would cost.

From as early as November 1948, therefore, we were involved in negotiations with the CIA's representatives. Their first job obviously was to find out as much as they could about the kind of work my organisation was performing. This took some time – to our increasing embarrassment, for by now we were on the horns of an increasingly uncomfortable dilemma. By February 1949 our financial position had become so acute that I found myself obliged to warn the US Army liaison officer attached to us that if the crisis persisted much longer I would have to cut back the organisation I had built up, and this would inevitably lead to a reduction in our efficiency. Soon afterwards I repeated this in a letter to the G-2 at SHAPE. I went so far as to offer my resignation, and recommended that in view of the imbalance between the modest means placed at our disposal and the tasks we were expected to perform, the Gehlen organisation should be disbanded. This cannot have fallen on deaf ears, for only very recently we had succeeded in penetrating and smashing the entire Czech spy network operating in West Germany, in 'Operation Bohemia': our Esslingen office had persuaded two Czech Intelligence officers to defect, and they had driven across the border in two cars loaded with a mass of files and details on the Czech networks, enabling the American authorities to move in and destroy them without trace.

At this time a very accommodating War Department colonel happened to be visiting us. He at once recognised the problem, but explained that the American defence budget was in some difficulty as a result of the Berlin crisis: it was the period of the costly Berlin airlift forced on the western powers by the Soviet blockade. He entreated me not, on any account, to disband or cut back our organisation, as we were doing such valuable work for the Americans. He gave his word that something would be done to help us. The good will of the American Allies was without doubt as fervent as ever; the real cause of the crisis was red tape, a phenomenon with which we in Germany were only too familiar.

An Intelligence service is a highly sensitive instrument. The moment there is any kind of upset at the top, the tremors are sensed by every link all the way down the chain even if the actual details do not become known.

The effect of the five-month financial crisis I have described was to increase the uncertainty of the climate in which our organisation had to operate. It was not until the late spring of 1949 that our talks with the CIA finally reached a positive conclusion; the terms were formally settled in English on 13 May and in German on the 23rd, in a new 'gentlemen's agreement'. This time it was put in writing. On 1 July, the beginning of the new American fiscal year, the CIA took over responsibility for us. But even now our difficulties were not really over, for the cracks could not be papered over as easily as that.

The CIA appointed a liaison staff to replace that of the US Army, civilian clothes now took the place of the familiar brown-and-buff American Army uniforms. The CIA liaison staff chief, Colonel M., turned out to be a particularly straightforward and forceful personality. There were inevitably some initial snags to be overcome before true mutual confidence grew up, but after that he did all he could to keep things moving and to help us. Even so, our financial problems continued to dog us for many months, and we resolved to make a virtue of necessity, and start a long-term shake-up in the organisation to refine it to the nth degree. This was made easy by the fact that the experienced CIA men were less interested in getting immediate results than in building up a really worthwhile and efficient organisation. My admiration for the individuals on that early CIA liaison staff is boundless: they for their part recognised that their own parent organisation was considerably younger than our own, and clearly regarded their job as being to learn as much from us as they could. This, in fact, is why I am not able to identify them here, for there is not one member of that CIA liaison team who has not now reached the highest positions within that agency.

We began the rationalisation process late in the summer of 1949. It yielded a crop of problems, all inter-related in some way. First we had to adapt the organisation to its reduced circumstances without any loss of efficiency; second, the organisation had to be restructured to conform by and large with the regular procedural and administrative methods of the CIA; and third, we had to start paving the way for policy discussions with the new West German government, which had been founded in September. If, as we hoped, the government agreed to take over our organisation as a nucleus for a foreign Intelligence service of its own, then our administration would have to conform with German standards as well.

Throughout this period Colonel M. radiated confidence and reliability. In harmony with his proposals we streamlined the organisation until by October 1949 we could show that we were putting our funds to better purpose than ever before. We merged offices, scrutinised every salaried position and shortened the links in our communications and courier networks. At the same time we remodelled our administration on the lines of the German government agencies, as far as we could without conflicting with the functions of the CIA.

An Intelligence service cannot always be run by the procedures adopted for other government agencies. Most government agencies have a purely administrative function; but an Intelligence agency has the vital task of procuring and evaluating information – the administrative aspects and the technical and

financial side of the agency are of less moment. For a secret
service (as with the armed forces) experience shows that an
excess of red tape will inevitably impair efficiency and finally
suffocate it altogether. It is one of the most important duties of
the head of the Intelligence service to combat excessive bureaucracy. (That is why at least one western government has found
it preferable to administer its secret service by Intelligence
experts with ancillary civil-service training rather than by civil
servants who are expected to grasp the ramifications of Intelligence operations.)

It is also essential to preserve the flexibility with which the
agency can use its technical and financial means, so that it can
put its operational decisions into effect quickly. Governments
are therefore faced in principle with two alternatives: either they
can force the Intelligence agency into the strait-jacket of the
existing civil service regulations; or they can make an exception
for it. In the former case, while the organisational pattern so
fervently desired by all higher civil-service authorities will have
been achieved, there will also be a significant reduction in the
agency's effectiveness. In the latter, the mobility of the Intelligence service will be significantly enhanced without any consequent loss of control over the application of public funds.
Every major country has opted for the second alternative; so
did all West German governments up to the time the socialist
coalition was formed in Bonn late in 1969.

Without going into tedious detail here, it will suffice if I say
that we adopted in the Gehlen organisation the same financial
practices as had the earlier *Abwehr* with the approval of the then
Reich Audit Office: we kept the most detailed accounts of all
personnel and capital expenditure just as any other government
department would; but the minutiae of Intelligence service costs
were represented by one lump sum, for which our operational
leaders had to account internally in detail. These secret accounts
were scrutinised by special inspectors reporting only to the head
of the organisation. With minor modifications this procedure

The Elend Lodge, a lonely mountain hut in the Bavarian mountains, which was Gehlen's hideout in 1945 until the Americans found him (See p. 127)

Gehlen's headquarters ('Foreign Armies East') at Zossen. Camouflaged in forests south of Berlin at Zossen lay the General Staff's headquarters in the second world war

Ernst Wollweber

was also approved by the Federal Audit Office in Bonn when we were later transferred to the federal service.

Life was not pleasant with the CIA at first. Their bureaucratic attitude towards the financing of our organisation, resulted in our shelving major operational plans for long periods since the question of whether or not we would be provided with funds for them could only be decided at CIA headquarters in Washington. The essence of the system was that the probable outcome of every operation and its requirements in time, manpower and money had to be submitted for clearance in advance. By the time clearance arrived at Pullach from Washington, the whole plan was usually long out of date. Our *Abwehr* experience led us to favour a system whereby the operational decisions and the allocation of resources would be left to our own upper command echelons. These would be given operational funds of their own for this purpose, and general guidelines and directives, except for instances where I reserved the right to make final decisions myself.

The infuriating and repeated delays while we waited for word from Washington resulted in yet another crisis of confidence within our organisation. The mood is well illustrated by a letter I received from one of my outpost leaders, Ritter, in October 1949:

I want to inform you personally of the situation in my unit. The attitude of the Allies over the devaluation of the Deutschmark, and the impotence of our present government and the pitiful plight of Germany can hardly be said to give us much enthusiasm for our work. On top of this there is very real uncertainty about the organisation's final relationship to the present government. Will the organisation be German or an all-American affair? We can be excused for beginning to suspect that the latter will be the case, since our friends are insisting on more and more information on what we are doing, down to the very lowest levels; or is this just a false

impression created by the tendency of those who have survived the *Chistka*[1] to give themselves a *raison d'être* by stepping
up the paper-war and reeling out more red tape?

It may well be that the provision of funds has been guaranteed until 1 January 1950, but the fact is that they are neither
so generous as to allow us to work properly, nor so inadequate that we can put our pens down with a clear conscience and do nothing. Besides, nobody knows for how long,
or at what rate, these funds will continue to flow, and this
makes any kind of proper planning utterly impossible. If I
could be sure that this financing would remain at this level, I
would cut my unit by a third or a half so as to be able to pay
those that are left a better rate and be able to ask more of
them in consequence.

After complaining about the impossibility of getting quick
decisions out of Washington and the resultant inefficiency and
demonstration, Ritter concluded:

Given the prevailing situation in our organisation I am
coming round to the view that it would be better to get out
now while the going is good. But as my own unit has been
built up on the basis of personal trust alone, I would prefer
not to go until I can be sure that those of my colleagues who
still wish to carry on with their work will be in good hands.
This is a crisis of confidence which extends much farther up the
organisation than the earlier ones. It is of course impossible
to conceal completely one's own sense of insecurity, in one's
dealings with one's colleagues; and often one does not wish
to anyway, because it would be doing a disservice to people
who put their trust in one.

I had a private talk with Ritter, explained the difficulties I
was meeting from our American friends and warned him they
would certainly last for some time yet. Unfortunately he was not

[1] Russian: 'purge', a perhaps over-dramatic word for the reduction of US
military personnel that became necessary in Europe at this time. – *Translator's
Note*

happy with the assurances I gave him and he resigned from the organisation some time later. I deeply regretted the loss of this experienced and likeable Intelligence officer.

His letter and subsequent resignation were not without effect on our American partners. Colonel M. intensified his efforts on our behalf and began an intensive investigation of the various ways of making our position easier.

A month before this letter, on 12 September 1949, Dr Konrad Adenauer had formed the first post-war government in West Germany. Germany was once again able to act as a state, as a nation of independent substance. This was of more than academic interest to us at Pullach. Now was the time for us to start thinking of approaching the new German government. Even though its absolute sovereignty still had to be recognised, we were under an obligation to inform the government of our existence (if nothing else) particularly since the 'gentlemen's agreement' laid down that a reconstituted German government should have the right to decide on our future.

As early as mid-August 1949, on the day of the first elections for the federal Parliament, I had spoken about our work to a certain Bavarian minister whom I assumed to have good contacts with what was likely to be the coming German government. One result of this was that I was able to brush up my contacts with the Bavarian authorities and particularly with their Prime Minister and his minister of the interior. On 12 October 1949 I made my first personal contact with the Bonn government, visiting Ritter von Lex (who was at that time a *Ministerial-Director* and later rose to the rank of state-secretary in the Federal ministry of the interior). It was through him that I established contact with the then minister, Dr Gustav Heinemann (who is at the time of writing West Germany's president). Through von Lex and Dr Hans Globke (the *Ministerial-Dirigent* in the Chancellor's Office) I submitted to Adenauer a memorandum with my proposals for a future foreign Intelligence service; I do not know how he received my ideas, but on 14 November I again travelled to Bonn for meetings with the Vice-Chancellor Franz Blücher and with Heinemann and Herbert Blankenhorn of the Chancellor's Office. The exchanges of views lasted about an hour this time. We discussed the organisation's history and its achievements, and finally I was able to expound the ideas I had been mulling over ever since the end of the war – ideas which for the first time could be expressed in the form of concrete proposals. The frank discussions went off exceptionally well, and I was well satisfied when I drove back to Pullach.

I began to feel that the selfless sacrifices of my colleagues had not been entirely in vain. The German government had begun to take an interest in us. Discreet though my approaches to Bonn had been, however, they aroused misgivings in our American partners. Colonel M. went so far as to forbid me to have anything further to do with German officials; this was in an edict on 21 December 1949, issued, I assume, on orders from Washington. I was instructed that the future of the organisation was a matter for the Americans alone to decide. Since this American veto flatly contradicted the terms of our agreement, I tacitly declined to bow to it.

Over the next few months there was some improvement in this delicate situation. The Americans no longer prevented me from pursuing my contacts with Bonn. Presumably the American authorities recognised that since they could not prevent this association indefinitely it would be better to sanction it and satisfy themselves with 'keeping informed' on the progress of our contacts. Early in 1950 I established the first official contact with Globke, who later became state-secretary in the Chancellor's Office. I got on well with him from the first moment, and gained the impression that he was in no doubt as to the importance of the Gehlen organisation. It was clear to me that he wanted to reserve contact with us strictly for his own office.

Globke promised us all the technical assistance we needed, and asked us to do what we could to help the security authorities in West Germany during the next few months, for previously public order and protection against extremist organisations had been exclusively the responsibility of the allies. I discussed the details of the aid we should give the Ministry of the Interior and its state-secretary, Ritter von Lex. I will return to this subject shortly.

It was not until 20 September 1950 that I had my first opportunity to meet Konrad Adenauer in person. I was summoned to see him at the König Museum, a science museum in Bonn which temporarily housed the federal government and Adenauer's office until the Palais Schaumburg was ready for occupation. Globke was also present. In the twelve years that followed until our temporary estrangement over the *Der Spiegel* affair, I came to recognise in him one of the greatest German statesmen of this century. My relationship with him developed over the years into one that went beyond the merely professional, into something approaching unquestioning mutual trust. I remember on one occasion when I had to report to him on a breach of security within the organisation, he asked me, 'Tell me, general, is there anybody you can still trust?' I replied, 'Where there is no trust, Chancellor, there can be no Intelligence service.' And I added, 'but we call it "a *watchful* trust" . . .' – a qualification which clearly amused him.

Of course I had prepared with some care for my first meeting with him, with all that it meant for the organisation's future. I was curious to see whether he was the old fox he was supposed to be, and whether the authoritarian paternalism with which even his admirers credited him would make any real dialogue possible between us. At least I was not coming to Bonn empty-handed: after all, we were the first German post-war organisation, and our roots extended back long before the establishment of the Anglo-American Bizone. I even felt that my own reputation as a 'legendary personality' – however little I felt like one myself – might rouse his own curiosity.

Adenauer welcomed me with a warmness and openness that cast my doubts to the winds. I did not even need to impress on him the basic need for a foreign Intelligence service – in fact over the years that followed he and Globke showed an unusual understanding of the difficulties facing my organisation. The Chancellor at once recognised the value of the instrument being offered him, and indicated that he would seize the opportunity while he could. I told him that I also proposed to advise the leader of the socialist opposition, Dr Kurt Schumacher, of our existence and to ask for his backing as well: the difficult mission of a foreign Intelligence service could only be accomplished if it was recognised to be strictly non-partisan in nature. Adenauer at once agreed.

I left the König Museum convinced Adenauer would give us all the help we needed. Here, I was convinced, was an outstanding German who was willing to put the whole force of his personality into the fight for the supreme goal that we at Pullach had set ourselves – the restoration of our afflicted Fatherland.

To work with Dr Globke was so pleasant and stimulating that I would not willingly have done without those years of joint effort which we shared until his retirement in 1963; I was glad to do what I could to defend him from the vicious communist smear campaign that was mounted against him later on – an infallible indication of the true value of this man for West Germany. Four years older than myself, he was the very epitome of the traditional German civil servant; he was the kind of man who would perform his professional duties without fear or favour. He was not what we would call an *éminence grise*, but he did endeavour to remain in the background. He had the machinery of the new government at his fingertips, and an infinite understanding for the complexities of foreign policy. It was this sense of judgment that enabled him to recognise at once the benefits to be gained from backing the Gehlen organisation.

I called on Dr Kurt Schumacher on the day after my visit to Adenauer. The socialist leader was probably one of the most tragic figures I ever met – his right arm had been shot away in the Great War, his left arm almost paralysed, and his left leg amputated above the knee during an enforced stay in a concentration camp. He had with him his deputy, Erich Ollenhauer, his confidential secretary, Annemarie Renger, the vice-president of the parliamentary assembly Professor Carlo Schmid and Fritz Erler, a leading socialist deputy. Schumacher wholeheartedly identified himself with Adenauer on the principle that ours must remain a non-partisan organisation – in other words, that we must have the support of all the political parties except the communists. It would clearly be unfortunate if such a sensitive instrument was to be passed from one set of hands to another each time the government in Bonn changed; if such were the case the uncertainty among our staff – of which I had witnessed more than enough over the last two years – would be intolerable. It would cripple the organisation, and achieve nothing but an influx of political opportunists into the upper echelons. I felt confident that I would be able to see eye to eye with Schumacher on any matters of importance. When I left him, he assured me his party would underwrite our work as well, and that it would in time support our transfer to federal control.

By now responsibility for internal security had been largely transferred to German control. On 14 April 1949 the three Western Military Governors had forwarded what came to be known as the 'Police Letter' to the parliamentary council (Bundesrat), or Upper House. This authorised them to set up an office for collecting and disseminating information on revolutionary activities directed against the future federal republic. The new body, however, would not be equipped with any kind of police powers. Shortly after my visits to Adenauer and Schumacher, a law was passed formally establishing a federal 'Office for the Protection of the Constitution' (BfV);[1] uniting all such internal security under one authority controlled by the Minister of the Interior.

For some weeks the question of whom to appoint chairman of the BfV was discussed within the Ministry. The State-Secretary Ritter von Lex, offered me the job; it was a difficult decision for me, but after much reflection I accepted, only to be told a few days later that my name had been turned down in favour of another. In a way I was relieved, since the job of glorified policeman would not have appealed to me; but I was less than enthusiastic about the man on whom the final choice had fallen. Dr Otto John, a forty-one-year-old lawyer, took up the appointment in December 1950. The Ministry of the Interior invited me to release a good officer from my own organisation to act as John's lieutenant. I gave him Colonel Albert Radke, a very conscientious officer who put the interests of the BfV first, from the moment he was transferred.

I admit that I felt many misgivings when I heard that Dr John's name was being canvassed for the BfV appointment, and I made no secret of this in Bonn. I verbally suggested to von Lex that the appointment would be more than tactless in view of John's 'past'. John had fled from Germany to Madrid and London after the bomb plot failed in 1944, and had then worked there for our enemies. He had served under Sefton Delmer for *Soldiers' Radio Calais*, broadcasting propaganda against our troops. He had interrogated many prominent German officers as prisoners – including several under me at Pullach and some who would now be expected to work with him. Even more disturbing for me personally was that Otto John had collaborated with the British team prosecuting Field-Marshal von Manstein, one of the finest soldiers of this century. I felt the position called for a man of a character different from John's.

---

[1] The law establishing a *Bundesamt für Verfassungsschutz* was enacted on 27 September 1950.

My objections were discounted. The British authorities and particularly Sir Ivone Kirkpatrick spoke well of him, and my American colleagues raised no objection themselves. Otto John announced his intention of paying his first courtesy visit to us at Pullach not long after. General Mellenthin, my deputy, circularised all staff that three themes were taboo during the visit: John's pre-1944 resistance work, his collaboration with Sefton Delmer, and his participation in the Manstein prosecution. To everybody's astonishment, however, at a social evening in our guest house in Munich that evening John himself brought the three forbidden topics up; he tried to suggest that he had gone out of his way to help von Manstein during the trial, but without success.

The work of Otto John's office and my own organisation inevitably overlapped, particularly where our own '*IIIF*' (counter-espionage) work was concerned. Claiming that *de jure* East Germany was an extension of his German 'beat', John extended his counter-espionage channels way behind the Iron Curtain in time; we received their reports and digests and we aided them all we could with the material supplied to us by agents we had employed within the Soviet and East German espionage headquarters, but I made no use of the liaison officer the BfV had seconded to Pullach, and I kept John himself at arm's length.

At about the same time yet another Intelligence agency came into being. In October 1950 an office was set up under Theodore Blank as 'Government Commissioner for the Reinforcement of Allied Troops in Germany', as a forerunner to a West German defence ministry;[1] Blank's security adviser, Gerhard, Count

---

[1] Another duty of the 'Special Connections' section headed by General Mellenthin had been to keep tabs on the most reliable former General Staff officers, so that when the day for the re-activation of West Germany's own armed forces arrived, we could at once supply the appropriate authority with detailed lists of which former officers were to be trusted, and which had developed a post-war leaning to the east. We sacrificed 56 of our best staff officers to the Bundeswehr.

Schwerin, appointed a former lieutenant-colonel of the *Abwehr*, Friedrich Wilhelm Heinz, to set up a military Intelligence service for the 'Blank Office'. I will not devote much space here to Heinz. He was more of a politician than a soldier, and had set up a freelance espionage office after the war in conjunction with a dubious Dutch Intelligence officer who later tried unsuccessfully to blackmail him over his contacts with Wilhelm Zaisser, head of the East German secret service, and finally committed suicide. Heinz eventually retired in October 1953. Two of my colleagues, from Foreign Armies East days, Colonel Gerhard Wessel and Colonel Josef Selmayr, took command of the Intelligence branches established within the new defence ministry.

By this time we had expanded our headquarters at Pullach considerably. From the air it looked like a housing estate with tidy green lawns and flower beds surrounding the lace-curtained villas and low administration buildings. But it was an estate with a difference: the approach roads were guarded with electrically operated steel-mesh gates, there were sentries and constant guard-dog patrols around the steel-fenced perimeter.

In 1949 I had moved with my family into a villa down a secluded lane near Starnberg. Among my personal papers I still have the results of the security investigation that was carried out on my orders into the character of the village that was to be my home: it named every potential source of trouble, and identified the local communists. But it was no easy matter to emerge from the official limbo in which I had lived since 1945. Officially I was an 'economic adviser' working somewhere in America; for me to settle in a village in post-war Germany, I needed papers, and I did not have any. Relations between the CIA and the State Department were so delicately poised that this harmless task proved impossible for them; so I ordered my own 'technical section' to produce the documents I needed. In no time I was the possessor of a long, folding Red Cross identity document forged complete with my real name and photograph and a dozen different border-crossings apparently authentically stamped upon its pages (the visa stamps were the hardest to obtain but eventually these too were affixed and cancelled). The document would probably have passed scrutiny by the KGB, and the local parish authorities certainly never suspected I was not the *commerçant* the document made me out to be.

I had to devote considerable attention to my own personal safety – not without reason, for in 1953 the windscreen of my car was shattered by a projectile which, as the Munich forensic authorities later established, was a bullet. Both I and my government service driver were always armed, and I practised regularly with my revolver at an American firing range. More than once we observed that my house was being kept under surveillance; on one occasion we returned home at 2 a.m. to see one man driving off hurriedly in a Volkswagen van – the police identified him from the registration plate as an under-cover communist from a nearby town. To my neighbours I had to explain somehow how I came to possess a car, and how I earned my living; so I invented a one-man firm and had a letterhead printed: *Patent and Idea Applications and Negotiation*, a firm which did indeed do occasional business, but of which the organisation proper was unaware. The camouflage was so good that when our activities were 'exposed' by a British journalist in 1952 and I was identified as head of the service, the local villagers knew better. The general, they told each other, really made his living from his patents company – the Intelligence work was just a sideline.

The organisation itself was at first set up like a large commercial undertaking, with its national head office at Pullach, and eight 'regional head offices' distributed throughout West Germany, each controlling between three and six sub-offices. These sub-offices supervised the activities of the local branches. Abroad, we established 'residents' in the countries which were of interest to us, each controlling his own network. Initially, equipment was so scarce that we had to employ ordinary tele-

printers for our communications from Pullach – an Achilles'
heel that caused me much anxiety; gradually we were able to
replace them with coded teleprinters and an extensive system of
couriers. The old-fashioned 'inverter' type of scrambler telephone, which offered no real protection (our own wartime
Ministry of Posts had unscrambled and recorded all the trans-
Atlantic radio telephone conversations from 1942 to the end of
the war, including top secret conversations between Churchill
and Roosevelt) was replaced by a modern communications
system with the various government agencies which is absolutely proof against interception. I myself communicated with
the outside world mostly by 'teleprinter-conversations'; or I
would dictate messages on to the plastic reels of an Ultravox
dictaphone on my desk: depressing one knob erased the whole
reel immediately. (We had special machines for erasing ordinary
recording tapes, and document-shredders for our classified
materials.) A constant stream of technical experts from our
particularly closely guarded technical laboratories visited my
first-floor office, bringing me the latest items of equipment for
approval; our investment in scientific research paid off, and I
was able to aid many Allied Intelligence services in this way.[1]

The overriding security principle was that of the 'watertight
compartment': members of one network or branch knew
nobody outside their immediate unit. Even at Pullach, the
compound was physically divided into different zones, and headquarters staff were allowed access only to certain specified areas.
They received their identity permits at the main gate, so they

[1] Professor Carstens, State-Secretary in the Chancellor's Office, paid particular
emphasis to the technical aspects of our achievements in his speech to me upon
my resignation: 'Scientific progress in electronics, cybernetics and automation,
necessitated new means of information procurement: they afforded the enemy
new means of safeguarding his secrets; a veritable arsenal of increasingly sophisticated tools and gadgets has been added to the conventional secret-service
artefacts of the past. You devoted special interest to the new scientific espionage
methods and to complex data storing and analysing systems whose introduction
could no longer be delayed; you were the first to recognise the importance of this
new branch of Intelligence activity, and devoted yourself wholeheartedly and
successfully to its systematic expansion.'

could not be lost or copied outside the compound. To enter a different zone they had to be given a special stamp in their permit; only my most trusted senior colleagues had all-embracing permits on a permanent basis.

We kept the identity of our sources our most sacred secret, and in this the physical detachment of the evaluation section from the Intelligence procurement section was most important. Within the latter section a department called *Sichtung* (Sifting) checked every report the section issued to ensure that the source could not be even remotely identified, and decided into what category the source could be placed. Our best agents' reports were given a *B*-grade, less reliable sources were given *C*, and untried sources were given *D*. *A*-grades were reserved for original documents of whose authenticity there could be no doubt, and which the Federal Chancellor had an automatic right to see. Under considerable pressure from the head of the Evaluation Section, I did grant him the exclusive right to approach the head of the Procurement Section in person for verbal information as to the nature of the source – whether the report came from a minister, a secretary or a cleaning-woman; if it came from a regular source of reports, the source's code-name would be attached to the report on a slip of paper for the attention of the head of the Evaluation Section alone. His section would then decide the probability that the report was true on the basis of other material at its disposal, and a code-number would be added to the grade letter, i.e. *B*-2.

It was the Evaluation Section which had to decide whether an apparently genuine report was being deliberately fed to us by the enemy; the evaluators gradually developed a 'nose' for this, and in this way we were usually able to detect disaster approaching a particular network a long time in advance, and flash a warning to its members to go to ground. We had a particularly brilliant 'source adviser' whom we dubbed *der Quellenpapst* – the 'Pope of the Sources'; he had long been an assistant of Baun, and he carried out the same remarkable task at Pullach from 1946 until quite recently, comparing the reports with other sources and with other reports from the same source, and asking himself the all-important question: how could this source come into possession of information like that? It was the kind of job that no electronic computer will ever be able to do, and the Americans showed particular appreciation of his work.

Very few of my staff knew me personally, and if they did deal with me they frequently did not know who I was. To encourage security-mindedness, I allowed my staff to address each other only by their code-names, which are secret even now.

Occasionally the tightness of our security measures produced remarkable results. I remember that on one occasion I entered an express train at Würzburg station, and found two journalists and a third passenger in the same compartment. After a while one of the journalists began talking about the Gehlen organisation, and commented that since its head must sometimes travel by rail or air, it must be possible to come face to face with him. Two days later, I received on my desk a written report on the whole conversation: the third passenger had been a director of one of my regional offices; since such officials were never allowed near Pullach, he had recognised me as little as had the journalists. Nor had I known him.

The first phase of the Korean war was fought while these developments in Germany were taking place. The war began with a severe set-back for the Americans, and it was only the outstanding leadership of General MacArthur, in an operation of classic strategy, that enabled them to recover their balance after an almost impossible start. This Korean conflict, remote though it was, led to a considerable increase in the demands made on the American and our own Intelligence services.

Our efficiency remained unimpaired by the internal changes that became necessary because of our future transfer to federal control. After meeting Adenauer, I had advised the American liaison team that in future I intended to keep both him and the leader of the Opposition *au courant* with the Gehlen organisation by means of regular oral reports. Any information we collected which had a bearing on the internal security of the federal republic we would pass on to Dr Otto John's new office. I went over the technical details of this with John and his superior, State-Secretary von Lex, on 13 December 1950. The day before, Dr Globke had confirmed to me that the federal government intended to take us over as soon as its sovereignty had been restored, and the necessary funds were available. Finance was still the real problem: perhaps Bonn was hoping that the Americans, who had so far been the main beneficiaries of our work, would continue to bear part of the financial burden for some time to come. My own view was that, with our transfer to federal responsibility, United States financial aid should be discontinued, so that there should be no question as to where our loyalties lay. This was one of several reasons for the delay of our final transfer until 1956.

From the end of 1950 onwards I briefed Dr Globke at the Chancellor's Office every one or two weeks in Bonn. We were *de facto* serving two masters now, one in Washington, the other in Bonn. We set up a special office at Pullach to process and forward to the German government any reports of particular importance and interest; in addition on 6 February 1951 we opened a liaison office at Oberpleis near Bonn to establish and maintain contact with the various federal agencies with whom we had to work – the Chancellor's Office, the Foreign Ministry, the Defence Ministry, the Ministry of the Interior, the Finance Ministry and the BfV. As a first step towards the federal take-over, I had ordered that, as of 1 January 1950, our accounting system was to be modelled on the practices adopted by the *Abwehr*. (Until that date we had followed the American system of double book-keeping.) All non-secret costs were now accounted for down to the last pfennig, in strict accordance with the old Reich (and now federal) regulations.

It would burden the reader too much were I to list all the

various stages of the negotiations between Bonn and Pullach which paved the way for our transfer to federal control. Globke, who showed particular sympathy for my insistence that the organisation be given a free hand and not be throttled by red tape, visited our Pullach headquarters for the first time on 7 May 1951; we showed him the individual sections at work, and he was able to form a clear idea of our structure and the kind of staff we employed. On 12 July there was a further meeting with Schumacher and Ollenhauer, attended this time by Generals Heusinger and Speidel, military advisers in the 'Blank Office' who were later to take up key positions in the West German armed forces. The principal object of that meeting was to discuss how the organisation would operate in such a way as not to conflict with Germany's defence interests.

Two senior civil servants from the Chancellor's Offices, Gumbel and Grau, were particularly frequent visitors to us from 1952 onwards; one outcome of these visits and the discussions which I and my colleagues attended in Bonn was that I was able to submit to Adenauer papers on the duties and organisation of my agency, on the procedure to be employed during our take-over by the government and on the other procedural questions that would arise in the course of the reorganisation. My memorandum of 21 May 1952 which is of particular interest, is annexed at p. 362. The documents contained roughly the following proposals:

　　1] The question of a future federal Intelligence service would have to be taken up with representatives of the main political parties;

　　2] As soon as the German Treaty[1] came into force, General Gehlen and a small staff should be transferred to the government as an 'Office of the federal Intelligence service', charged with establishing a federal Intelligence service from

---

[1] The "Convention on Relations between the Three Powers and the Federal Republic of Germany" of May 26 1952, by which sovereignty was restored to the West German state.

the existing organisation and from other individuals and agencies in accordance with directives issued by the federal Chancellor's Office;

3] At the same time special sections should be set up within each ministry concerned to assist in the organisation's smooth transfer to government control;

4] The transformation of the Gehlen organisation into the federal Intelligence service should proceed in such a manner that the flow of Intelligence work could continue unimpeded and the continuity of reporting would not be impaired; and

5] Simultaneously, any other suitable groups should be merged into the organisation, and their work taken over.

As time passed, of course, these proposals underwent constant modification and refinement until the General Treaty signed in May 1952 finally came into force three years later. But these were the general bases on which we worked. The reader will have noticed that I referred to the need to merge 'other suitable groups' into our organisation. In this connection neither Bonn nor I was referring to the BfV offices at either federal or provincial level, so much as to the small, German-staffed Intelligence agencies created and financed by the western Allies on German soil. When the time for our transfer came, we were duly offered a strange assortment of such agencies; but with the exception of a particularly capable group of economic Intelligence analysts operated by the British in northern Germany, I did not consider it expedient to accept responsibility for any of these groups.

With the Treaty signed, we now began to think in terms of transferring the Gehlen organisation to government control with effect from 1 April 1953.

7. Setbacks and successes

A lot has already been written about the attempts of the communist secret services to blacken the Gehlen organisation in the eyes of the public before it could become a federal government agency. Probably in no other period since the end of the war was such an intensive Intelligence battle fought on German soil as in the early 1950s, with Berlin as its focal point, affording the newspapers every opportunity for exciting, not to say sensational, reporting. The fact was that so much Intelligence activity was crammed into a short space of time, with attack and counter-attack, that even the most superficially informed writer could hardly fail to distil the requisite colour and drama from those events and come up with a story for his editor.

This was a very damaging climate for a fragile organisation to grow in. In our organisation's early formative years we had tried to steer well clear of any kind of publicity, choosing our camouflage with care and acting very circumspectly in public. The handful of confidants among the leaders of the democratic political parties in West Germany kept the secret of our existence closely. The communist secret services – and particularly that of East Germany, which was controlled by Wilhelm Zaisser – also kept silent since they wanted to expand their knowledge, while at the same time awaiting a suitable opportunity to launch a massive attack on us. From later events it is not difficult to demonstrate that this waiting game, played by the communist secret services *vis-à-vis* an enemy Intelligence had been ordered at the highest political level.

So the east kept quiet, and it remained for a western journalist to turn public attention on to my organisation. On 17 March 1952 the well-known newspaperman Sefton Delmer published an article in the London *Daily Express* under the headline HITLER'S GENERAL NOW SPIES FOR DOLLARS. This opened the flood gates to a deluge of other articles. Delmer was well versed in German affairs as his father, Professor F. Sefton Delmer, had lectured in English at the University of Berlin and he himself had worked as the Berlin correspondent of the *Daily Express* from 1928 to 1933. As a war correspondent in the Spanish Civil War, in Poland and in France, and then broadcasting from the spurious Soldier's Radio Calais later in the war, Sefton Delmer had pumped out propaganda against Hitler's Germany. But now his continuing hostility towards Germany had evidently blinded him to the fact that our country had been recognised by our former enemies, the three western powers, and that we were now their partner in the fight against the corrosive forces of communism. In 'exposing' our organisation, as Sefton Delmer must have known, he was attacking one of the few institutions that had been fighting for the interests of the free world since long before the 1952 treaty was signed. In his article, Delmer branded the organisation as a danger for the future of Europe, and in doing so, unconsciously provided the slogan which the press hounds of both east and west were waiting for. He followed up his exposure by alleging that, under my control, the Gehlen organisation had already infiltrated every government agency of the federal republic, and that it was trying to enlarge this foothold and exert improper influence on government policy. He further charged us with deliberately shielding former Nazis and SS men from prosecution.

Although Delmer offered no proof for his attacks on the organisation and no competent or well-informed western authority associated itself with them, his allegations were given further currency by both German and foreign newspapers. Sometimes blown up into unrecognisable and spiteful proportions, Delmer's 'disclosures' were kicked around from one sensation-hunting journalist to the next, each more injured than the next at the thought that his nose for news had wholly failed to scent the existence of the Gehlen organisation until then. I retaliated in the way I thought most suitable. I established contact with a number of leading journalists representative of every political point of view, and did what I could to set the record straight. Out of these early talks emerged a regular policy of the organisation (and later of the federal Intelligence service) to maintain a proper basis for collaboration with selected representatives of the press and other news media. I will refer to our cautious public relations work more than once in the pages that follow, particularly since our organisation was both the object of much envy and the victim of misunderstanding because of these connections with the press.

The timing of Delmer's bombshell strongly suggested that he was acting – perhaps unwittingly – on someone else's order.[1] It has always been the custom of hostile propaganda agencies to arrange for the publication in some third country of either spurious or genuine allegations about inconvenient adversaries, and then to follow this up with additional material themselves, while ostensibly referring to the original disclosures. Delmer's actions, which he explained as having been prompted by his private fears about the future, could hardly have tied in better with such communist designs.

Despite this unwelcome public attention attracted to the organisation, preparations for its transfer to federal control pressed ahead. They received a great boost from the incorporation of West Germany into the western alliance under the terms of the General Treaty of May 1952 and by the agreements on the setting-up of a European Defence Community. This alliance between the German federal government and the western

---

[1] The conservative newspaper *Christ und Welt* repeated this suggestion on 19 August 1954: 'It may well be that Sefton Delmer is not a communist, as has repeatedly been claimed. It may not be his intention to play into the hands of the Russians. But that is just what he is doing.'

powers put an end for the time being to Soviet attempts to draw the western part of Germany into the communist sphere of influence. The demarcation line which had been drawn across Germany at Teheran and Yalta was thus confirmed anew as the front line of defence for the western hemisphere.

The Soviet Union recognised that its German policies had collapsed, and accelerated the total expropriation of its own zone of occupation. From now on, East Germany became one of the most important elements in the Soviet campaign to dominate Europe. Even though the Soviet-occupied zone was later transformed into a state of its own as the German Democratic Republic, and as an economic power, reached a position within the communist bloc second only to the Soviet Union, it is its importance as a forward military area that has made it prominent in every Intelligence appreciation up to the present day.

Stalin's death on 5 March 1953 occurred at a time when the Soviet attempt to mobilise their zone of occupation for the conflict with West Germany was approaching its climax. The sudden demise of this dictator, a man later to be condemned even by Moscow, raised new hope throughout the world that the Soviet policies of subjugation and suppression would be relaxed in the communist empire. In the Soviet zone of Germany there were numerous signs in those first months after Stalin's death that a process of liberalisation was taking place – but it was impossible to reconcile this process with the unwavering demands made on the zone's economy and labour force. In May 1953 the work norms were suddenly increased, and the growing aspirations of greater personal freedom were tempered by the resentment of the workers at the continuing deterioration of their working conditions.

In the middle of June, Berlin construction workers protested in the streets of the capital. On the following morning, 17 June, this wave of protest erupted into a general strike. The anti-Ulbricht movement spread like wildfire, with large sections of the population throughout the Soviet zone joining in the uprising. For many hours the fate of the lords of East Berlin seemed sealed. Then the Russian troops came to their rescue, and the national uprising was put down by force. Soviet tanks crushed the defenceless citizens, and the zone's population fell back from the brief ecstasy of freedom into the grey and lethargic existence of life under communist dictatorship, sorrowing for those who had lost their lives in the uprising. Lacking central guidance and searching in vain for signs of assistance from abroad, the East Germans on that 17 June lost all hope of seeing Germany reunified.

There are many indications that the national uprising, which is commemorated in West Germany every year with reverence and sorrow, was in fact a spontaneous act comparable only with the revolutionary movement that swept Hungary three years later. But the Russian authorities immediately attempted to indict the Gehlen organisation with having planned the 17 June uprising, and this alone was proof enough that from now on we were going to be the main target for a vindictive and persistent communist smear campaign. Two months before, in April, the East German Foreign Ministry had still been blackening the Allied Intelligence services as such and blaming them for the increased tension in Berlin; after 17 June, the big guns swivelled round on to my organisation. Wilhelm Zaisse was dismissed as chief of the East German state security service (SSD) a few weeks later. He was replaced by Ernst Wollweber.

Before this, an even more startling change occurred, of which we were the first western Intelligence service to learn. Lavrenti Beria, chief of the Soviet MGB, was overthrown and executed in Moscow.

I still have a number of papers which reflect the disturbance this caused in West Germany. One of my senior colleagues wrote in an internal memorandum,

Our views on the struggle for power in the Kremlin and the conflict on the new line in foreign policy have been confirmed with unexpected crudeness. The consequences are incalculable.

And he posed the following questions for our agents to investigate:

On the basis of what internal shifts of power could Beria's overthrow have been possible? Did his own security apparatus get out of hand? Is the influence of the party machine now greater than that of the security apparatus? Did the ultimate decision-making force, the Soviet army, back up the provisional victor [Malenkov]?

We had to investigate why Beria alone had been kicked out and not, for example, Molotov, whose political line was not unsimilar. Was it coincidence that the *Pravda* leader attacking Beria's record was redolent of Vyshinski's speeches in the purge trials of the thirties? And above all, we had to find out what the consequences would be for Soviet occupation in the communist zone and the SSD, still controlled by Zaisser: 'Are there signs of strong disagreements between Zaisser's organisation and the party political authorities?' We ordered our agents to report on the relations of the Russian MVD troops and offices and the conventional armed forces, and to keep watch on the MVD headquarters located within the forbidden zones in Berlin's Grunau suburb, particularly at Ragatastrasse and the barracks compounds at Bohndorferstrasse and Wuhlheide. Any signs that the Soviet Twenty-Fourth Airborne Army was being put on to full alert were to be reported to us at once.

Before we had time to appreciate the full significance of Beria's overthrow, we learned that Zaisser had been replaced by Wollweber.

For the next five years he was to be my most determined adversary – a man notorious throughout the world as a professional revolutionary and expert on sabotage, one of the most unscrupulous figures in Ulbricht's government. He scrupled at nothing in his war against my organisation, and at one stage he put a price of a million marks on my head; I never met him, I never saw him in film or newsreel, and as far as I know I only ever saw one photograph of him – a paunchy figure with dark eyes deep-set in a fleshy face, beneath thick black eyebrows. But it was his campaign against us that delayed our transfer to federal control for three long years until 1956. Neither his predecessor Wilhelm Zaisser, who had distinguished himself by service on the republican side in the Spanish Civil War, nor his successor Erich Mielke, came anywhere near matching Wollweber's notoriety.

When Wollweber took up his new office, he had waited a long time to emerge from the shadows and climb to this new exalted rank, as Moscow's favourite spy-hunter. He was by no means unknown to my organisation; we had followed his career with interest for a long time. Born in 1898 near Hanover, he had won his spurs as a revolutionary while a sailor in the battleship *Heligoland* in the Kaiser's navy, playing a leading part in the mutiny at Kiel in 1918. He joined the German communist party, later becoming a member of the Prussian assembly and of the Reichstag prior to Hitler's seizure of power in 1933. Meantime in the Soviet Union he was put through an extensive schooling in sabotage work, specialising in the destruction of large merchant ships. He built up an International Seamen's Union, and used it in the 1930s to organise attacks on important merchant vessels of various flags: tens of millions of pounds' worth of damage was inflicted on the British, French, American and German merchant fleets, as their largest, newest and most costly vessels suddenly caught fire in port and burned out with their cargoes. As chief of Comintern in Copenhagen, Wollweber continued this campaign, and from Stockholm after the war broke out he headed a major espionage and sabotage network until his capture by Swedish authorities in 1940. He was sentenced to three years' imprisonment for illegal entry, but the Soviet Union successfully applied for his extradition and thus recovered their saboteur for further employment.

He surfaced again in 1946, as Director-General of Shipping

in the Soviet-occupied zone of Germany, with Moscow's recommendation that he be assigned wider duties. Wollweber returned to form, resuming his anti-shipping sabotage and establishing schools to train scores of saboteurs. British shipping was a special target. On 1 May 1953 he had become State-Secretary for Shipping, but now, barely two months later, garlanded with past laurels he took over from Zaisser as head of the SSD. His primary task was to destroy our organisation and to prevent its transfer to the federal government by fair means or foul. He knew from Zaisser's example – the victim of savage criticism over his handling of the attack on our organisation – what to expect if he should fail. In the first few days after taking office, he swept aside his unfortunate pre-decessor's subtle plans and poured scorn on Zaisser's efforts. To the newcomer it only seemed necessary to round up all the people suspected of working for the Gehlen organisation in the Soviet zone in one fell swoop, and then broadcast the results with a blaze of publicity.

Within barely two months of taking office, he had already mounted his public onslaught on the organisation. As the end of 1953 approached he initiated a series of sudden and co-ordinated swoops on what he described as 'Western espionage, terrorist and sabotage groups'. Hardly a day passed without fresh raids being announced. By the end of October ninety-eight arrests had been reported in this series of 'victory communiqués' – all those arrested, allegedly members of various western Intelligence agencies, though from early November 1953 onwards Woll-weber's spy-hunters were apparently rounding up only 'Gehlen agents', for there was no longer mention of any others.

I had done all I could to make my organisation watertight and security-conscious. In Germany and abroad I travelled under different names, and in each of the three sub-sections in West Germany I was known by a different name. In the north it was Dr Schneider; I had also had an American passport issued in the name of Garner, and another identity card in the name of

Gross. I felt it better to assume the dignity of 'Doctor' since then I could be addressed anonymously as *Herr Doktor* – the less use that was made of any name the better. I knew the over-all shape of the organisation's structure, and from time to time I would be shown area charts of our operations on the other side of the Iron Curtain, but I took care not to learn too much about identities or the minutiae of the organisation's undertakings. Probably nobody knows less of the operational incidents which seem to fill the pages of modern spy books than the director of an Intelligence agency; but, conversely, the man in the field knew only what was happening at his immediate level, and could betray few other people if he was caught. I myself could always have been kidnapped, and modern science knows ways of breaking the silence of any man. If one of our agents was caught, we had ways of learning almost immediately, and we took all possible steps to tip off anybody else who might have been compromised and extract them from the Soviet zone by one or other of our pipe-lines. The taking out of one cell, or the loss of important agents, was a tragedy, of course; but I regarded my organisation as a living tree – as one branch collapsed or was cut down, another was already growing elsewhere. The tree itself survived.

Wollweber's onslaught on the Gehlen organisation reached its climax during November 1953. At an East Berlin press conference on the 9th a certain Hans-Joachim Geyer was produced to the newspapermen, and introduced as having worked for us in the Soviet zone since 1952, and then allegedly as deputy-manager of one of our Berlin offices. It is true that Geyer, author of a number of popular detective stories, had offered to operate for some months in East Germany as a 'collector' of volunteers, but for security reasons he was then relieved of that position and recalled to West Berlin, where unknown to me at the beginning of 1953 he was given a job as assistant in the one-man bureau of an agent leader. This re-employment contravened a strict embargo I had placed on permitting operatives who had been recovered from the Soviet zone to continue working in certain sensitive jobs. Geyer had indeed become a double-agent by the time of his return. At the end of October 1953, his partner asked him to obtain a new female secretary; Geyer interviewed the short-listed applicants at a restaurant – he could hardly invite them to the office – and since he could only answer evasively about the nature of his 'business' one of the girls became suspicious and reported to the police that Geyer might be engaged in some kind of white slave trading. The vice squad police called at his apartment in his absence; hearing of this on his return, Geyer feared the police were from the counter-espionage and bolted back to East Berlin, no doubt in accordance with SSD instructions.

It was only then that we realised that Geyer had been recruited and turned round by the SSD long before his return to West Berlin – and possibly even before he volunteered to work for our organisation in the Soviet zone. At the spectacular press conference on 9 November Geyer described himself untruthfully as 'deputy-manager of Gehlen's West Berlin branch' and recited a number of statements put into his mouth by his communist bosses. He had changed sides, he said, 'because his conscience troubled him', and as a dowry he had taken with him original files and personnel records from the West Berlin bureau.

I need scarcely add that I and my colleagues did not delay in taking every conceivable step to prevent similar mishaps in future. I issued instructions demanding that my security regulations be more stringently observed, since there were bound otherwise to be disasters in an organisation employing as many operatives as we did. We introduced new security precautions as quickly as we could, since we fully expected Wollweber to continue with his campaign. Geyer's treachery had meanwhile unleashed a wave of carefully-prepared arrests throughout the Soviet zone: it was later established that the majority of people rounded up in this purge had nothing to do with either our organisation or any western Intelligence agency. They were just people who had fallen foul of the government in other ways, and so were arrested. The Ministry of State Security announced the arrest of 546 spies, saboteurs and terrorists employed by the Gehlen organisation – a fantastic figure which should itself have sufficed to convince any impartial observer that this was pure propaganda; it reminded me of the RAF and Luftwaffe claims in the Battle of Britain. Even if our security had been very slack indeed, Geyer could never have picked up information about more than a fraction of the army of agents the other side was now bragging about having captured. The truth was that in his tiny bureau, which was only one among dozens of similar bureaux in West Berlin, he would have been able to put the finger on only a handful of our operatives in the Soviet zone with sufficient detail to ensure their identification and arrest.

A second, and this time more painful, blow was struck by Wollweber only four nights after the Geyer press conference, even as our efforts to make the Intelligence procurement arm of the organisation absolutely watertight were at their height. On the night of 13 November 1953, the agent-leader of one of our other cells, Major Werner Haase, vanished into thin air near the border between East and West Berlin. From the clues left behind it was clear he had been ambushed by an SSD snatch squad on West Berlin territory and hauled into the east. This was very different from the Geyer affair: Geyer's was a cowardly defection exploited to the full on the communist propaganda stage; in the case of Haase it was the daring of one dedicated officer that resulted in this further injury to the organisation.

A particularly reliable and imaginative agent, Haase had been ordered to reconnoitre a possible route for a secret telephone cable across a canal running along the sector boundary between East and West Berlin. We had expressly ordered that the actual laying of the cable was not to be risked until explicit instructions to that effect arrived. We planned to maintain contact with our agents in East Berlin by means of this cable, what is now referred to as a telephone-sluice; it would obviate the need to rely on the increasingly hazardous courier service. Although Haase was aware of the implications of the Geyer incident and of the security precautions I had ordered throughout the organisation, he decided to go ahead with the laying of the cable on his own initiative. Under cover of darkness he proposed to feed the cable across the canal using a toy steamboat, helped by an agent from East Berlin on the other side. Only later did we find out that this agent had shortly before responded to the SSD's widely publicised offer to western agents promising them amnesty if they surrendered to the authorities.

Haase was ambushed and kidnapped, and after a show trial in East Berlin he was sentenced to life imprisonment on 21 December 1953. In numerous interrogations beforehand and under cross-examination during the trial he was forced to make statements on matters we knew he could not possibly have learned in the course of his own limited Intelligence work. But he also managed to colour his testimony in such a way as to deceive the enemy on many matters, while allowing us to recognise from the trial reports that he had so deceived them. He could have faced the death penalty, a fate meted out to many of my agents in the early years; later on the communists recognised their mistake, for dead agents cannot be 'turned round'. After protracted efforts we finally managed to exchange Haase for a communist agent early in 1957. I expressed to him the organisation's boundless admiration for his intrepid work and for his exemplary courage during his trial.

At the end of the same month, November 1953, the Soviet zone's Radio Germany and communist newspapers published what they claimed was the 'interrogation report' on a 'recently captured Gehlen agent', Wolfgang Höher. We knew that Höher, another of the organisation's workers in West Berlin, had disappeared some nine months before; at the time his defection to the communists had been camouflaged as a kidnapping. According to the version fed to our organisation, a stranger had lured him into a well-known West Berlin bar, had laced Höhers' drink with some kind of powder and had then dragged out the unconscious agent, explaining that he was intoxicated. It was easily believed, because it was something that had actually occurred before on more than one occasion. (The Allied Public Safety Officer listed more than a hundred and fifty instances of political kidnapping in West Berlin during the 1950s, in which the communists resorted to 'luring and entrapment'. We know, for example, that in April 1954 the Soviet secret service in concert with the SSD succeeded in kidnapping Dr Alexander Trukhnovich, the eminent leader of the Russian émigré organisation NTS[1] in West Berlin and conveying him to the eastern sector rolled up inside a carpet. On another occasion, an SSD attempt to lure an important Gehlen organisation official – whose wife had been kidnapped – across the sector boundary by means of a fake telephone message from the Soviet zone, was happily a total failure.)

The Höher case was different. We were able to establish almost at once that he had been recalled by the SSD to East Berlin, evidently to prevent his imminent unmasking as a double-agent. It was characteristic of Wollweber's methods that he had kept Höher on ice for nine months after his defection, before producing him as a 'star witness' against the organisation. But again Wollweber and his men committed serious blunders which were bound to discredit this kind of sensational revelation, at least in the eyes of Intelligence experts. Höher described himself as the organisation's expert for espionage operations against France, and claimed that we were shadowing French personalities and were operating a 'vast and complex' network of agents in the Saar – all of which was completely untrue.

Ernst Wollweber did not get everything his own way. He needed a steady flow of incidents to feed his publicity campaign against our organisation. In mid-November he splashed in considerable detail the story of a number of arrests at the Baltic ports of Rostock and Warnemünde, and branded the

[1] The Russian initials for *Death to the Tyrants*.

organisation with responsibility for an incident with which it was entirely unconnected. In fact the arrests had taken place eighteen months earlier. It was not difficult for us to point out that these 'fresh arrests' trumpeted by Wollweber in the newspapers were *identical with those made in May 1952* – except that at that time the three men now described as 'Gehlen agents', caught red-handed installing explosive devices in the port areas, had been described as members of the 'Battle Group against Inhumanity', an organisation from whose methods we had always firmly dissociated ourselves. (The League of Free Jurists was another such idealistic but extremist organisation backed by the Americans.) The 'Battle Group' caused us most trouble: it was German-controlled, but furnished with material and financial support by the Americans; we considered the sabotage operations it conducted immoral and futile – the agents were committed to activities which might have had some point if there was a full-scale war, and they were properly co-ordinated with military operations, but which in peacetime injured only our fellow-Germans behind the Iron Curtain; bridges were blown up, public installations were set on fire, and many agents were caught and executed. Armed with the reports procured for me by Colonel Metz's department[1] I raised a constant stream of objections to the 'Battle Group's' operations with the American authorities: I tried to point out that quite apart from the clumsiness of the planning, the communist counter-measures were affecting my own networks too.

Three years later, after our transfer to West German government control, the Americans offered us control of these groups: but I could not sympathise with any kind of sabotage operations

---

[1] Colonel (later Brigadier-General) Lothar Metz had served in Foreign Armies West under von Roenne, and had joined my organisation on 22 October 1948 on the counter-espionage Intelligence evaluation side; Intelligence procurement was later attached to the same department as far as counter-espionage was concerned. From 1958 Metz was attached to our liaison office at Bonn, and from then until his retirement in 1965 he dealt with our relations with Allied Intelligence services at Pullach.

in peacetime, so I turned down the offer. These groups did not fight cleanly. All that we later took over was the personnel card-index of the 'Battle Group', but not the people themselves. We did make extensive use of American commando-training facilities (for their Rangers) in Bavaria, to teach our agents how to live off the land when parachuted into hostile territory; this training we considered necessary in case there was an attack from the east. But again these were strictly espionage agents, not sabotage. I resisted all American pressure to undertake sabotage operations behind the Iron Curtain, and I refused to invite their sabotage agents to carry out spotting missions on our behalf. The two kinds of operation must always be kept strictly separate. My own view was that in the long run only he who fights with a spotless shield will triumph – a legacy of my contacts with Canaris.

Our very effective replies to his allegations whipped Wollweber into a new frenzy of action. By the end of November 1953, it was clear to him that, even by employing the entire Soviet propaganda machine for his purposes and despite the widespread publicity in his favour throughout the other communist countries in eastern Europe, he had failed to convert the individual and local successes he had admittedly scored in his fight against the Gehlen organisation into anything like the total annihilation he had promised. At this point he made his infamous offer of a million Deutschmarks for any man who succeeded in handing me over to him, dead or alive. I know that a reward was offered not only for my head but for those of others too, for my organisation was by now well placed to secure accurate details of this kind of internal East German government pronouncement.

For several years, my organisation had employed an important agent in Wollweber's very office. At the end of November I considered the time was ripe for this man to be extracted – both for his own safety and to damn Wollweber still further. Walter Gramsch, a high-ranking civil servant (*Ministerial-Rat*),

HITLER'S GENERAL NOW SPIES FOR DOLLARS

BONN, Sunday.

WATCH out for a name which is going to spell trouble with a capital T.

It covers what in my view is some of the most dangerous high explosive in Western Europe today.

The name is spelt Gehlen and is pronounced Gale-enn.

Ten years ago this was the name of one of Hitler's ablest staff officers. General Gehlen was the Chief of the anti-Soviet Espionage Department in Hitler's Military Intelligence Headquarters. "Chief of the Department of Foreign Armies East" was his official title.

Today Gehlen is the name of a secret organisation of immense and ever-growing power.

When the Hitler armies collapsed in 1945 General Gehlen managed to escape westwards with the most important of the secret files of his department.

He kept in his control many of the top secret lists of German agents planted in the Soviet Union and the eastern neighbour States which subsequently became the satellites of Soviet Russia.

He had the key to the espionage network built by Canaris, Himmler, and Schellenberg.

So impressed

THE Americans took Gehlen prisoner. He did not remain a prisoner for long. The American Intelligence chiefs were much impressed with his ideas and the documentation he was able to put at their disposal.

They set him up in a little office of his own. He was allowed to pick out a small staff of former Abwehr officers (Admiral Canaris's German Intelligence Service).

Most of these men, needless to say, were equipped with good anti-Nazi records.

Within a few weeks Gehlen

...and he makes it pay so well that he could cast off U.S. help

Sefton Delmer's NEWSMAP

—which also brings you up to date on the riddle of the airman and Barbara

TURNER   BOBRO

was providing excellent reports on Soviet military and political activities in the Eastern Zone of Germany.

The Americans, delighted with his work, were only too ready to let him expand both his staff and the scope of his activities.

As he expanded, plenty of former Nazis, S.S. men and S.D. men (Himmler's Secret Service organisation) crept into his staff where they enjoyed full protection.

Today Gehlen is the head of an espionage organisation which has agents in all parts of the world. Many "sources" which had been planted in Hitler and pre-Hitler days have begun to work again—for Gehlen.

The Americans supply the funds. They are giving Gehlen $3,500,000 a year (£1,250,000).

Reserves

BY clever business deals Gehlen is able to multiply this sum to many times its original value.

It is believed he has already succeeded in piling up a substantial reserve which would enable him to carry on

---

independently should the Americans cease to support him.

The material collected by Gehlen, I am told, is of first class value. The interpretation of it, done by Gehlen's skilled analysts at their headquarters in Munich, has impressed not only the Americans but British and French experts as well.

The danger of the organisation lies in the future. For Gehlen's network already today has become an immense underground power in Germany. It has key men in all German Government offices, in the police, in newspapers, radio stations trades unions—everywhere, in fact.

They have even penetrated the Adenauer Government's new Secret Police office, fittingly called "Office for the Protection of the Constitution."

For the present the Gehlen organisation is only using its underground power to expand its influence still further, get its members into strategic positions, and cover ex-Nazis and S.S. men from any persecution.

Gehlen himself, I am told, is not ambitious for political power. His hope is to become the Intelligence chief of the European army.

But there are many ex-Nazis and ex-officers high up in his machine who are ambitious. They represent a real danger.

Sefton Delmer's original exposure of the Gehlen Organization in *The Daily Express* of March 17, 1952.

(See p. 178)

Stashinskyi's wife

Stashinskyi

The victim: Stefan
Bandera

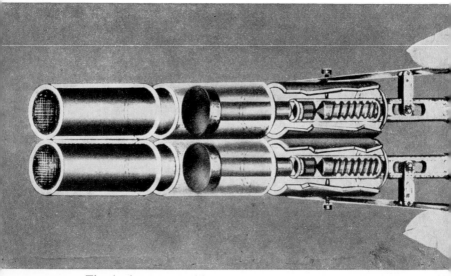
The hydrogen cyanide gun. Pressure on the levers detonated th
capsules which pumped the contents of the ampoules out of th
tubes. (See p. 265)

had been an intimate colleague of Wollweber since 1946, when Wollweber himself had been appointed director-general of shipping. In Gramsch, the latter had seen an outstanding expert on transport matters and over the years had relied more and more upon him as a general factotum. He had continued to heap praise on him, most recently in a letter dated 28 March 1953 in which he thanked him for his magnificent service on the Central Transport Commission. The manner in which my organisation recruited 'Brutus', as we code-named Gramsch, and his subsequent extraction from the Soviet sector, must remain two of the organisation's most fascinating untold stories.

Gramsch started by supplying important documents on the whole field of transport behind the Iron Curtain, and soon he was sending regular reports on the secret service work of Wollweber as well. For years he had despised Wollweber for his unscrupulous methods, and saw in him the real obstacle to the eventual reunification of Germany; so he passed on everything he could learn to our organisation, convinced that in doing so he was thwarting the plans of the Ulbricht régime and serving the cause of the German people. After the crushing of the uprising on 17 June, the flow of material from Gramsch redoubled. We were forced to discontinue 'Brutus', however, when we detected the first signs that people were becoming suspicious of his activities.

But other branches of the tree remained. At the same time as we were extracting 'Brutus' our organisation controlled two female informants of considerable significance. These were women employed in particularly important positions by the communists, and they showed unparalleled devotion to the free world's cause. One of the two must and always will remain cloaked in secrecy; suffice to say that she was a senior official of the Soviet zone's Free German Youth (FDJ) movement, an organisation primarily devoted to undermining West German youth organisations and securing footholds for penetration of the federal republic. The other, Elli Barczatis, was personal secretary to the East German Prime Minister Otto Grotewohl; the reports from her were given a very high grade, B-2, and when they emerged from the Procurement Section a slip was attached to them for the benefit of Colonel Herre, chief of Evaluation, code-naming the source as 'Daisy'. (For a long time Herre thought the material too good to be true, but when *der Quellen-papst* ordered a thorough de-briefing of the secretary, she explained convincingly how she had come into possession of the documents, and was subsequently believed.) It was one of the supreme ironies of the situation that we were receiving top-level documents and information from 'Daisy' at the very same time as Wollweber was bragging that he had annihilated the Gehlen organisation.

What she and others accepted by way of risk and personal sacrifice may sound incomprehensible, since working for one's country out of sheer idealism is nowadays a matter for contempt in West Germany. In recent years the Russians have repeatedly honoured their own spies working in non-communist countries with medals and public eulogies – a form of recognition which may well seem misplaced to some. But I would like here to place on record my gratitude to 'Daisy', for her devoted and successful work for Germany. She supplied us with carbon copies of Cabinet documents, and incidentally with a quantity of material incriminating political figures in the west, of which, however, we were unable to make any formal use. In the end her over-eagerness to help us led to her being caught out, she was tried in secret for espionage and guillotined. I will have cause to refer to her once more when I come to describe the conflict between Grotewohl and Wollweber, which led to Grotewohl's elimination.

Another of the informants our organisation could rely on at that time was none other than a former Deputy Prime Minister of East Germany, Professor Hermann Kastner. As joint founder and chairman of the Liberal Democratic Party (LDPD) he had been given a high rank in the government so as to bestow on it some semblance of bourgeois respectability (as had the long-standing chairman of the Christian Democratic Union in the Soviet zone, Otto Nuschke, who was also a Deputy Prime Minister under Grotewohl, and the Foreign Minister Lothar Bolz, chairman of the National Democratic Party (NDPD). These 'bourgeois parties' had been created by the Soviet authorities for the purpose of simulating for the benefit of foreign countries some kind of alternative to the principal government party – the Socialist Unity Party (SED). These sham parties had their government deputies nominated in advance, however, and they never attained a political status comparable with that of the SED.

Kastner placed himself at the disposal first of the Americans and then of our organisation, after a series of tedious arguments with Ulbricht and other SED officials had shown him that his own political ambitions would never be fulfilled. He had managed to preserve his excellent contacts with the Soviet occupation authorities – and particularly with the Russian Commander-in-Chief in Germany, Chuikov – but not even these could keep him on top in the East German government, though they did keep him alive. They did, however, make him a particularly valuable source of Intelligence to our organisation. Kastner decided to help first by supplying us with Intelligence material, in which his wife was of great help to us. Later on he agreed that, if we could get him out of East Germany, he would emerge in the public eye as a kind of antipodes to Ulbricht. By this time life had become intolerable for the Kastners in the east: although they possessed two villas, a service car and a chauffeur, they were constantly shadowed, and we learned from our sources that only their Soviet contacts kept them alive. Frau Kastner was almost hysterical with fear. Eventually we decided the risk they were running was too great. I put to Dr Adenauer the idea of promoting Kastner, if we could get him out, as the most prominent refugee yet to flee East Germany, and he expressed a strong interest. We arranged a date with the Kastners, and told

Frau Kastner she would be able to take only her jewellery with her – she must leave everything else behind. We spirited the professor and his wife out of East Berlin in a dramatic smuggling operation: one of our agents guided the couple through two empty buildings into West Berlin, a particularly risky operation with two refugees. We immediately flew the couple to West Germany.

We wanted to make immediate capital from their flight: we wanted Kastner to deliver a major speech to the German people, attacking Ulbricht and his régime. But while one section of the press saw Kastner's defection as a serious blow to East Berlin, others dismissed him as an opportunist who had basked in the limelight of the Ulbricht régime as long as he could, and who should not, accordingly, be allowed to make political capital in the federal capital. We were not able at that time to reveal the extent to which he had co-operated with our organisation while in office. The sniping came mainly from the Free Democratic Party whose approaches to Kastner's similar party in the Soviet zone had earlier been rebuffed. His first wife, who lived in Munich, was also less than enchanted at the prospect of the emergence of Kastner with his new spouse, and caused us many difficulties.

As the hostile clamour in the newspapers increased, we recognised it might rebound on us. We had to cast Kastner adrift, and the government decided to drop its plan for Kastner to deliver a public denunciation of Ulbricht. We would exploit his knowledge and experience in some other way. A few months later Kastner died of a heart attack in Munich's Central Station.

The increasingly noisy communist campaign against the Gehlen organisation was inevitably an embarrassment to the authorities in Bonn. While government spokesmen officially pooh-poohed the campaign and announced on one occasion that the Federal Cabinet had discussed my organisation 'for several seconds', in private it was clear that there were reservations about the early incorporation of the organisation into government service. On 11 December 1953 I was called on to testify before the EDC committee of the Federal Parliament, and Fritz Erler, the socialist deputy-chairman of the committee, put to me a number of distinctly hostile questions on the Geyer affair. That enabled me to deliver a lengthy speech on the role of the organisation and on its structure and methods, and to report in detail on the Geyer case as well. At the end of the three-hour session, Erler congratulated me and encouraged me to carry on as before. Several of the other committee members afterwards told the press they were 'deeply impressed' by what they had heard.[1]

By this time it had become increasingly plain to us that the immediate target that Wollweber had been set was to disrupt the foreign ministers' conference which was to take place in Berlin during January. Throughout December the Soviet zone newspaper and radio published a barrage of mostly outdated 'revelations' about the organisation, in a campaign of unusual scope which became explicable only when examined in the context of the Soviet political offensive that followed. I should stress here that until Wollweber personally ordered the publication of these voluminous disclosures about the organisation it had been the unwritten law of all Intelligence services to keep quiet about any important findings on the enemy's Intelligence service in order to keep the enemy guessing and to prevent him from making running repairs on his organisation. The first clue as to Russian intentions came on 11 December 1953, even as I was addressing the EDC committee in Bonn. The Soviet zone's Radio Germany accused Dr Adenauer of planning to disrupt the meeting of foreign ministers in Berlin; and at the same time,

[1] The *Hamburger Abendblatt* of 15 August 1954 reported, 'Most of them praise his confident and collected manner, his intelligence and versatility. They gained the impression that Gehlen is an expert, and his organisation is kept pure of political influence. He shows no trace of political ambition.' – *Translator's Note*

the Russians tried to brand the western Intelligence agencies as the permanent enemies of peace.

A few days later, my organisation scored an important coup in the fight against the co-ordinated Russian and East German smear campaign. One of our cells procured from the Soviet embassy in East Berlin an original copy of a so far unpublished Russian-language 'White Book'. It was a nasty piece of work, listing just about all the lying allegations that had ever been made against the western Intelligence agencies. We found out that it was intended to circulate this amongst the four foreign ministers (Molotov, Dulles, Eden and Bidault) during the conference; the main attack was to be concentrated on the Gehlen organisation. We were depicted as a dubious association of former *Abwehr* officers and ex-Nazis, and our war-mongering activities were described in bloodthirsty detail so as to disgust the conference's participants. Once again we were painted in lurid colours as an organisation whose tentacles extended right across Europe, engaged in espionage, sabotage and all manner of underground activities. Patent as the purpose of this White Book was, it was equally implicit in this onslaught that, to Moscow, the organisation over which Wollweber had spoken the last rites so frequently was still very much alive and kicking.

On receiving this book I held a series of intensive discussions with my closest colleagues at Pullach during the days before Christmas. We decided to answer the Soviet litany of allegations with a White Book of our own. Like theirs it would not be intended for general publication, but for confidential distribution to the foreign ministers meeting in Berlin if need arose. Obviously we would only use information in our White Book which we could afford to see published. The final decision on whether or not to include specific matters was one that I took on myself. Throughout that Christmas there was feverish activity at Pullach, as page by page the Soviet brochure was translated and analysed, and page by page I cleared the final text of our reply, the 'White Book on the Soviet Communist

Offensive against the German Federal Republic'. In the first part we illustrated the enemy's political activity and organisation by means of specific instances of propaganda and infiltration; and in the second, we reported on the work of the communist secret services operating against West Germany and on its soil. Whereas the Soviet publication took as its theme the alleged espionage and subversion operations of the West, our own reply contained extensive material proving that East Berlin was being used as a base for operations against the federal republic. We attached particular importance to laying bare Soviet tactics and techniques for use in Germany and to exposing their current goal – the fomenting of a popular revolutionary movement in West Germany.

When the Four Power talks began in Berlin on 21 January 1954, the Russians were advised through suitable channels that a reply to their White Book had been prepared. They thereupon decided it might be better not to circulate their own confidential brochure. Our organisation's document of rebuttal stayed locked in its safe as well – it had served its purpose merely by its existence. The conference itself ended a month later with the foreign ministers still not having made the least headway towards reaching a settlement of the German problem.

In the mid-1950s we scored another success – though admittedly more by insult than injury against the Soviet secret service through what was in fact a massive deception operation.

We called it operation 'Uranus'. It started at the uranium mine at Aue in Saxony, in the Soviet zone. From here our organisation received a number of valuable mineral samples from an agent who later transferred to East Berlin, where he surrendered to the headquarters of the Soviet secret police in the suburb of Karlshorst. But he did so on our organisation's instructions, and with our knowledge. We provided him with the material to enable him to convince the Russians that he had managed to infiltrate a (wholly fictitious) 'main controlling office' of ours in West Berlin. This ostensible double-agent persistently warned his Russian controller, the later notorious Colonel Petrov, that there was a large number of 'Gehlen agents' functioning throughout Saxony. So vivid a picture did he paint of their effectiveness that the Russians took hasty steps to smash the spy ring. After strenuous preparations, for the Russians were particularly sensitive about the area around the uranium mine, they sprang their traps simultaneously throughout the province, only to find this spurious army of agents evaporate before their eyes. This was one Gehlen network in which there were more holes than net.

In the case of Emil Bahr – no relation of Brandt's later State-Secretary – Wollweber burnt his fingers even more unpleasantly. Bahr was one of our agents who fell into Wollweber's hands immediately before the Four Power talks in Berlin were due to begin. To the press of the Soviet zone this was indeed manna from Heaven. Bahr's 'revelations' were broadcast by the radio system of the Soviet zone throughout 24 January 1954, the day before the conference began, and they were published in every newspaper there, by way of welcome to the western delegates. Since Bahr's supposed confessions included damaging details of 'widespread preparations being made by the Gehlen organisation to disrupt the conference', there could be no doubt but that the communists saw his arrest as a curtain-raiser to the distribution of their 'White Book'. A witness like Bahr, who could be persuaded to pass himself off as a sorrowing sinner, willing to expose his former bosses, was obviously worth his weight in gold – at least so long as he was to hand. We can readily imagine the discomfiture of the SSD's boss, Wollweber, when Bahr – whose presence in East Berlin had of course been exhibited to the foreign press – slipped his leash and escaped to West Berlin. Here this inter-sector commuter declared to the world that he himself had not uttered one word of his supposed confession, and that his 'testimony' has been faked from start to finish by the SSD to fit the pattern they had desired.

During the rest of 1954 it became clear even to the loyal communist in East Berlin that Wollweber had not attained his objectives. The Gehlen organisation had not been crushed – indeed, from his expostulations and statements I and my colleagues had frequently been able to make Intelligence deductions as to the chinks in our armour; we had been able to correct our earlier errors and constantly improve on our security precautions. The morale of our agents in the field remained high: steadfastly they continued to work for us, unimpressed by the communist propaganda. He had succeeded neither in destroying the organisation's machinery nor in discrediting us in the eyes of the federal government in Bonn. Though the transfer of the organisation to government control was still shelved for the time being, the very fact that I had addressed the EDC committee during December 1953 marked a further degree of indirect recognition of our organisation's existence and capabilities.

Thanks to the early contacts I had established between Pullach and the publishers and editors of selected West German newspapers and magazines of every shade of political opinion we had also succeeded in neutralising a number of press channels which had initially displayed an indecent readiness to repeat communist propaganda about us. On various occasions we were able to use the friendlier organs to put the truth in its proper context in reply to the muck raked by these irresponsible journals, and this in time served as a warning to others who might otherwise have felt inclined to publish uncritically material emanating from communist sources.

Ernst Wollweber's attempts to smear the organisation in the eyes of Allied and neutral countries of the west also proved a futile exercise. His countless distorted or lying accusations frequently defeated their own purpose, so exaggerated was the form in which the 'revelations' were publicised. In the end the SSD did itself more harm than good, because by their clumsy methods they often unmasked agents of their own, and their show trials in the long run rebounded more on the prosecutors than on the defendants in the dock. At the end of this first campaign, *Neues Deutschland* published an item which cannot have pleased Wollweber. On 24 February 1954, the East German national newspaper reported under the headline GEHLEN TO ENTER BONN'S SERVICE the somewhat premature news:

... Meanwhile it has been anounced in Bonn that the Gehlen espionage organisation, which has hitherto operated under American orders in collusion with the federal government, is to be transferred in its entirety to federal responsibility, in other words to the control of the Adenauer government.

In printing this, the official organ of the Socialist Unity Party *de facto* admitted that the broadsides the SSD had fired to prevent the federal government from taking over the organisation had failed to strike their target.

8. Transferred to federal control

Originally the transfer of the Gehlen organisation to federal control had been planned for 1952 or 1953, but this had proved impossible. The communist smear campaign and the setbacks of 1953 stirred misgivings in the politically-minded West German public, not to mention some members of the Federal Parliament, as to whether the organisation would live up to its reputation and act for the good of the federal republic if it were to enter government service.

The principal figures of the federal republic – especially Chancellor Adenauer and his State-Secretary, Globke, who had succeeded Lenz in October 1953 – refused to be deterred by the communist campaign. They remained convinced, as did the leaders of the opposition parties, that the Gehlen organisation would have to be taken over by Bonn as soon as possible. Both my American colleagues and I agreed that the proper time for this would be when West Germany's political sovereignty was restored; and this would occur when the Occupation Statute legalising the residual rights of the Allies in West Germany was rescinded (with certain exceptions[1]). This condition was met on 5 May 1955 when West Germany was accepted for membership of NATO and a mutual defence pact was signed with the United States. By then three years had elapsed since the signing of the General Agreement; and the long period of waiting before the organisation was formally taken over had been in many respects

---

[1] After the Occupation Statute lapsed, the Allies retained certain residual rights in West Germany, e.g. the sole authority to monitor private telephone conversations.

something of an endurance test. I know many of my colleagues, anxious for their futures, would have preferred the transfer to have taken place earlier. As it was, however, the organisation had been able to avoid the many teething troubles which beset the civil service at that time. By 1956, when the date for the formal transfer finally arrived, the maturing process in the federal authorities was largely complete, a circumstance which went a long way towards ensuring a smooth transfer.

The Office for the Protection of the Constitution (BfV) chaired by Dr Otto John had been under federal control since its inception in 1950 as a part of the Ministry of the Interior. This federal agency and its provincial subsidiaries was very different in character from my foreign Intelligence service. Dr John's job was to provide a defence against internal dangers like seditious agitation, espionage, sabotage and the like. His was purely a reporting function; his agency had no powers of arrest comparable with those of the Federal Bureau of Investigation (FBI) in the United States. Where the BfV uncovered the necessary evidence, it was for the regular authorities to institute the arrests. Unlike my organisation, therefore, the Office of the Protection of the Constitution had a purely domestic function. Provided the functions of the two agencies were clearly defined there should have been only a few exceptional cases of significant overlapping.

It is untrue to suggest that my organisation at any time cast covetous eyes on the BfV. A foreign Intelligence service like mine has only one task – to gather information on other countries which will be of importance in the shaping of foreign policy. If this seems a truism, it will be equally obvious that we would also obtain useful information by keeping the activities of the various international communist organisations under surveillance, and this in turn justified our operating on West German soil as well as abroad. Where the Intelligence we obtained through these sources touched on the internal security of the nation, we passed it on to the BfV as the responsible agency. This study of international communist organisations was of far greater importance for us in our analysis of Soviet foreign policy, which may explain the communist-inspired attempts to blacken my organisation for having been involved in 'domestic espionage', as they described it. Clearly I had to insist that the organisation should remain strictly impartial on internal matters, an attitude which our first Federal Chancellor did not always appreciate. I remember Adenauer more than once invited me to put our watchdogs on a certain Social Democrat official.

I would never have favoured a merger of the two organisations: the surveillance of subversive activities in West Germany calls for co-ordination and co-operation between us, not for amalgamation. In nearly every country of the world the two organisations do in fact operate independently of each other. The Soviet government takes particular pains to avoid any squabbling over jurisdiction between their espionage and security agencies.

Of course relations between my organisation and the BfV were put under a severe strain by the tragedy of the Otto John affair. Late on 20 July 1954, under circumstances which are still a matter of controversy, he crossed or was conveyed across the sector boundary into East Berlin and participated in a spectacular press conference there in August – to all appearances a defector, a top-level Soviet agent who had been recalled by his paymasters. Some time before, John had paid an official visit to the United States; I had sent a private warning to my colleagues that it would be unwise to show him too much, and this prescience on my part was now recognised by the Americans to have been justified. The fact remains that in *my* organisation it would have been unheard of for a senior official, let alone the head of the organisation, to visit West Berlin; nor is it possible to forgive him for his actions once he was in East Berlin. It was for *these* that he was later sentenced by our Supreme Court to a period of imprisonment for treason, not for the dubious circumstances of his border-crossing. In East Berlin John broadcast over the radio the favourite communist lie that my organisation was carrying out espionage against France, and suggested that West Germany was on the threshold of a new Nazi revival. He seems to have regarded me as his great rival for the role of Adenauer's Canaris; unfortunately Dr John was inclined to see all his real friends as enemies, and – far more dangerously – vice versa.

In mid-December 1955, even as a parliamentary commission of inquiry into the defection was resuming its sittings, Otto John reappeared in West Berlin. Our organisation played no part in retrieving him. Adenauer certainly had no affection to spare for the returning prodigal, and is said to have announced the news to his Cabinet colleagues with the words: 'I have an item of information which will fill you with mirth. Dr John has defected.' Ollenhauer, the Opposition Leader, privately described John as a case for psychiatrists rather than for politicians, which is an over-harsh assessment in my view. I consider Dr John deserves our sympathy for suffering a hideous personal tragedy. His eighteen months in communist hands must be attributed at most to a momentary aberration, a *Betriebsunfall* (technical hitch). He has served his sentence and there I propose to let the matter rest.

Meantime, the problem of restoring West Germany as a military power could no longer be ignored. This was accomplished in several stages. First, General Count Schwerin was appointed military adviser to Adenauer. Then a special office was created under the later Defence Minister, Blank, to pave the way for the establishment of a *Bundeswehr* – the federal armed forces. As the Gehlen organisation did not yet come under the government's aegis it proved necessary for Bonn to activate within the general framework of the *Bundeswehr* a modest military Intelligence agency with a limited scope for carrying out Intelligence evaluation. This was looked after by the Americans as well. With Minister Blank's approval the Chancellor's Office ordered this agency to collaborate as closely as possible with our organisation until such time as we were in a position to take on that work too. As a result of his detailed exchanges of ideas with the Chancellor's Office and his regular talks with me, Minister Blank willingly identified himself with my own concept of a uniform foreign Intelligence service, and over the years that followed he threw his weight behind our efforts to secure the closest possible collaboration between the Blank office and our Intelligence service. Meantime the man who has twice been my successor, Gerhard Wessel, became the liaison officer between Blank and Pullach, and he later accepted the position of G-2 to the *Bundeswehr*.

The question of transferring the organisation's headquarters from Pullach to Bonn never arose. The selection of Pullach as the site for our headquarters in 1947 had been pure chance; it had happened simply because the location answered our immediate needs and could be vacated without serious problems merely by moving out one Allied agency, a point which was not unimportant at that time. Our geographical separation from the nation's capital by some 350 miles did not hamper us in our work at all: if we were called upon to be in Bonn in person, there were railroad sleeping cars, or good airline connections, or, if need be, even motor cars. In addition I saw to it that our liaison office just outside Bonn was well staffed with high-grade and experienced experts who were available for immediate discussions if need arose. In another sense this remoteness had one great advantage: our organisation and its staff were far from the political bustle of the capital, and could attend to their work without distraction. Many another government department had cause to envy us that immense advantage.

The most complicated problems were, of course, those connected with the transfer of our staff. Would it be possible to transfer them all to government service? Whose services would we have to terminate – an unpleasant decision for any superior concerned with the welfare of his men? What would be the status of staff involved in the transfer? Would their earlier employment within the Gehlen organisation be credited to them as public service employment, and what would the effect be on them if it was not? Some of the more stubborn questions in this field remained unresolved to this day.

On the other hand we had been able to convert our permanent salaried staff to the same scale as applied to other public service officials as early as February 1953, so that at least as far as salaries were concerned we were in line with other federal agencies three full years before we were taken over by the government. This made it necessary for us to arrange our staff into the same groupings as in other departments. This was not often easy, and my colleagues and I were grateful for the advice of the Federal Audit Office on how to have things done our way, without contravening the spirit or letter of the government regulations. The net result, to our understandable pleasure, was an increase in our incomes, and this was not without its effect on the recruitment of fresh staff.

At the same time we began to convert our Pullach head-quarters to exclusively official purposes: families had to move out of the compound, and internal facilities like the kinder-garten and school were closed down. These unavoidable measures brought problems of their own: homes had to be found, and given the prevailing housing shortage the new accommodation was frequently some distance away, since, for security reasons, the village of Pullach was out of bounds. Many of the staff we had hitherto been employing had to resign, and this in turn brought the headaches of finding replacements, with whom we had still more security problems.

All these innovations were not without psychological con-sequences. Hitherto we had been, so to speak, one large family – the enforced togetherness by night and day, at work and off duty, had brought us all close to one another. Everybody knew everybody else – though very few of my staff knew me – they shared each other's sorrows and excitements and helped each other wherever possible. Naturally there was friction too; it is unavoidable in even the smallest family. But I am happy to be able to record that over all the years, the sunny side of community living far outshone the bickering. Now all this was coming to an end. The hour had struck, and we were soon to become a government agency. While it would certainly make our daily work more businesslike, it would also mark the disappearance of the indefinable something, the inner warmth and sense of real solidarity that had pervaded the Gehlen organisation since its foundation a decade before.

Since late 1950 the attitude of our American friends to the future of the Gehlen organisation had undergone a remarkable change. The two CIA directors, General Walter Bedell Smith and then, from January 1953, Allen Dulles, had recognised that my 1945 plan was bound to come to fruition, just as General Sibert had accepted in his 'gentlemen's agreement' with me. They concluded that they should support the transfer of the organisation to federal control. Over the following years American representatives had therefore held many conversations with the Chancellor's Office in Bonn in which the technical details of the transfer were thrashed out, and by various means they prevailed on their other Allies to accept what had formerly been an American-controlled agency. The expectation was that my organisation would continue to work in close collaboration with the western Allies, and the CIA was moreover convinced that this readiness on their part would pay for itself later by cementing the future political partnership between Bonn and the western Allies. In this they were not disappointed.

The lasting comradeship and trust that was born then bore rich fruit for everybody concerned. The results of a balanced joint effort between several Allied Intelligence agencies will always far exceed the sum of the component efforts. Given a regular exchange of Intelligence, facts can be double-checked, faulty conclusions can be avoided and the chances of preventing enemy infiltration of one's service reduced to a minimum. Obviously I am not at liberty to give individual examples of how our collaboration with the other NATO agencies grew up and was continually improved between 1953, when Dulles became Director of the CIA, and 1956; but I can assert that in every important crisis like the Berlin uprising of 1953, the Suez conflict of July 1956, the Berlin incidents of 1958 (in which Khrushchev demanded the withdrawal of Allied troops) and the Cuban crisis, as indeed during several episodes in Asia, our co-operation with the other western agencies stood the test.

In the course of my work I met Allen Dulles many times, both in Germany and later in the United States. We would limit ourselves to discussions of top-level policy. He pleased me by his air of wisdom, born of years of experience; he was both fatherly and boisterous, and he became a close personal friend of mine. Once he made me a gift of a small carved wooden statuette – a sinister figure with cloak and dagger whose nameplate betrayed his American nationality: 'Fnu Nmi Lnu' (the American index-card abbreviations for 'first name unknown', 'no middle initial', 'last name unknown'). This anonymous gentleman still graces my desk today. In all the years of my collaboration with the CIA, I had no personal disputes with Dulles; there were minor problems caused by different American concepts and procedures, particularly in financial affairs, but I have no cause to criticise these allies.

Nor was this close collaboration impaired by the transfer. It gained in importance from the fact that, after 1952, the West German federal government had repeatedly sent us requests for Intelligence work. These inquiries were not limited to Iron Curtain countries alone, but applied to every country in the world. Eventually there was not one country in which we did not have our sources. I regarded the growing federal interest in us as recognition of the work we had done so far, and I took good care that these inquiries were answered as promptly as could be arranged.

A natural consequence was that, to an increasing extent, the Gehlen organisation was called upon to furnish material as a basis for foreign policy appreciations whenever Bonn faced discussions of a particularly momentous character. I admit that we had at first to overcome certain misgivings from professional diplomatic quarters; given their unhappy experiences with some representatives of the *Abwehr* and the Reich Main Security Office (RSHA) during the war years, they showed a marked reserve which was only natural. But the principal officials in the Foreign Ministry set great store by our reports; and they repeatedly encouraged us, especially after our transfer in 1956, to draft summaries analysing certain specific themes. These we were able to produce in the distant tranquillity of Pullach, to the Ministry's ultimate satisfaction.

These initial misgivings did on occasions lead to grotesque situations. For example, a German ambassador once asked one of his foreign colleagues about an Intelligence report supplied by us to the Foreign Ministry, and passed on to him for his information. The report concerned some exceptionally secret activities in which the foreigner was engaged. Of course the latter – who was incidentally himself a former member of his country's Intelligence service – indignantly denied the accuracy of the report, whereupon the German ambassador reproached the Foreign Ministry with this and asked them not to bother him with such nonsense in future. A frantic search for our organisation's source immediately began in the country concerned. The facts he had provided, were incidentally, of the greatest value. About two months after this episode his report was confirmed in every respect.

As the demands from Bonn on our organisation multiplied, so, from as early as 1952, I had to set up special sections to work almost exclusively for the federal republic. From 1954 onwards the volume of work they handled intensified.

Parallel to our discussions with the various government departments, including the BfV which had been directed by the former attorney-general, Hubert Schrübbers, since the Otto John affair, we made a point of establishing contact with the provincial (*Land*) governments. For various reasons the Americans had built up these contacts in their occupation zone during the early years of the organisation's existence, while in the French and British zones the links were rudimentary at best. In Berlin they were channelled through the Allied garrison headquarters. Due to a number of tactless actions, there had been some unpleasant friction between the provincial governments and the Americans. The latter were therefore happy to see me begin to pay visits to the Prime Ministers of the various provinces. I briefed these local dignitaries on the Gehlen organisation and on my plans for a federal Intelligence service and I outlined to them how the provinces could best help us. It was in these meetings that the ground-work was done for the appointment of 'liaison experts' between my service and the provincial governments, an arrangement which was to prove exceptionally useful. I well recall my visit to the Prime Minister of Hesse, Herr Zinn, and his Minister of the Interior, Schneider, on 20 February 1953. They displayed a keen interest in the work of the organisation, particularly since various careless slips by our American friends had caused them offence in their own province. They listened avidly to all I told them, and in later years we received considerable support from them. We established outstandingly good contacts with both Prime Minister Ehard of Bavaria and his successor Högner. Without their sympathetic support we should scarcely have been able to overcome many of the obstacles that confronted us during the period of our organisation's construction.

On 5 May 1955 West Germany was accepted by NATO as a member with equal rights, and on the same day her sovereignty was restored to her. Thus the last formal obstacle to the organisation's transfer to federal responsibility was removed. We could hasten our preparations and set our hand to the main problems that were left.

The transfer could have been effected in two different ways: a law could have been passed, or the transfer could simply have been ordained by the government under the powers granted it by Article 86 of German Basic Law. The two possibilities were debated within the government, and the parliamentary committees concerned discussed them with my colleagues and myself. It is true that a special law would have anchored the future Intelligence service firmly within the structure of the government and thus have obviated a lot of the ambiguity and vagueness that later gathered round it; but on the other hand, it would have cramped both the government and the service in their dealings with each other. The service would immediately have become an inflexible body, virtually incapable of change, because any structural alterations which might have proved necessary in the future would have been sanctioned only by the passing of new laws. With opposition approval – an important requisite in my view – the government therefore opted for the second alternative. On 21 February they decided that a new agency should be set up with the style of 'federal Intelligence service',[1] attached – not subordinated – to the Chancellor's Office. Adenauer directed that the formal transformation of the Gehlen organisation into this new service should begin on 1 April 1956, the beginning of the new financial year.

The government's choice of the second alternative did not preclude the possibility of its reverting to the first at some later date, and then entrenching the new service's position by statute. As it was, the simple Cabinet decision left the government and the service's directors flexible in their approach, while at the same time enabling us to take our operational decisions without red tape while still keeping within the broad directives issued to us. Our *attachment* to the Chancellor's Office gave us something

[1] *Bundesnachrichtendienst* (BND).

of the status of a central government agency, such as the Federal Press Office; had we been *subordinated* to the Chancellor's Office, its current head would have become *de facto* the responsible superior of the federal Intelligence service and he would then have had to shoulder responsibility for all our actions and omissions.

Now, all countries have adopted the cardinal principle that their Intelligence services be granted the utmost discretion to perform their duties – obviously within the broad framework of the Cabinet directives. The requirements of security are one obvious reason for this; further, it would be unrealistic to hope that such services could be adequately supervised by lay civil servants. But the operations of Intelligence services can produce embarrassing situations which, under certain circumstances, can strain the government's relations with foreign countries – the kind of incident which even the greatest circumspection can never entirely prevent. (One has only to consider the U-2 affair in 1960, which Khrushchev swiftly exploited to torpedo the Paris summit conference in which he had lost interest. At the time, President Eisenhower stood up for his secret service chief Allen Dulles – there could be no better witness to the soldierly bearing of that outstanding president. But it was not typical of the common usage in such cases and even in America it attracted strong criticism. The British and French governments would have acted very differently.)

It is the occupational hazard of every Intelligence service chief and his senior colleagues that, in incidents of this kind, they will have to carry the can. *Raison d'état* demands that they cannot expect either public support or approbation for their actions. Every government must be able publicly to dissociate itself from incidents where an Intelligence service has 'exceeded its discretion'. It was this kind of political consideration that prompted the solution of attaching, rather than subordinating, us to the Chancellor's Office; in effect, I was *personally* responsible to the chief of that office, and hence to the Chancellor himself. An added blessing was that I could discuss matters directly with the various federal departments concerned, or with the provincial governments, without having to go through any intermediate bureaucratic stages. This direct line of communication with other departments proved vital for the rapid evaluation of the information we obtained.

Lastly, the 'attachment' process also made it possible for the federal Intelligence service to be used – as were the services of other countries – as a channel for putting out unofficial feelers before the diplomatic service itself was resorted to. This method, which in some circumstances enables a service to exploit its links with other friendly services, has the advantage that delicate matters can be explored in advance without committing the government officially. It was the method Adenauer used when he first explored the possibility of a *rapprochement* with France; even before our transfer to federal control, my organisation was employed to approach our French opposite numbers to prepare the basis for an *entente*. The advantage is that such feelers can be broken off by either side at any time with no consequent loss of prestige. Adenauer made use of these channels on more than one occasion, and he grew to appreciate them.

On only two occasions did I become involved in Intelligence contacts with the Russian secret service; I am reluctant to enlarge on them in too much detail as they are liable to be misunderstood by a West German public unversed in the requirements of Intelligence. It was through a Russian agent whom we had turned round that we received the first news that Lavrenti Beria, head of the Soviet secret service, had been liquidated – news so incredible that at first we did not know whether to take our source seriously. We prepared to exploit this man as a direct channel of political contact with Moscow, but his superiors must have suspected something, for after a year of working for us he vanished without trace before we had been able to put our ideas into operation. Although the *III F* (counter-espionage) part of this case was known at Pullach, our attempts to use him as a link were known only to Adenauer and myself; the whole affair was of such sensitivity that I destroyed all papers relating to it in person.

On another occasion a former Panzer colonel, Bogislaw von Bonin, who had been chief of the German Army's operations branch after 1944, called to see me late in 1955 and told me that he had been invited by the Russians to discuss the political future of the two Germanies, in a meeting at their headquarters in East Berlin. Bonin asked whether he ought to admit that he was a personal acquaintance of mine (though not in any sense a member of my organisation). I advised him to tell the Russians that, and also that our organisation was aware of his invitation to Berlin and the nature of the proposed unofficial talks. Nothing came of this approach – the talks merely confirmed that the gulf between the eastern and western standpoints on Germany was as wide as ever. Frankly, had I apprehended that these particular feelers would ever have borne fruit I would have sent someone more diplomatically personable than a former Panzer colonel.

For eleven years after that the Russians kept the secret of these unofficial talks, before disclosing it in characteristic style in an attempt to discredit me in the eyes of our government.[1] This piece of trickery failed, however: I had taken the precaution of recording my conversations when von Bonin visited me, and I had immediately sent the tapes to the attorney-general at that time.

The organisation's staff were transferred to federal service not *en bloc* but individually. The whole transfer took about two years to complete, and we took the opportunity of screening every member of the staff once more with respect to his ability, security record and character.

At the time the question of the Nazi past of some of the staff

[1] A retired colonel in the Soviet secret service, Vladimir Karpov, summoned *Der Spiegel*'s Moscow correspondent and revealed the story early in 1966.

was also of importance. During the post-war years we had of course recruited nobody who had not passed the proper deNazification procedures, but in some cases where staff had been members of certain Nazi Party formations we considered it appropriate to vet them once again. In the following years we repeated the vetting process several times, particularly where the few former SS members employed by the organisation were concerned. The organisation had sent certain former members of the SS who had a clean political record on special missions overseas; this was done with the full approval of the American authorities. For example, we found the Arab countries particularly ready to welcome Germans with an ostensibly 'Nazi' past. There were not many of them in our employ; the various accusations that have been made against us, of having large numbers of former SS officers working for the organisation, are mere fictions. Most of these allegations emanated from East Germany though occasionally they were echoed by the less informed sections of the western press. This was a matter that was also repeatedly raised in the special parliamentary committee established to liaise with the federal Intelligence service.

It was I who had proposed that a small parliamentary committee should be set up to look after our affairs, and this was probably in State-Secretary Globke's mind as well, for the aftermath of the Geyer affair showed how much my organisation needed to gain the confidence of the parliamentary deputies. The result was the birth in 1956 of the 'Confidential Committee', a committee consisting of the leaders of the parliamentary parties, who in due course displayed the utmost understanding and readiness to assist the service wherever it was important that they should.

And so on 1 April 1956, the Stars and Stripes were hauled down for the last time outside our Pullach headquarters, and the black, red and gold federal flag was hoisted to the adjacent masthead. All of us knew that the most exacting phase of our existence had begun: now we should find out whether the organisation was adequate in structure and concept for its new role as an official German government agency. Looking at the empty flagpole, it occurred to me that it might be a pleasant idea for the flag of Bavaria to be flown at Pullach too. I telephoned Prime Minister Högner in Munich, and the Bavarian government sent a blue and white flag soon after. It was dedicated at a small ceremony in Högner's presence, and it has flown ever since then next to the federal flag. It was wholly improper from the federal point of view, of course; but then there is much that happens in an Intelligence service that is not strictly according to the rules.

Part 3

In the service of West Germany

Knowledge of the future can not be acquired from the Gods or demons; nor can it be obtained by comparisons or measurements or calculations. Knowledge of the enemy is acquired only by human agencies.

The kinds of spies that are used are five in number: there are the native spies, and there are the spies within; there are the spies that return from the other side; there are the spies of death and the spies of life.

If all five kinds of spies are employed, then nobody will ever learn their secret ways; that is what we call a divine secret. It is the most priceless possession of the Lord and master.

The lord and master must control his spies' work in person. The spies that return are those that render the best knowledge of the enemy, so show particular nobleness unto them.

– Sun-tse, *Treatise on the Art of War*

9. The Intelligence service

I propose to preface this part of my book, which is to be an account of the work of the federal Intelligence service, with a chapter on the general character of such services. At its head I have set a quotation from Sun-tse's *Treatise on the Art of War*.[1] This Chinese philospher lived from 550 to 470 BC, and his treatise is the oldest complete theoretical work on war to have survived. It is some 130 years older than Xenophon's *Anabasis* and was written at about the time of the battle of Thermopylae, a classical struggle which was decided in the Persians' favour by an act of treachery – the antithesis of espionage. Sun-tse's treatise has found countless commentators, and their writings, together with the original teachings of the master himself, can serve even today as a comprehensive and timeless set of guiding principles for the establishment, organisation and direction of a foreign Intelligence service. That is why we can regard this service as being one of the oldest professions in the world.

One thing is common to all these legends: that Intelligence procurement is regarded as being a self-evidently necessary occupation. It has attracted a completely unjustified notoriety through its automatic association with 'treachery' in the public mind. Treachery, of course, always has been regarded as a despicable act, customarily punished by death, while 'high treason' was not necessarily so, the offender being usually 'sent to the Tower' – in Germany a fortress like Landsberg. Both crime and punishment were almost honourable. Treachery and

[1] Published by the East German Ministry of National Defence, 1957 (translated from the Old Chinese into Russian and thence into the German language).

espionage are, however, regarded as indictable offences and are subject to severe punishment in every country.

The man legally convicted of 'treason' can expect as little clemency from his judges as can the captured spy. He must accept responsibility for his actions in court irrespective of whether they were motivated by idealism or by greed. In my own life and chosen profession I have learned not to be too hasty with moral condemnation in such cases, so far as I can judge them from the human angle. Particularly in view of the recent past, I have come to recognise that each act – including even espionage and treason – must be considered in the light of the motives that inspired it, and these are completely distinct from what legalistic minds may later pronounce.

Another such case of an idealistic agent was Alfred Frenzel, a Social Democrat Member of Parliament who was arrested for treachery in 1960. Born in Czechoslovakia, Frenzel had emigrated to Britain in 1938 and eventually joined the RAF. He entered the parliament in Bonn in 1953, and sat, *inter alia*, on the committee investigating the Otto John affair, the Party's internal security committee and the parliamentary defence committee. For four and a half years he supplied the Czech Intelligence service with top secret West German defence plans and documents. My own view was that he had been recruited by the Czechs long before he entered parliament; there was certainly great alarm among the Czechs at the time of his arrest that Frenzel might give away a top agent they had infiltrated into a German news magazine (whom the BfV never managed to identify). Born as they are of deep-rooted convictions, I find it ethically difficult to condemn such acts, irrespective of whether they are committed in the interests of the enemy or ourselves, and irrespective of their consequences.

If we are to apply the same criteria regardless of nationality, it is obvious that Oleg Penkovsky and other agents sentenced to harsh penalties in communist countries for working for the west are not alone in deserving our admiration and sympathy.

We must reassess in this light the acts of Soviet spies like Klaus Fuchs, the Rosenbergs, Richard Sorge and many others, applying standards other than the purely legal ones by which they were condemned. These agents also knew that their acts exposed them to prosecution, but they still committed them, motivated so far as can be seen purely by their communist convictions. I have always regarded communism as a deadly danger, and I totally reject its ideological edifice; but nonetheless we must differentiate between the agent who risks life and limb out of political conviction and the man who is motivated purely by greed. The former, however, are the more dangerous as well as the more admirable – the ones that can be unmasked and captured only after years of painstaking work. It is hardly necessary for me to add that such an abstract and ethical approach could never under any circumstances be allowed to interfere with the due processes of law in punishing all traitors, whatever their motives.

The purpose of these remarks was to attempt to disarm some of the prejudices against secret services. They do not all work with bribery, blackmail and drug addiction; above all they need human material of the highest possible calibre. People in West Germany accused Kastner of disloyalty, but it was the far higher qualities in him that we respected. Some Intelligence services distribute cash on a lavish scale and expect to obtain results like that; but we always preferred to rely on *V*-men, volunteers, the kind of agent who would work for nothing more tangible than his expenses. It will suffice to say that numerous such people came forward, willing to risk their freedom, their health and their very life to work on behalf of West Germany, acting out of a sense of duty towards their country and out of hatred for the totalitarian system of the communists.

Much has already been written on the history of secret services, so there is no need for me to enlarge on it here. In general it is claimed that in the Dark and Middle Ages and until comparatively recent years they served a primarily military purpose.

In my view this view is erroneous, as should be obvious from the fact that (apart from in Byzantium after the decline of the Roman empire in the sixth century AD) for almost nine hundred years there were no standing armies against which espionage work could have been carried out. Only in brief periods of crisis was conscription introduced. It follows that such espionage as was conducted in those centuries must have been for political ends. Of course it was not a rigidly disciplined espionage, but it *was* centrally controlled – controlled in fact by the chancelleries of the monarchs themselves precisely as Sun-tse recommended.

Thus we know of Louis XI of France (1461–83) who smashed the tyranny of the French nobility and was the first Continental European monarch to maintain a small standing army (of Scottish bowmen) which he formed into a large permanent network of agents in the principal cities of Europe. These agents served two purposes: they culled information from various sources, and at the same time they had instructions to influence public opinion in France's favour. So even the 'influencers' now so favoured by the Russians and British are by no means a modern invention.

Other monarchs, and notably the British kings, acted similarly to Louix XI of France. Frederick the Great of Prussia employed among his official emissaries to the European courts a number of agents of his secret service with orders to keep an eye on the situation independently of the accredited ambassadors. During the Middle Ages and until the beginning of modern times the two Italian city-states, Venice and Genoa, ran regular political Intelligence organisations of a covert nature. As is shown by the secret reports filed by the diplomatic representatives and other emissaries of these states, these were in every respect the forerunners of a modern secret Intelligence service (they even used codes and secret inks). After the Italian city-states the British have the Intelligence service with the longest tradition – its roots go back some six hundred years. As an island nation, Britain was cut off from the general flow of events and the Intelligence bound up in them, and this may well have obliged the British Crown to lay its hands on additional first-hand information by whatever means it could. To this end the British service employed people of high social standing who would have access to the notables – and hence to the primary sources of Intelligence – of the countries concerned.

As in so many other fields of activity in Britain, there is an unbroken tradition in their secret service too. Time and again we came across evidence of this. This is why in my view the British Intelligence service – which may not be the biggest in the western hemisphere – is certainly one of the most efficient; indeed, only those now run by the United States and by Israel come anywhere near the British in effectiveness. The British get by with a minimum of red tape, but at the same time their SIS is treated with a high degree of confidence by both government and parliament. It is always referred to with the utmost dis-cretion – not even the name of its head may be mentioned. This discretion is of course observed by the entire British press, irrespective of whether it is a mass-circulation daily or a serious magazine, and irrespective of whether the newspaper inclines to labour or conservative opinions. Their so-called D-notice system deserves particular attention: these are confidential standing instructions circulated for the advice of editors on matters which the government of the day requests them not to publicise. The British press observes this agreement without exception. Would that such a system were workable in West Germany!

Various authors have put their hands to writing histories of the German secret service, including Colonel Walter Nicolai[1] the head of the service during the First World War and, more recently, Dr Gert Buchheit.[2] Its history differs little from that of the other European services except that, unlike them, the

[1] *Der Nachrichtendienst* (Berlin, 1920).
[2] *Der deutsche Geheimdienst* (Munich, 1966).

German service has had to wage a constant war against the tendency to ignore and neglect it. In this respect it can be compared with similar agencies of the United States in the interwar years.

The First World War had shown that in an age in which war is a paramount activity of Man with the total annihilation of the enemy as its primary aim the gathering of secret Intelligence is more important than ever before. At any rate, it proved no longer sufficient to scout around for largely military secrets; the rapid procurement of information on the enemy's foreign policy, his economic potential and his morale, attracted greater attention than before. Just how crucial such Intelligence could have been is shown by an instance from the First World War. Our High Command was unaware of the depths to which French morale had sunk after the failure of their Nivelle offensive in 1917. Had this crisis been recognised in its full extent, it might have encouraged an offensive against the main French front, instead of an attack in a minor theatre of war, namely Italy, and the returning of Lenin to Russia. Thus France gained the breathing-space she desperately needed. The Allies, on the other hand, were more precisely informed about morale in Germany: they succeeded in gauging exactly the rate at which the German will to resist was ebbing, a process heralded by the big munition workers' strike and the first of the naval mutinies; and they were thus enabled to reject the various peace feelers extended to them in 1917 with an easier conscience than if they had been wholly ignorant of Germany's precarious internal situation.

At any rate, the First World War taught us how vital it was for all one's Intelligence agencies to work in close co-ordination – assuming it was not possible to bring them all together under one roof. That was how it had always been in Britain; and in France the Deuxième Bureau of the General Staff had always performed this duty. But by the Treaty of Versailles of 1919 Germany had been expressly forbidden to establish or maintain an independent Intelligence service; so we did what we could by means of expanding the *Abwehr* (literally, 'Defence') organisation into a highly efficient Intelligence service under its successive heads, Gemp, Patzig and Canaris.

The interwar years and the Second World War confirmed the lessons of the First World War and these in turn were amplified by the lessons we and the Allies afterwards learned in the fight against the Russians – namely that sabotage and counter-espionage operations also rightfully belong within the ambit of secret-service duties. Since 1945 it has become universally accepted that only a uniformly-controlled foreign Intelligence service embracing every facet of a nation's interests has any prospect of justifying the expectations held out for it. This service must feed to the political leaders every item of secret information that they may need for the formation of policy or for the security of the nation. The information must be such as will confirm or modify the existing premises on which the government bases its decisions; but it must never be used as the sole basis for decisions – only as one source which may in certain circumstances be sufficient to tilt the balance one way or the other.

The Intelligence service's digests must be strictly non-partisan and objective. I am reminded of an episode in 1959, when Fritz Erler, the socialist politician, who was by no means complaisant about our service, paid a visit to Pullach in his role of parliamentary watchdog. During this visit he expressed his doubts about the objectivity of our *Weekly Digest*, a regular summary of the political situation. Its main section, 'Soviet foreign policy', was always read with great respect in Bonn as it was the only such condensed but easily comprehensible account of its kind at that time. Erler thought this digest reflected the subjective opinions of whoever was its author, and doubted whether its contents were based solely on Intelligence sources at our disposal. 'If that is so,' he told me, 'then it is clear you are attempting to bring pressure to bear on Bonn.' I was convinced of the objectivity of my official's analysis, but it was equally clear that I must now prove it beyond question to Erler. I sent for the official and Erler reiterated his scepticism. My man invited the politician to select any of the countless weekly digests, and undertook to provide the complete file of documentary sources used within half an hour (of which he would need ten minutes to get back to his office and another ten minutes to return). He was as good as his word. Erler was visibly impressed by the balanced and cautious picture the digests presented, when he compared them with the documents on which they had been based. I subsequently learned that from that moment on he always based his own political judgment on the *Weekly Digest* and defended it against other sceptics.

A western Intelligence service will report to its government on the plans and potential prospects of events in the countries under observation and on current and future trends in politics, arms technology and military planning. It will also report on that country's morale. It will supply facts on anything from new weapons to production statistics, military movements, the utterances of top officials and the like; it will procure secret documents, such as reports of conferences and organisation plans, and it will prepare assessments of the fighting quality of the country's armed forces. In forwarding such information every service accepts a considerable responsibility; that is why a detailed background knowledge of every factor involved, including the national character and political ideology, is indispensible. How far are the actions of communist governments conditioned by their ideology? Or how far is ideology resorted to only as a smoke screen? What part do the ties between the various national communist parties play in Soviet foreign policy? Above all, an Intelligence service's operatives must never apply their own western values in their speculations about what the enemy may do; for nothing will lead more frequently to false conclusions.

Of course, the government will always want to be briefed as

comprehensively as possible on events with which it may have to contend. Sometimes it will ask for details about the exact date and time that a certain event which the service reported as being probable is likely to occur. Complaints that this or that service has 'let us down again' are usually sparked off by developments which have taken at least the public – if not the government or its Intelligence service – by surprise.[1] But secret Intelligence on political and, to a certain extent, also on military affairs is largely a matter of prediction. That something *may* occur does not necessarily mean that it *will*.

Every political or military action can be split up into three parts: firstly the decision to act; secondly the preparation for that action; and thirdly its commission. A secret service can usually detect only the second of these stages, the preparatory stage. From its further observations it will detect what progress is being made and finally the completion of preparations. Of course there *are* occasionally great coups in which a service pulls off a master stroke and ascertains the actual decision or even the date set for an operation to commence. For example, our federal Intelligence service was in a position to report in good time that Khrushchev had decided to break up the Paris summit conference of 1960. But instances like these are the result of the purest good fortune. They do not prove the quality of an Intelligence service; this can be judged only by the consistency and regularity of its reporting.

Nor, I might add, is the value of a prediction solely to be judged on the basis of whether that prediction comes true. It is perfectly possible for certain intentions to have existed in the enemy mind at a time an Intelligence report is made, only to be revoked later because, for example, they are known to have been compromised. For instance, on 10 January 1940 documents revealing that Hitler planned to attack the western powers including neutral Belgium seven days later fell into Belgian hands. Hitler had no option but to cancel the operation

[1] The erection of the Berlin Wall was a case in point.

on the 13th. What the Belgian Intelligence service reported at the time was true, even though it was not borne out by immediate events. Unfortunately the reverse of this situation is more frequently the case: reports reaching an Intelligence service are dismissed as irresponsible by their political recipients, since they do not dovetail neatly into their own view of the situation – all too often shaped by wishful thinking. I write of this with some feeling, in view of my own wartime experiences in connection with the November 1942 Russian offensive which resulted in the encirclement of the Sixth Army in Stalingrad, and the thwarting of our operation 'Citadel' the following summer.

A major headache in the organisation of a secret service is the controversy of effectiveness versus accountability. It should hardly be necessary for me to emphasise that Intelligence work is essentially a secret pursuit: it takes place behind closed doors. That is why it is necessary to scrap the dogma prevailing for the rest of government, including the armed forces, of the accountability (*Transparenz*[1]) of public bodies for themselves and for their activities. The basic principle must always be this: whereas every other organisation must be open and everybody must know precisely what his function is, in an Intelligence service exactly the opposite applies; the organisation must be as *opaque* and *confusing* as possible to outsiders. Security considerations demand that the internal structure must contain so many watertight compartments that on occasions certain problems can be kept under scrutiny by two separate sections, acting entirely independently and in ignorance of each other, so as to bring possible sources of error to light. If the organisation of the service is easily detected by the outsider, it will not be long before the enemy finds his way in.

[1] *Transparenz* was the word under which Professor Horst Ehmke, Minister in charge of Brandt's Chancellor's Office, pressed the reorganisation of the Federal Intelligence Service. – *Translator's Note*

For similar reasons experience has shown that the organisation in the field should not be entrusted to a few large networks; it is far better to work with numerous small cells of up to ten men. Large networks lack the necessary flexibility of response; the smaller and more versatile the unit the better its security will be. They force the enemy to disperse his counter-espionage activities, and from the purely budgetary standpoint, they are more economic to run: their transport, security and so forth are cheaper. Moreover, the service's structure must constantly undergo gradual change, so that anything the enemy's counter-espionage may have learned yesterday will be obsolete and useless by tomorrow. The 'industrial' camouflage of my organisation, with its head office at Pullach and its local branches, regional head offices and 'representatives', was discarded years ago. Obviously this constant change is expensive, but security and camouflage can never be got for nothing. For similar reasons the Intelligence headquarters must never make direct contact with its operatives from the field. None of our real agents ever saw the inside of Pullach; they were met at distant rendezvous, often hundreds of miles away.

In its final, perfect form, each cog in the secret service machine must mesh so perfectly with the next that no one unit can function entirely independently of the others; if an individual unit is being manipulated by the enemy, the whole machine will sense it after a while. In this way errors and security lapses are automatically brought to the surface.

In short, if the governments of our Allies give their secret service heads a free hand to organise their machines as they see fit, they do so with good cause. The best example of this is the way the Americans run their secret service, and its history. Until the Second World War, American Intelligence had led only a skeleton existence, consisting of separate agencies for each branch of the armed forces and the State Department. But during the war, and with the active assistance of their British allies, an Office of Strategic Services (OSS) was founded under

General William J. Donovan, and by 1945 this employed some twelve thousand people and embraced the work of the other agencies referred to. To the OSS must go the credit for having recognised at a very early date the importance of science and technology for modern Intelligence work.

Before the end of 1945 the OSS was disbanded, but the need soon arose to co-ordinate the various other agencies including the FBI so as to prevent overlapping of efforts and mutual obstruction. This was achieved by the passage of a National Security Act in 1947 which set up the Central Intelligence Agency (CIA). The act established a National Security Council headed by the US President himself, to advise him on all matters of external and internal security.

The 1947 Act created the CIA as a foreign Intelligence service for the United States. Its director is nominated by the President with Senate approval from among the serving officers of the armed forces or leading civilian figures; his pay is also determined by the Act. He has the task of co-ordinating every other agency working in the Intelligence field or processing information. He is permitted to hire and fire CIA officials, alter its organisation and structure as he sees fit and fix staff salaries (bound by the sole proviso that he may not raise any salary to a level higher than his own). The CIA is supervised by its own internal inspecting authorities. In consequence the director of the CIA has all the freedom of decision that is vital to the efficient running of an Intelligence agency. In Britain and America it is an accepted fact of life that however outstanding a senior civil servant may be he will be incapable of taking over a high-ranking position in an Intelligence service if he has not benefited from years of solid experience in Intelligence work. In Germany this has been overlooked: after my retirement the position of vice-president of the federal Intelligence service was handed to Dieter Blötz, an outsider who had distinguished himself in the management of the Hamburg office of the Social Democratic Party.

The freedom of the CIA from political interference has been entrenched in an Act of Congress. Perhaps it will even succeed in outstripping the performance of the British SIS, which is an example to the entire western hemisphere. In particular, the director of the CIA is ultimately responsible to the government for all Intelligence operations, and particularly those of his own agency, and this fact explains his unusual privileges and prerogatives. Where the safety or protection of his sources is at stake, it is proper that he should not be bound by the regulations binding the rest of the public service. In all major Intelligence services of the world, except the West German since its reorganisation by the Brandt government, these matters are settled in a similar way.

I have concentrated on only a few basic aspects of the theory of modern Intelligence services. Even if these are ignored, the resulting service may still for some time outwardly resemble a hard-working and efficient machine. But even if the enemy does not succeed in penetrating it, its output will little by little deteriorate until instead of providing (sometimes inconvenient) Intelligence digests pieced together from every conceivable source, it will offer information that is wholly superficial and inadequate to justify the man-hours and funds expended on the service.

Elsewhere in the west the foreign Intelligence services are high-powered organisations answerable only to the head of state or prime minister himself. They are absolutely independent of party politics; to obviate the need for a reshuffle at the top each time the government changes, they are separate from the bodies concerned with national security, which can never free themselves entirely from the maelstrom of domestic politics.

A foreign Intelligence service is comparable with a costly scientific instrument: it must be operated by specialists of the highest order if it is to obtain the undistorted picture needed to permit a sound assessment of the potential of an enemy (or for that matter of an ally). I know for a fact that when one western prime minister took office in 1964 virtually his first act in office was to spend a whole day with his foreign Intelligence service, to obtain a briefing on the world situation as they saw it. This is one example – and there have been many others – of the exceptional importance attached by other governments to their services.

10. The Intelligence worker

Much has been written in this book about the Intelligence worker. I particularly want now to emphasise the qualities of these men and their achievements, frequently accomplished under the most adverse conditions. The subject seems so important that it deserves a chapter to itself, for it is an obvious dictum that any Intelligence service can only be as good as its best men or, to put it more fully, a service is only as good as the men who work in it, sustain it and mould its character.

Unhappily, it is with the image of the 'spy' that the members of Intelligence agencies, and particularly the staff employed by my own service, are most closely identified in the public mind. The astounding feature has always been that the people who accept this stereotype are not just addicted cinema-goers or constant readers of spy thrillers but otherwise judicious people.

Obviously the influence of films, television productions and spy novels on public attitudes cannot be ignored. In the James Bond films, or films like *The Spy Who Came in from the Cold*, film-goers are shown acts of spine-tingling horror and sadism. Few and far between are the films or books which rise above this level, and they reach only a limited audience; among films of this latter type I am thinking of the film *Canaris* with the veteran actor O. E. Hasse in the title role. It deserved particular credit for its content, message and portrayal, which was rich in conviction and verisimilitude.

The agent who fits the popular image of the super-spy, complete with false-bottomed suitcase, silenced pistol and

various items of facial camouflage, is as much a figment of the
Hollywood imagination as the beautiful female spy. Invisible
inks, dead-letter-boxes, hidden microphones and other technical aids which are also the stock-in-trade of every spy film,
are indeed tools with which no Intelligence service running
'genuine' agents can dispense; but even so they are no more
than props for the real work. Yet these illusions are dangerously
refurbished in the public mind by apparently authoritative
'insight articles', memoirs and 'scoop' literature. Above all, the
memoirs of famous spies in recent years need to be taken with a
pinch of salt. I will mention the memoirs of the Briton Philby
later, but here we need only recall the Lonsdale Papers, manufactured at breakneck speed by the Soviet KGB after the
Russians had learned of the Americans' intention of publishing
the Penkovsky Papers. (The latter were, broadly speaking,
genuine; but naturally certain items were woven into the text to
deceive the communists.) It need scarcely be pointed out that
documents published in this way are not the best material on
which to base an investigation of historical truths – nor, I might
add, are the biographies of retired Intelligence service chiefs!

The same is true of books and pamphlets emanating from the
communist side and purporting to deal with the western
Intelligence agencies. Seldom are such concentrated collections
of lies and distortions to be read as in this Soviet propaganda.
I have already described how the object of these publications
was for a long time part of a systematic smear campaign
against our service, designed to undermine our authority and
prevent the federal government from taking us over. It is all
the more unintelligible that magazines and newspapers have
reproduced entire sections virtually verbatim from these
communist pamphlets, including the fake photographs they
contain.

What are claimed to be objective histories, as those published
in East Berlin by Dr Julius Mader with titles like *The Grey
Hand*, *Secret No Longer* and *Who's Who in the CIA* are

typical products of this kind of tendentious and frequently lying publications. I do not propose to waste much time on them. In one case, however, which does not relate to my own service, I feel honour-bound to expose the fraud, since it reveals even to the layman how truth can be twisted. In his *Who's Who in the CIA*, Mader lists virtually every member of the United States diplomatic service by name, and labels each one simply a 'member of the CIA'. Yet, with a few exceptions, officials who are known to occupy senior posts at CIA headquarters are not listed at all. The purpose is simply to discredit the entire US diplomatic service throughout the world.

When we talk of 'Intelligence workers' we are referring to the permanent employees at headquarters, the operatives at home and abroad, and the agents working for the service in foreign countries. It is impossible to generalise about the latter: the agents are so heterogeneous and individualistic, conditioned by local circumstances and the requirements of the particular job that no generalisation could possibly include them all.

In the early years of the Gehlen organisation we adopted the principle that we would work on enemy soil only with agents who had volunteered out of sheer idealism to join in the fight against communism. We had, however, to abandon this principle as the years passed, for as the standard of living in East Germany improved so the flow of people volunteering to work for the west was reduced. And as the service's task expanded, the ranks of agents were now joined by a new type who sometimes worked for payment. Increasing use was made of foreigners as well as Germans. Sometimes too, we could recruit people by other means. I well recall the case of a detective who was guilty of a minor embezzlement; we were able to persuade him to work for us in return for the dropping of the charges against him. Since we concentrated on the ramifications of international communism, we also tried to recruit disaffected communists in other countries.

During the 1960s, even in the case of those agents who had started working for us for purely idealistic reasons, material considerations began to play their part. An agent working for us in East Germany would do so in the knowledge that at the end of his service he could reach the west and find secure employment. Where we did pay cash, it was always genuine; I do not believe that 'Cicero's' claim that he was paid in counterfeit notes was anything more than a refined confidence trick. No Intelligence service could afford to dupe its own workers in that way.

The West German press has now picked up the parrot cry that the Intelligence service must become 'accountable' and even goes so far as to suggest that it has become so under its new management. I must reiterate that I have always considered that there must be limits on how far an organisation and its procedure can be open to inspection. A secret service, by its very nature, should not become involved in public controversy, with the exception of a few controlled 'public relations' operations. It was because I believe the latter can be beneficial that I gave my encouragement to the television film that was produced about our service in 1964. But a *transparent* secret service is a contradiction in itself.

Service in the 'Service' is something of a sacrifice. Great is the capacity for total commitment and self-effacement which is expected of its members. They must be prepared to perform actions above and beyond the call of duty. I have already described the conditions under which we were obliged to recruit our staff during the early years of the Gehlen organisation. At that time, while we obviously undertook certain inquiries into a future operative's basic education and background, we were primarily interested in ascertaining whether he had the experience and knowledge of the communist countries of Eastern Europe that were necessary for espionage work. Apart from the criteria of being a good security risk and politically unobjectionable, these were the basic considerations on which we based our decision.

We decided whether an applicant was politically unobjectionable on the basis of security vetting, in which his political past would be the subject of detailed investigation. The deNazification procedure was not in itself enough to clear or to disbar a candidate, as we soon discovered that there were obvious shortcomings and loopholes in it. As an example of this, one only had to consider the deNazification verdicts on former officers of the General Staff, a group strongly represented in the post-war Gehlen organisation. Not one of them had belonged to the Nazi party, but without exception they were classed as Group I and II offenders, as being former members of the War Department (*Kriegsministerium*) and of senior *Wehrmacht* agencies. Many of them had to suffer property disqualification and severe penalties before they were finally deNazified and graded either as 'no longer implicated' or 'not affected' by the deNazification Law.

No candidate can be properly vetted without considering the danger to which he or his family may be exposed. If these dangers cannot be discounted, or at least reduced to an absolute minimum, the candidate must be rejected even if he appears to be otherwise particularly highly qualified. This was the basis of one of my most inflexible principles – that we would under no circumstances employ anybody who had only recently arrived from behind the Iron Curtain. During the 1950s and 1960s my orders in this respect were obviously more concerned with refugees from the Soviet zone than from anywhere else. Those who volunteered for the organisation were turned down on principle, since there was always the risk that before their 'escape' they had been assigned espionage missions in West Germany by the enemy's Intelligence service. In certain cases we had reason to believe that individuals who had had time to settle down in West Germany had been approached by the enemy's Intelligence service, blackmailed over relatives left behind the Iron Curtain, and forced to work against our service.

For the same reason we were reluctant to employ former prisoners of war returning from the Soviet Union, or from other communist countries. Hard though I tried in many instances to ameliorate their plight upon returning, we found time and time again that the Soviet secret service had been recruiting prisoners for espionage work in West Germany shortly before their release, either by threats to detain them for a few more years (most of them had been in Soviet prison camps for ten years already) or by blandishments.

In cases where people volunteered their services from West Germany or other western countries I always made the final decision myself. Obviously we could not advertise in the press for staff. Initially we recruited by word-of-mouth recommendation, and from members of our own families. I still maintain that this system will always prove the best as far as security is concerned; at that time there was anyway no alternative. Of course, this led to allegations of 'nepotism', but these left me unmoved. Certainly there has never been the slightest shred of evidence offered for the suggestion that relatives employed within the organisation received privileged promotions; as any relative who has ever worked under me could testify, the relationship is a disadvantage rather than a blessing! There can be no charge of 'Jobs for the Boys' against the federal Intelligence service either: the personnel file of every candidate for employment who was not rejected straight away was considered simultaneously by several different sections within the organisation. The greenhorn had to prove his worth, and his promotion depended solely on his capabilities.

As soon as we had the chance I tried to recruit fresh blood from various walks of public life, particularly for the higher levels of the service. Critics of our methods never revealed how they would have preferred us to recruit specialised staff: perhaps they were thinking of using the local labour exchange, or inserting discreet advertisements in the national press? I myself am convinced that the West German service – like most of the Allied services – must employ a number of 'contact men' in various walks of public life, particularly the universities, and that these must pass on regular tips as to people they believe will make good Intelligence workers. Unfortunately, in West Germany it is at present difficult to work with the universities; but in the United States they have brought this co-operation to a fine art. During my own period of office a number of outstanding academic personalities, including particularly the late Professor Bergstraesser, showed complete understanding of our needs and did all they could to help.

The conclusion is inescapable; in future the Intelligence service will have to attach the greatest importance to recruiting qualified staff from civilian, and particularly from academic walks of life, using whatever methods seem appropriate at the time. The latter will be required more for the technical sections of the service than for the administrative sections (which will be the province of those with legal training). Obviously for the technical sections certain specialised skills are needed before a candidate can be considered for recruitment to the service.

It is not easy to be specific about what is required of workers in the procurement and evaluation sections. The nature of Intelligence work differs so greatly between headquarters and field, and between home and abroad, that the worker must be a man of many qualities. Initiative and character, energy and tenacity, creative thinking and clever application, improvisation and imagination – these, coupled with specialised knowledge, are what will help an Intelligence agent to get ahead. Secret data will only dot the i's and cross the t's of an existing appreciation; they may confirm it and enlarge on it; and in extreme cases, which will always remain the great exceptions, they may even cast an entirely new light on events.

From what I have said it should already be clear that an Intelligence service must not only be in a position to procure secret information. If the raw facts it gathers are to be properly sorted and analysed, it needs an immense background knowledge, and this in turn means that the service's analysts must have at hand all the most important publications and that these must be reviewed in conjunction with the secret data when it comes to drafting the final situation digest. For example, a local newspaper in the Caucasus reported a speech by a Russian general to NCOs at a local sporting event; yet western Intelligence services last knew of him as a Soviet military commander in Rumania. We assumed that he would hardly have travelled to the Caucasus to address NCOs, and that therefore he must have been given a local posting there. The Americans were reluctant to believe us, since their attaché in Bucharest reported having seen him there quite recently. Some time later, our own deductions were confirmed by another source. I have always held that only a systematic and expert review of the entire body of public and classified material will enable an Intelligence service to turn out digests that are consistent in quality and up to date. In short, a really comprehensive Intelligence agency must dispose of top-grade specialists of every kind, for the analysis of the material that comes into its hands.

The senior analysts carry a responsibility no less marked than that of their colleagues on the procurement side. While in the latter field one's constant concern is for the agents in one's charge, often operating under the most adverse field conditions in foreign countries, the paramount requirement governing all analytical work is that of objectivity. It is an unwritten law of the Intelligence service that none of its members, not even its head, may attempt to bring influence to bear on the decision-making processes of the government. This in turn calls for a willingness and ability to set aside completely one's own personality and opinion. But equally, the job calls for a degree of moral courage, for sometimes the service is obliged to put before the government facts which are disagreeable in the prevailing climate of affairs. It is only right that anybody contemplating taking up Intelligence work – which can entail as much deprivation as it offers fascination – should know all this.

Since my retirement in 1968, much has been written about the need to reduce the average age of the service's staff, particularly of those in senior positions. Such a public debate was regrettable to say the least: at all times I gave every one of my juniors the promotion that accorded with his qualifications – it was an obvious provision for the future. But there is one limitation, which ought to have occurred to those who – presumably out of ignorance – have been clamouring most vociferously for this 'rejuvenation'. In Intelligence work, as elsewhere, you cannot get far without a full measure of experience. There may be 'vertical take-off experts' in politics, but in Intelligence work development is slow and unspectacular. If, as has happened, senior staff are appointed to responsible positions from outside the service, with inadequate experience and little background knowledge, they represent a danger. I do not deny that in certain professions, and for example in the *Bundeswehr*, special circumstances may call for a frequent turnover of staff in particular positions. In various other government departments there are certain jobs which impose gruelling wear and tear on the older staff. This again calls for a steady transfusion of younger blood. But for a foreign Intelligence service these rules do not apply.

On the contrary, it may be expedient to employ certain specialised and proven workers far beyond the normal retirement age. I am thinking of some of my senior colleagues at Pullach who were personally familiar with the communist countries under our surveillance, and were fluent in their languages. As an example, I recall that two of our finest agents (who have since died) operating behind the Iron Curtain did their best work for us long after they were both seventy. Just as the physician gains in experience with his years in practice, and his success in treating patients increases, in many cases the senior members of an Intelligence service assemble a volume of experience which no service can afford to dispense with lightly.

A man's ability to lead others is often closely related to his experience. It is of decisive importance in the field of Intelligence procurement where it is essential for him to set the agents entrusted to his command a good example, and to give them a sense of security while spurring them on at the same time to ever greater achievements. But leadership is equally important in the field of Intelligence analysis, where a group of thoroughbred and sensitive individuals has to be tactfully and patiently made to work as a team for the good of the common effort. With orders alone one can achieve little; the application of purely military command methods is quite unsuitable. One instance involving the American Intelligence service deserves mention as a warning to others. A distinguished military officer, an admiral, was appointed head of the service; within a short time he had completely failed, simply because he tried to direct the service by military and parade-ground methods. The important thing is to issue broad directives and guidelines of sufficient clarity for the agents concerned to recognise not only the headquarters' intentions, but also the sense and Intelligence purpose of an assignment.

The fact that I have mentioned only men as Intelligence workers might seem to confirm the widespread public belief that women do not make the best workers in important Intelligence positions. Here too the picture has been distorted by a number of frivolous books and films on great female spies like Mata Hari, *Mademoiselle Docteur* or *The Cat*. During the 1960s there was also a number of espionage cases in which female agents working for the communist Intelligence services in ministries in Bonn were captured and put on trial; these were eagerly seized upon by the newspapers and worked up to fit in with the popular image of the female spy. My own experience has been that many women have been able to apply themselves to the most diverse jobs, both at headquarters and in the field, with great distinction. In employing them I made it a rule that only their capability and not their sex should decide the positions they were given.

In my twenty-six years in Intelligence I established close personal relationships with many of my colleagues. I suppose that Admiral Canaris and my old friend Allen Dulles were the most outstanding of these men; but there were others among my acquaintances who are still alive today and who came close to the example set by these two men. Virtually every Intelligence service chief has distinguished himself by decades of experience in this work, and commands an unrivalled background knowledge. I, at any rate learned to value the capacity of my foreign counterparts: balanced and imperturbable, they won confidence by their far-sighted and methodical leadership, and sustained it through many vicissitudes.

The head of an Intelligence service must be able to influence his staff by force of personality but even more by his expertise and personal talents. These qualities are very different from political sleight of hand. It is he alone who ultimately decides which particular items from the vast influx of reports and other data are worth forwarding to the government. So he bears a responsibility not only for what he reports, but also for what he suppresses. His judgment, based on the labours of his staff, may be of crucial importance in the decision-making processes of his government. Obviously if the government does not have complete trust in the loyalty and ability of its Intelligence service chief and in his organisation, it would be impossible to place such a responsibility in them.

It goes without saying that all the qualities of leadership called for in the senior staff of an Intelligence service must be present in its chief. For both him and his deputy there can be only one principle: he must control the organisation trusted to his care on the basis of the confidence he can personally generate towards himself. The proper assignment of work and the delegation of authority – without going too far and losing control altogether – are the foundations which will enable him to keep a clear head for the decisions that really matter. Above all, he must control his staff appointments in person. I used to spend one hour every day reading through our personnel files. It is from him that the staff expect most knowledge and the greatest familiarity with Intelligence work in all its aspects; they will expect him to be interested in all the technical and scientific questions, and to display a complete mastery of the administrative regulations and the necessities of his staff. Last but not least, he must also show a compassionate attitude towards all welfare problems, including medical and psychotherapeutic care, which play a major role in this strenuous profession. (In one year alone we had thirteen heart-attacks at Pullach; I established a medical unit for the staff, and next year there was only one such case.) To be indifferent to such considerations would be enough to disqualify one for supreme office.

11. The BND at work

With the transfer of the organisation to federal control in April 1956, the American liaison team moved out of Pullach, and I moved my office from the small brownstone house we had occupied since 1947 into the big main building on the other side of the street: it was a red-roofed building set in a magnificent garden, surrounded by a rose-covered pergola and a steel fence; on the ground floor there were spacious reception rooms and halls, and my own room was on the first floor – a room about twenty feet square. By one of those freaks of the changing fortunes of foreign policy, it was panelled in a rich light brown timber that was part of a pre-war Russian shipment to Hitler from Moscow. (I need hardly add that I had a special section check the woodwork regularly for Russian 'bugs'.) The only concessions to our special profession were the folding wooden window-shutters *inside* the room, and a box of cigars that graced my desk: a humorous former colleague who had left to join the tobacco industry had presented them to me, and it was some time before I noticed that the cigar bands had been printed with the word *Geheimdienst* – 'Secret Service.'

I hesitated a long time before deciding to include in this book any chapters on the work of the federal Intelligence service (BND) itself. For twenty-six years I occupied a senior position in Germany's various Intelligence services, and for the last twenty-two years I was head of the Gehlen organisation and of the BND that succeeded it. The twelve years in which I headed Germany's foreign Intelligence service have remained indelibly in my memory, and it has not been easy to make a selection from the superabundance of impressions, from the ups and downs of many dramatic years.

Two features distinguish me from the small number of contemporary authors who have purported to write about my organisation: I know the *true* facts in all their details; though in the interests of national security there is much that I regretfully feel unable to relate. None of my foreign counterparts – I am thinking of Allen Dulles particularly in this context – has ever reported in detail on the secret foreign operations of their services.[1] Even many years after the event the disclosure of operational plans and episodes could provide the enemy Intelligence agencies with important pointers, and do untold damage to one's Allies. Nevertheless I am very conscious of the fact that many readers will expect me to narrate certain well-known episodes in far greater detail than have been given in published sources. They will hope that I will correct previous versions of incidents which, by design or ignorance, have been wrongly reported hitherto, with consequent public controversy and loss of confidence in the service.

I will try to strike a golden mean between the requirements of security and the justified curiosity of the public, and describe a few particularly important events as they occurred, and the part my service played in them. Nearly all the episodes I will describe belong, as is only natural, to the great conflict between Communism and the free world. Virtually all of them have as their background areas which I – regarding them from a purely Intelligence viewpoint – term 'permanent crisis zones'. The first of these is Central Europe, with the special conditions created by the division of Germany and the isolation of Berlin. Then comes Eastern Europe, its recent history scarred by bloody uprisings in the name of national liberation and the brutal Russian measures of repression; the Middle East, where

[1] Allen Dulles's book, *The Craft of Intelligence*, (London 1963) reveals little about the CIA.

latent tensions have twice forced the world to hold its breath, in 1956 and at the beginning of the 1970s; Asia, where the Vietnam war has followed that in Korea and where Red China has steadily increased in influence; and Central America, where the communists have succeeded in establishing a base in Cuba from which to subvert the whole of Latin America and which can be expanded into a military bridgehead from which to launch an assault on the United States at any time that the political situation may call for it.

Prior to the transfer of our service to the federal republic in 1956, my directives to our Intelligence procurement section were that they should concentrate mainly on espionage in and observation of the communist empire, both its military strength and the important changes it was undergoing. After our transfer to federal control, however, our terms of reference were enlarged to include the activities of international communism in the other crisis zones. This significant expansion was executed stage by stage until its completion in 1960; eventually I had agents watching the communist movement in virtually every country of the world. Only in the United States did we refrain from establishing a network of our own, for the FBI functioned perfectly and we needed only to address our inquiries to it to learn all we needed. I attached particular importance to establishing contacts in even the remotest regions, to ensure that we had some opportunity of gleaning information independently of our Allies. It was in these remote regions, where intensive espionage would have proven very costly and even then incomplete, in view of the vast areas involved, that the work of our analytic section came into its own. Our evaluators pieced together their reports from a multitude of scraps of information until the whole mosaic was complete.

I need scarcely add that I tried to put to good effect all the latest technical aids in expanding the basis of our Intelligence work. I took a personal interest in finding out and testing as much as I could of the modern processes and equipment. I was fascinated by some of the items involved – the codes, chemicals and inks. I made a point of reading all the scientific journals, and visiting the laboratories where special devices were developed and tested, both in West Germany and the United States. We carried out advanced electronic research, so that our workers in the field would be properly equipped; and a computer was installed at Pullach, not only to aid our code-breakers but as a data bank (at the time of my retirement we had still not solved all the problems connected with computerised data processing). I also had experts studying the part that could be played in Intelligence work by various specialised skills like medicine and psychology. I had in mind the possibility of compiling psychological studies of leading enemy figures, as the British SIS did with notable accuracy in the case of Khrushchev for example.

All our most important Intelligence reports were transmitted by coded Telex to Bonn, either to the Foreign Ministry or to the Federal Chancellor. Globke later told me Adenauer was an avid student of all our reports, reading up to ten pages of them every day and taking them home to study in further detail. About once a week I would drive to Bonn and report in person to Globke or Adenauer. Sometimes we at Pullach would receive an Intelligence report which we considered wrong, but we were bound to forward it just the same if it was important, while making clear in the commentary we attached the reasons why we discounted it. If Adenauer went abroad he turned to us rather than the Foreign Ministry for details about that country.

There is one thing I must however make quite clear about our espionage activity. The German press has repeatedly claimed that we carried out intensive domestic espionage on West German political figures, although our legitimate duty was purely foreign espionage. It is absurd to believe I would be so foolhardy as to risk the future of the BND by getting mixed up in internal political espionage, which is the duty of the various offices for the Protection of the Constitution. Obviously before there was a federal government and before the BfV was established we kept the communist party in what became the federal republic under surveillance, but we discontinued this as soon as the proper authorities began to function. Moreover, every report which emanated from Pullach was filtered through a special section attached to my own office, which had strict instructions to ensure the non-partisan nature of the reports. I believe it did its job magnificently, and I am convinced that not one report containing BND material on domestic political affairs was forwarded to Bonn during my tenure of office.

Of course I am only too well aware that the communist countries have repeatedly raised this allegation in the hope of injuring the service. They have employed the most diverse channels to air these allegations, supported by what appear to be actual examples, and West German newspapers have frequently followed up these claims in good faith and given them publicity. We certainly never shadowed Ollenhauer, as has recently been suggested – a man whose absolute integrity was conceded even by his staunchest political opponents. On the other hand in the years prior to the establishment of the BfV we had naturally kept an index of all known communists in West Germany at our headquarters in Pullach – we would have been failing in our job if we had not. Our preparations for the period of transfer to federal control and the associated reconstitution of the organisation as the BND were to stand us in good stead. The new federal Intelligence service was able to flex its muscles that same year.

In two different theatres, a hot and arid summer heralded the storm that was to come later in 1956. In the Soviet-dominated part of Europe, the signs multiplied first in Poland and then in Hungary that there would be manifestations of the same yearning for liberty as we had seen crushed by Russian tanks in East Germany barely three years before. While the security forces succeeded in localising the unrest that flared up in

Poland, in October 1956 the floodgates of revolution burst in Hungary. As we had secretly predicted in Intelligence appreciations some time before, the people suddenly arose in a violent insurrection and seized power in the first days of the uprising. But the Russians moved swiftly, threw several divisions of troops into the unhappy country and subjugated it for their satraps to rule again.

A flood of Hungarian refugees descended on Austria and Bavaria, and they brought with them the real possibility that the Russians' tanks might not halt at the Hungarian frontier but – under the pretext of stamping out the rebels' nests abroad – continue to roll westwards into the free half of Europe. The agonising question of whether they would do this was what the federal government were now asked to answer. We had a wealth of Intelligence material relating to this, and we were able to follow the precise course of the Russian military movements and operations and see how they fitted in with the context of Soviet power politics. I myself became convinced that the Russians (just as in 1953 in Germany, and again in 1968 when they invaded Czechoslovakia) were solely concerned to demonstrate their military might, so as to quieten down their restless satellite empire. We were accordingly able to advise the government that there was no call to fear that the Soviet military operations would spill over into Austria and Bavaria.

The Hungarian tragedy, of course, occurred in the very heart of our Intelligence area. The growing Middle East crisis brought the first extension of our Intelligence effort to a non-European area, strategically placed between Europe, Asia and Africa. Almost simultaneously with the Hungarian uprising, the Israelis attacked Egypt; and when it seemed likely that the fighting on the Suez front, which was complicated by the intervention of the British and the French, might spread to a military conflict on an international scale, our service was in a position to report rapidly and accurately, with newly acquired contacts dramatically proving their worth to us. For several days Bulganin issued ultimata which culminated in his threat to subject London and Paris to rocket attack; a constant exchange of ideas proved necessary between the Allied Intelligence agencies and ourselves. In these discussions I recognised with considerable pleasure that our service's 'launching' into the Middle East had been a complete success. While many contacts built up there by our Allies in their traditional hunting grounds had been hampered and sometimes completely crippled by the watch kept on their diplomatic missions (the British came off better than the Americans) our own agents, working with unorthodox methods, were able to preserve their unrestricted freedom of movement.

I chanced to meet my American colleague and partner Allen Dulles at the height of the Suez crisis. His own assessment of the over-all situation was perhaps somewhat more pessimistic than my own, but we both agreed the Soviet rocket bombardment threats should be regarded simply as sabre-rattling bluster. We were both convinced that Moscow was a long way from actually putting her finger on the button.

Thus the events in Hungary and on the Suez Canal were the first real tests for the new federal Intelligence service. I have therefore related them before an event which decided the international flavour of the 1950s as no other. This was the ceremonial launching of the dangerous Russian policy of 'peaceful co-existence', which began to make itself felt during that crisis year of 1956.

Ours was the first, and so far as I know the only, Intelligence service to obtain a complete transcript of Nikita Khrushchev's secret speech to the Twentieth Party Congress on 25 February 1956. In it the communist party leader announced what he described as a new policy towards the Soviet empire and her neighbours. According to him, 'peaceful co-existence' would lead not only to a relaxation of the permanent confrontation between the power blocs of east and west but would also guarantee a future in which they could live together without fear of strife. It was not long before it became clear that all these promising noises were nothing more than the familiar Soviet ploy of embracing the enemy and softening him up for the final kill, as Lenin had always advocated. While outwardly the Russians continued to propagate this principle they simultaneously rearmed their forces for the resumption of the conflict between the world's power systems – but using other methods and other means.

The whole complex communist machine throughout the world was now called on to support Soviet foreign policy under this new slogan of 'peaceful co-existence'. It was hardly surprising that there were people in every country and even non-communist governments who accepted the new Moscow message at its face value and put their faith in it. The Russians seemed to be achieving their first aims almost without effort. But Khrushchev's speech was immediately subjected to detailed analysis by the Soviet experts we employed, and they concluded that the danger to the free world was now greater than ever. I warned many of our correspondents abroad of the results of our analysis and of the grim consequences of taking Khrushchev at his word. The experts among them had already reached the same conclusion themselves, but in West Germany there were many people who were reluctant to heed our warnings; they regarded us all as incorrigible 'cold warriors'. Many were as entranced by this creeping Soviet poison of 'peaceful co-existence' as a rabbit that has been hypnotised by a snake.

It was only when the Russians smashed the Hungarian uprising eight months later that it became plain even to the most diehard optimist that the Russians were not prepared to extend their much publicised 'peaceful co-existence' to their own sphere of influence. Seldom can a lie have been so swiftly exposed. It is incomprehensible that most people have contrived to obliterate these tragic events from their memories so quickly –

just as they have already virtually forgotten the Soviet invasion of Czechoslovakia in 1968.

If 1956 had barely allowed the new service respite to consolidate itself as a government agency, the following year was marked by a calm that bordered on the monotonous. In the field of diplomacy the troubled waves of the previous autumn had subsided. In West Germany the political parties and the public began to get accustomed to the idea of a federal Intelligence service.

At the beginning of 1957, however, the BND was once again the target of an East German smear campaign. No one who had lived through the propaganda barrage against the Gehlen organisation of the early 1950s could be taken by surprise. But, *Neues Deutschland*, the principal organ of the Socialist Unity Party in East Berlin, fired the first shots on 27 January with an article headlined GEHLEN AIDED THE COUNTER-REVOLUTION IN HUNGARY. This was wholly untrue; promoting insurrections is the kind of makeshift which achieves nothing except to expose the bankruptcy of one's own policies. This did not prevent them from printing fictitious evidence to suggest that the service had been spinning its recondite web in Hungary, and had sent in agents to support anti-government forces in their insurrection, just as we had allegedly done prior to the uprising of 17 June 1953 in East Germany.

The new smear campaign was reminiscent of Wollweber's earlier assault on the Gehlen organisation by the mass media of the communist bloc, aided by the communists' and their fellow-travellers' publications in the west. Wollweber had frequently exploited isolated arrests of our agents as a foundation for the most fantastic allegations against us; as this flow of 'suspects' had dried up, he had satisfied himself with inventing wholly fictitious fresh sins for us to commit. In time he had even begun to snipe the prime minister, Otto Grotewohl. Initially Grotewohl had been able to restrain his ambitious and unscrupulous rival, but he suffered a severe setback when Wollweber was able to use the affair of Elli Barczatis as a trump card against him (this was, it will be remembered, the personal secretary of Grotewohl, who was in our employ). When she fell into Wollweber's hands the secret service chief had Grotewohl just where he wanted him.

By the end of 1957, however, Ernst Wollweber, the professional revolutionary and sabotage expert of the 1940s, had come to the end of his road. On 1 November he was demoted from the Central Committee of the Socialist Unity Party, his espionage organisation in ruins as a result of his barren and unimaginative management. This abrupt downfall represented a severe censure for the officials and functionaries who had shielded him. In February of the following year Grotewohl and his two top officials, Schirdewan and Oelssner, lost their positions in the Socialist Unity Party's *Politbüro*. For Grotewohl the overthrow of Wollweber was sweet revenge, but he himself was already a broken man. He had been the leading member of the post-war socialist party in East Germany, which had merged with the communist party to form the Socialist Unity Party, and it was he who had long tried to keep senior members of the 'bourgeois' parties in his Cabinet to shore up its reputation. Grotewohl had tried to steer a relatively moderate course and there were numerous feelers from him to the West German government; but he never managed to build a bridge that was quite strong enough to enable him to bail out as did his Deputy Prime Minister Professor Hermann Kastner.

As for Wollweber, it is probably one of the most remarkable episodes in the history of East Germany that the minister who for years had been built up as our great adversary finally attempted to apply his revolutionary experience to bringing about the downfall of his own comrades. There can be no doubt but that he was planning to dispose of Walther Ulbricht, according to the information reaching us. That his last actions before dismissal have been cloaked by the East German govern-

With a newspaper Heinz Felfe covers his face from the cameras. Felfe (below left) and his accomplice Hans Clemens (right) were put on trial in 1963 before the Federal Supreme Court. (See p. 271)

Gehlen in his uniform as a Lieutenant-General of the Bundeswehr

ment in an almost impenetrable darkness is something that can be understood only too well.

In the autumn of 1958 the world's attention was once again focused on the former German capital, Berlin. On 27 October Ulbricht announced that 'all Berlin' was 'the sovereign territory of the German Democratic Republic'. This claim was at first regarded by most of our politicians in Bonn as little more than a one-man *coup de théâtre*, and shortly afterwards it was followed up by equally aggressive posturing by the Soviet party leader Khrushchev. On 10 November Khrushchev called for the 'repeal of Berlin's Four-Power status', and two weeks later he repeated this demand in a note couched in identical terms. In East Germany these claims were clearly recognised for the threat they were; scores of refugees arrived in the west, spreading anxiety and fear throughout the country as so often on earlier occasions. But the government was able to counter this with its own sober appreciation, in which it was aided by the Intelligence we supplied. We recognised the initiative as a renewed attempt to exploit Berlin's 'lever effect', which the Russians had put to such impressive use earlier in the 1950s; the city had retained its importance as a pivot of Soviet foreign policy ever since. During those autumn weeks of 1958 the federal Intelligence service was repeatedly pressed to give its opinion; we replied that while Khrushchev and Ulbricht would push the Berlin crisis as far as they could, they would not take it to the point of a violent solution.

In January 1959 it became clear from the Soviet proposals for a German Peace Treaty that the Russian leaders regarded their campaign for a settlement of the German and Berlin problems as by no means over. They seized their next opportunity to act during the Four-Power foreign ministers' conference at Geneva, which was to last for almost three months that summer. But despite unsubtle Soviet threats to sign a separate peace treaty with their puppet government in East

Germany if the western powers continued to oppose them, the Geneva talks ended without profit for Ulbricht. From the reports which reached Pullach, it was clear that disappointment in East Berlin was keen: all the greater was the effort they now determined to invest in the celebration of the tenth anniversary of the foundation of the German democratic republic in an attempt to secure its *de facto* recognition by western countries.

Ulbricht personally took charge. He dispatched his emissaries not only to the capitals of the communist-bloc countries, but to London and Paris as well, to persuade their most noteworthy politicians to attend the celebrations in East Berlin. One of the most important of these emissaries, E., had already volunteered years before to work for the Gehlen organisation, and through him we now learned every detail of the preparations. The first acceptances of former French premiers and of well-known British Parliamentarians soon arrived; by their presence as guests of honour, it seemed, they would show the world that Ulbricht's was a regime worthy of international recognition.

Seldom have I had to take a harder decision, as head of the service. Our informant was one of our most valuable sources, with exceptional opportunities for access to secret material in East Berlin. Ought I now to discontinue him, extract him to the west, in the hope that we could prevent the appearance of the prominent French and British politicians in East Berlin? I put the whole matter to the Federal Chancellor, Dr Adenauer, and secured his approval before I decided on the appropriate counter-move: we would evacuate E. with his family to the west, and dispatch him immediately in secret to Paris and London again, this time with the job of persuading those he had so recently invited to East Berlin to cancel their acceptances. The coup was successful: East Berlin had to celebrate the coming-of-age without any prominent visitors from London or Paris. As for E. himself, he now lives in the west, a free man.

While for West Germany and its Intelligence service these two years had been overshadowed by the international dispute over the German problem, by the beginning of 1960 we observed the first dim outlines of a far graver confrontation looming up over the Soviet Union. An increasing volume of Intelligence flowed in, confirming what had at first been little more than vague prophecies by politicians about a growing aggravation of the relationship between the Soviet Union and Red China. I will refer in more detail to this greatly over-estimated conflict elsewhere; it will suffice to say here that for many years to come it was to destroy the united front of international communism, and for a time even to jeopardise the supremacy of the Soviet Union. Our organisation was the first western Intelligence service to report in detail on the coming rift with Red China, but I was always at some pains to keep it in perspective. I recall how Globke once told me after Adenauer returned from his visit to Moscow that the Russian leaders had assured the Chancellor that their real problem was with China; it took some effort on my part afterwards to persuade the Chancellor that this was not really so.

We at Pullach recorded our opinion on this permanent trial of strength in numerous subsequent analyses. At first some of the most experienced observers we employed doubted whether there really would be any split between the two communist super-powers: after all, the supreme maxim of international communism, which they had observed most recently in the Korean war, was that the ultimate defeat of the capitalist enemy was attainable only by the combined efforts of communist movements throughout the entire world. These early doubts seemed confirmed by indications we received of 'voices of reason' speaking out among the top communist hierarchy, urging immediate steps to seal the widening gap between Moscow and Peking. But we soon received unshakable documentary evidence that the conflict was becoming more bitter, and we learned many details of the mutual hatred felt by each side for the other. The BND was unable to sit on the fence any longer. We concluded in our reports that the dispute would be a long one, but that a major armed conflict between the Soviet Union and Red China was *out of the question*. We could not credit China with the slightest chance of overcoming her crippling backwardness in arms technology and economic development in the foreseeable future.

This was an opportunity the western world should have grasped. In my view it was of the utmost importance to put out feelers to Peking with the aim of securing a *détente* in Russia's rear. If we were to strengthen our hand in dealing with the Russians, then we had to come to terms with their potential enemies. It was a mystery and disappointment to me that the west hesitated for too long. The consequence of this lack of unity in the West has been, in my opinion, that this split between the giants of the communist camp has been only inadequately and marginally exploited by the west.

Seen against this awkward background, it is easier to understand what a godsend the U-2 incident of 1960 was for Khrushchev, a brilliant opportunity for him to distract attention from his own difficulties with Red China. The American Intelligence service had been flying photographic reconnaissance missions over the Soviet Union since 1952, using very high-altitude U-2 aircraft; the results wholly justified the high political risk involved in such an unusual operation. Unfortunately, a U-2 piloted by Francis Gary Powers was shot down over Soviet territory on 1 May 1960. He was put on trial and imprisoned, and two years later exchanged for the KGB 'resident' arrested in the United States, Colonel Rudolf Abel. For a long time it remained a matter for speculation whether the aircraft had been downed by a chance shot from some modern Soviet anti-aircraft missile system, or whether the incident had been planned a long time before and only awaited the order to be issued for its execution. Suffice to say that at Pullach we received enough information to indicate that the shooting down occurred at a moment which was not exactly inconvenient to the Russians. Khrushchev used the incident as an excuse to break off first the summit meeting in Paris sixteen days later, and then the Geneva disarmament talks shortly afterwards. It is obvious that his almost orgiastic outburst in Paris was caused by more than mere indignation at the incursion of an enemy reconnaissance plane.

East Berlin continued throughout 1960 to prosecute with undiminished vigour its smear campaign against my Intelligence service. In November a book was published in which were concentrated all the attacks that had ever been made on us. The author of this book, *The Grey Hand*, published by Kongress Verlag, East Berlin, was the notorious Dr Julius Mader. With *Squaring Accounts with Bonn's Secret Service* as its sub-title, it contains such incredible distortions and allegations and is enriched with such clumsy forgeries that it would not be possible to answer them all in detail even if I felt it really necessary. As the head of a sinister undertaking with evidently inexhaustible opportunities for sprinkling poison and toppling politicians – friend and foe alike – I myself am portrayed in the book as some shadowy mastermind, compared with whom the great manipulators and intriguers of world history pale into insignificance.

When I was asked about this standard textbook of defamation, I limited myself to the statement that it was intended to discredit the BND as a whole and myself as its head in particular, in foreign eyes, and to undermine our Allies' and colleagues' confidence in us. (This was clearly the purpose of the 'evidence' that was served up of our espionage work in western countries.) Of equal importance was the aim of bringing the service into disrepute in West Germany itself. We were depicted as a state within a state, 'politically ambitious', dominated by adventurers of dubious past who were recklessly sacrificing their agents' lives behind the Iron Curtain: in short, the sooner the BND put the shutters up the better. It speaks well of the sense of responsibility of the larger part of the West German press that they saw through these transparent claims and recognised the real purpose of East Berlin's *Agitprop* experts. For the communists the consequence was an embarrassing failure, and *The Grey Hand*, which they had distributed with such tumultuous publicity, was totally disregarded in the west.

One of the incidents whose effects on world events were to be felt in full only later was the collapse of the seaborne invasion of Cuba launched by a force of Cuban exiles bent on the overthrow of the Castro regime early in 1961. After the end of the débâcle, there was powerful public criticism in the west of the American Intelligence service, not all of which was unjustified. Allen Dulles's CIA was accused of having failed completely, and of having neglected to provide sufficient aid for the anti-Castro elements that had launched this operation to liberate Cuba. These accusations were backed up with claims that the over-optimistic reports supplied by many 'native informants' (i.e. based on Cuba) to the effect that large sections of the population would rise in support of the invaders, were palpably untrue. There have been allegations that the CIA originally promised large-scale military aid from the United States mainland for the invasion operation, and that this was not forthcoming; but so far there has been no absolute proof one way or the other. One is entitled to assume that the Cuban exiles mounting the invasion would hardly have hazarded their lives unless the United States *had* promised them some such support.

One thing is beyond dispute, however: had the United States taken its courage in both hands and made the decision many people in the free world expected of it at that time, the world would have been spared the real Cuba crisis of eighteen months later. The truth is that there were certain overriding reasons why the United States deemed it appropriate to the interests of world peace not to react as the Russians would certainly have reacted under similar circumstances. Moreover it is not improbable that Washington underestimated the significance of this island nation, and that this played a contributory part: they believed that though Cuba might be right on their 'doorstep', it was too diminutive a nation ever to cause real trouble.

As we read the incoming cables at Pullach at the time, I remember describing it to my colleagues as incomprehensible that the United States should fumble this unique chance of military intervention to eliminate Castro. This was the result of our own in-depth analysis of the future role Cuba might be expected to play on the international chess-board. Oddly enough, I suspect that the Americans were themselves largely to blame for Castro's overthrow of the dictator Batista. It is clear that the Americans did not move a finger to aid Batista, while in Castro, who was known to have had a devout Jesuit schooling, they believed they could see a leader who would restore democracy. But now, by mid-1961, his Cuba had become a grave danger to world peace in two respects. First, the Russians could equip her as a kind of outsized 'aircraft carrier'; where they could base not only their aircraft, but their missiles and submarines. Second, she could be used as a base for the communist subversion of Latin America.

After the Bay of Pigs fiasco of 17 April 1961, only eighteen months passed before the United States was forced to the brink of war to halt the placing of Soviet missiles on Cuban soil. Since then the presence of Russian military advisers in Cuba has become an accepted fact of life. And the realisation that young East Germans are being trained in Cuba for infiltration into West Germany has meantime been brought home to the German public with sufficient emphasis. Thus Cuba represents a latent military threat to North America, and a real psychopolitical threat to the south; her tentacles have penetrated so deeply into the countries of Latin America that it is only a matter of time before she secures impregnable bases on the mainland.

At Pullach I issued the necessary orders for this communist activity emanating from Cuba to be placed under surveillance. We intensified the efforts of our espionage network against the spread of world communism in South America, particularly in Chile, and reported the results in our regular analysis of Soviet strategy in the west.

The most vociferous criticism of our service occurred whenever sudden actions by the communists in East Berlin were allowed to succeed apparently without resistance. I repeatedly had to calm down my colleagues, who often reacted with great bitterness to the lack of understanding and to the unjust criticisms from the public, and there were times when I would have dearly liked to contradict the falsehoods published about our work. It has always been the lot of the Intelligence services to be blamed for anything that goes wrong, even when other things are going right, and I do not suppose that the future will be any different in this respect.

The gravest of these criticisms, a criticism with which some politicians identified themselves, was that we failed to provide warning of the communist plan to build the Berlin Wall in August 1961. The truth is that in countless individual reports before that date, we indicated that the situation at the authorised crossing points in Berlin was worsening, and that East Berlin would have to stem this mass flight of labour which was costing them far too many of their skilled workers and specialists. Otherwise the Ulbricht regime would face catastrophe. Many items of information showed that it would not be long before the communists had to take rigorous steps to constrict this flow. Then we learned from a reliable source that the Russians had given Ulbricht a free hand, so that only the date was left open to conjecture. We reported to Bonn that a *totale Absperrung*, or total shut-down was imminent. We received and passed on further reports of an imminent sealing of the sector boundary, particularly within Berlin itself, and of the stockpiling of light materials suitable for the construction of barriers. (Later it was claimed that our agents did not detect the stockpiling of the necessary heavy building materials – steel girders, stone slabs, and concrete – that were used to construct the wall in its final form. This claim ignores the fact that the wall was erected in its solid form only at the end of an operation lasting about a year. In the beginning, the barrier was a light and temporary structure, which could have been withdrawn at the least sign of force from the three western Powers.)

We could not predict the actual date they would start; it was known, we later found out, only to a handful of top party officials. When the day dawned, barbed-wire barriers were put up at first. It was only when they saw that the tanks of the protecting Powers in West Berlin made no move to flatten these barricades that more permanent material was unloaded; and even then the barrier that was constructed was nothing like the Berlin Wall we know today – with its tank traps, minefields, watch-towers and other permanent defences.

This example illustrates lucidly the limitations of Intelligence work. Working against dictatorial regimes with all the means of a police state at their disposal, active Intelligence will frequently succeed in learning of the enemy's preparations for particular operations. Often it will be possible to deduce the approximate date as well, from second-order information such as economic fluctuations, weather conditions or known political events. But when the precise date is kept a closely guarded secret, it will seldom, if ever, be ascertainable (particularly since in a rigidly disciplined organisation it will generally be announced only at the last moment). In this particular case, it is difficult to see how knowledge of the *exact* date would anyway have altered the situation.

In view of the criticism that was voiced against us, I ordered a complete file to be drawn up later that year. This established that the service had more than performed its duty in warning the authorities in Bonn in good time. The leader of our parliamentary assembly, Dr Eugen Gerstenmaier, and many other politicians who were permitted access to the file, all vindicated us from the allegations levelled against us.

A few days before the first barbed-wire barrier went up, the West German public was shocked to learn of an affair that ought to have unmasked the true face of communism to them and imprint the image indelibly on their minds. One day, a KGB agent, Bogdan Stashinskyi, turned himself over to the West Berlin police and confessed that he had murdered two well-known exiled Ukrainian politicians. He had killed the politician, Lev Rebet, on 12 October 1957 in Munich, and Stefan Bandera, a former Allied agent and leader of the anti-communist group OUN[1] which Stashinskyi had infiltrated four years before, on 15 October 1959 in the same city. He claimed he had carried out both assassinations on the direct orders of the Soviet KGB; he had shadowed both these 'targets' for a long time in Munich on the orders of the KGB chief Nikolayevich Shelyepin (about whom we shall be hearing more), and finally disposed of them with a specially designed poison-dart pistol provided to him by Moscow. This was a silent gas pistol which fired one capsule of hydrogen-cyanide into the victim's face, poisoning him immediately. Stashinskyi himself had been given a pill to swallow beforehand, as an antidote to any cyanide fumes he might himself inhale. On each occasion, after perfunctory medical examination, the deaths had been ascribed to heart failure. Shelyepin had personally bestowed the Order of the Red Banner on him for these deeds.

The whole affair was so monstrous that after the first numbing

[1] Organizatsia Ukrainishikh Nationalistir (the organisation of Ukrainian nationals consisting of anti-Communist emigrés).

sense of outrage that such crimes should have been committed on German soil, in the heart of Munich, there were numerous sceptical newspaper reports. The consensus of opinion was that the peace-loving Soviet Union could not have been responsible. The deaths of Bandera and Rebet were now accepted as unnatural, but they were comfortably labelled as the obvious outcome of 'internal power struggles within the émigré organisations', as in a similar case in which the exiled politician Czermak opened a parcel addressed to him at a Munich post office, and was blown up by the bomb it contained. We knew that, like Bandera, Czermak was one of our men, so we were in no doubt as to who had mailed this present to him. Two days after the West German authorities made public the news of Stashinskyi's confession, the communists called a press conference in East Berlin complete with the familiar contrite 'ex-Gehlen agent', and announced that the truth was that the orders for the elimination of Bandera and Rebet had been issued not from Moscow, but from Pullach. This hint was taken up by a number of western publications.

But Bogdan Stashinskyi, who had been persuaded by his German-born wife Inge to confess to the crimes and take the load off his troubled conscience, stuck resolutely to his statements. His testimony convinced the investigating authorities. He reconstructed for them the crimes precisely as they had happened, revisiting the crumbling business premises in the heart of Munich where Lev Rebet had been entering the office of a Ukrainian exile newspaper, his suitcase in his hand, when the hydrogen-cyanide capsule had exploded in his face. He showed them too how he had left Rebet slumped over the rickety staircase. The case before the Federal Court began on 8 October 1962, and world interest was revived in the incident. The outcome was a foregone conclusion. Passing sentence eleven days later, the court identified Stashinskyi's unscrupulous employer Shelyepin, as the person principally responsible for the hideous murders, and the defendant – who had been able to give a highly credible account of the extreme pressure applied to him by the KGB – received a comparatively mild sentence. He served most of it and was then released. Today the KGB's 'torpedo' is living as a free man somewhere in the world which he chose in the summer of 1961, a few days before the Wall was erected across Berlin.

12. 'Moscow calling Heinz Felfe'

The Stashinskyi affair taught us a multitude of different lessons. Thanks to his confession and his co-operative behaviour, we were able to establish beyond all doubt in the eyes of the world that two political assassinations had been planned and executed in the west for which the head of the KGB, Shelyepin, was responsible. The careful planning and perfection of the means employed permit us to conclude that similar methods and devices must have been used to eliminate inconvenient anti-communists in other cases. Several political assassinations in the west, which had remained unexplained until then or whose perpetrators had been allowed to escape for reasons of expediency, could now be explained without much difficulty: they were 'special operations' by the Soviet secret service, or those of the other satellite communist countries.

It was no novelty for our Intelligence service to be blamed by communist propaganda for having liquidated these prominent émigrés ourselves; we were repeatedly accused of using the most brutal forms of sabotage, intimidation and murder. I wish to emphasise that every one of the Intelligence organisations I ever controlled always dissociated itself from any kind of violence. Nobody has ever produced a shred of evidence to the contrary. This is why one of my most disagreeable memories is of the way in which East Berlin used the death of the Liberal Parliamentary Deputy, Wolfgang Döring, to impute to the BND some kind of mysterious involvement in the deaths of many well-known politicians. Many are the contemporary politicians who would like to be able to eradicate all memory of the murders of Bandera and Rebet in Munich from their minds. How else could they even contemplate inviting Shelyepin – the man identified by the German supreme court as having commissioned the assassinations, but now promoted to leader of the Soviet Trades Union Congress – as an honoured guest to West Germany? Not all of us can boast of consciences as easy as the politicians'. 'Why bother about the Past?' they ask themselves. 'We have got to learn to live with the Russians, and Life Must Go On.' In the Stashinskyi affair, to display such an attitude was not only an offence against public propriety, it was downright incomprehensible as well.

It was equally unintelligible to me that our government did not utter the smallest squeak of protest to Moscow about the murders committed on its soil. Bonn has no sense of sovereignty. This was brought home to me with even greater force a year later when a leading French opponent of De Gaulle, the OAS Colonel Antoine Argoud, was kidnapped in the heart of Munich and left next day in a van parked outside a police *préfecture* in Paris. In France he was a wanted man, having been sentenced to death *in absentia* for political offences. (We ourselves had had tenuous contacts with the FLN movement in Algeria, and De Gaulle's government had made use of these channels in its early dealings with them.) We were in no doubt but that De Gaulle himself had sanctioned Argoud's abduction, but we waited in vain for Bonn to register a formal protest at this violation of our sovereignty. So the BND raised its own complaint through secret service channels: I instructed our colonel – who was attached to the embassy in Paris – to lodge a stiff protest with my opposite number in France. In the interval we had learned that an independent French secret service group was responsible, and we had no hesitation in identifying them sufficiently in our protest to compromise the French minister concerned. If a formal protest is properly made, and clearly justified, then it need not affect one's long-term relations with a neighbour, and our own co-operation with the

French SDECE remained exceptionally close. Its head, General Grossin, used to visit us about twice a year in Pullach.

By this time I had a far more worrying problem on my desk, one of the most damaging episodes in the entire history of the federal Intelligence service. This was the affair of Heinz Felfe, a top Soviet agent who we discovered had been working for ten years in the headquarters of the BND at Pullach. For week after week the affair continued to hold the newspaper headlines: his character, his Nazi past and his subsequent treachery were grist to their mill, resulting in increasingly exaggerated reports about us and not infrequently in astringent criticism as well.

There can be no doubt but that Felfe was an extremely adroit and intelligent worker; he was mobile, slight in build, and active. His complexion always seemed pasty, as though he suffered some chronic internal disorder. He was a man of few friends, but no enemies either; the type constantly and unsuccessfully seeking contact with his fellow men, who instinctively brushed him off without being able to explain to themselves why. He was married, and lived at first in a small apartment in a residential part of Munich. At the time of his arrest, Felfe was working as an assistant adviser in the section which handled counter-espionage work against communist networks in the west. He had risen to the modest civil service rank of a probationary *Regierungsrat* and was known internally only by his code-name 'Friesen'. Whereas other Soviet double-agents arrested in West Germany had been fed with 'bait material' of only limited value, on Shelyepin's orders Felfe had been given secrets to feed to us which can only be described as unique in the history of the Intelligence war between east and west. This was their way of ensuring that he was rapidly promoted within the Gehlen organisation and subsequently the BND. After he in turn had won the confidence of his communist employers by furnishing them with important documents and other 'deliveries' from Pullach, Felfe was kept well supplied with priceless political Intelligence to pass on to us. These reports sometimes contained important state secrets of the East German government; the Russians sacrificed their satellite government to build up the traitor's prestige within the BND and to give the impression that he was one of our most dependable Intelligence procurers. It will demonstrate the ruthlessness of the KGB if I reveal that at one stage, to speed up his promotion still further and to enhance his access to classified material, the KGB sacrificed one of its own political agents in West Germany; a step rare even for the Soviet secret service. Through Felfe they fed to us in cleverly regulated doses the clues that led to the arrest and conviction of C. A. Weber, the editor of the magazine *Die deutsche Woche*, an agent who acted for the Russians out of mistaken idealism and had long been under observation. Thus the agent who was of the greater value to Moscow was permitted to deliver his less important colleague to the sword.

For many years Felfe had been able to work without attracting serious suspicion. But experience shows that if a flow of reports is on balance 'too good to be true', it will in the end bring suspicion on and the downfall of the officer who procures them. This, broadly speaking, was where Felfe first went wrong. During 1960, one of the analysts working in our counter-espionage section tipped us off that something about Felfe's work was wrong. Now we put Felfe under the microscope without his being aware of it. Nothing the Russians could do could block the painstaking internal security investigation which was put in hand by our security section. The secret was from start to finish confined to myself and five others – neither my vice-president Hans-Heinrich Worgitzky nor my personal assistant was aware of it. Under my direct supervision the security section began a screening process which was to last many months until the mosaic of evidence was complete.

We learned that Felfe had purchased an expensive house with grounds at Oberaudorf, and had begun boasting of the financial transactions with which he had raised the funds for this; but (although he undoubtedly received large sums of money from the Russians) almost immediately we discovered to our chagrin that he had indeed taken the precaution of financing the house purchase with a regular home loan. Our first inclination then was to send our experts in to search Felfe's house during his absence – in other words to break in, without leaving any signs of having done so. This might have provided us with the confirmatory evidence – a photographic laboratory or wireless transmitter – that we needed to pull him in. But our experts explained that this would be illegal, and that any evidence found by such means would have no legal standing in a trial.

Thus our hands were tied for many months by our quaint West German laws. We could not act against the man, although we were convinced he was an agent for the other side. The strain of going on working with this senior colleague can be readily imagined. As the security section's file of circumstantial evidence grew thicker, I had to find some means of restricting Felfe's freedom of movement within the compound without arousing his suspicions. I instructed his immediate superior to pick a quarrel with him, and to see that Felfe was given no new cases to deal with for the time being. We intended Felfe to attribute his 'shelving' to the bad odour the row had provoked. All my instincts suggested we should find some pretext to dismiss him forthwith, despite his civil service status: the fact that he had concealed his Nazi past from us would have been grounds enough, and Globke would have done the rest. Only Moscow and the KGB would benefit from a public scandal involving the BND. But as the investigation unearthed evidence of the extent of his treachery, it became clear his arrest and trial were inevitable. There was no attempt to sweep the affair under the carpet as has been claimed.[1]

---

[1] Recent publications have talked of an 'anti-Felfe group' at Pullach, who insisted on formally warning me that Felfe was a traitor very early on, and that my private secretary took written notes of their warnings. It is further claimed that after Felfe was arrested, I arranged for the destruction of these notes. This

For several months prior to his arrest, we deliberately fed certain material to Felfe in the knowledge that this would be taken as authentic in Moscow, so we did not entirely lose by the affair. Felfe continued to suspect nothing. Indeed, he approached the personnel section and pointed out that his three years' probation as a *Regierungsrat* were over. He asked for a permanent civil service grade, and applied for a transfer to the post of security officer in our ComInt section (Communications Intelligence) – our most sensitive area. I was able to block this, and also prevented the award to him of a gold medal for ten years' service to which he was now formally entitled.

By the end of October 1961 the evidence was almost complete. We had even intercepted wireless messages from the KGB to its agent at Pullach (whom we now of course believed we had identified) asking for advice on how to handle the propaganda campaign against the Stashinskyi confessions. We set the normal legal procedures in motion, and without any hesitation I ordered that the affair be brought to its distasteful conclusion. At the attorney-general's request neither I nor my deputy were present when Felfe was summoned to the office of General Wolfgang Lan'kau, head of our strategic Intelligence section and the senior ranking officer after us, and arrested. In his possession were a number of microfilms of our classified documents, and a miniature recording tape. Two accomplices, one of whom was not a BND employee, were arrested soon after. I have always held that such black sheep will be found in the best of families, and the Allied Intelligence agencies certainly recognised that none of us was proof against such affairs, however rigorous the security precautions. One Allied service cabled: 'Congratulations. We are still looking for the Felfe in our own ranks.' It would be uncharitable for me to say which service sent it.

is incorrect. My secretary has moreover confirmed separately that there was no such 'group' and no such notes.

The federal investigators now revealed the full extent of Felfe's treachery and its probable consequences. In the interrogation it was disclosed that he had been recruited by a fellow ex-SS officer called Hans Clemens who had been persuaded by a KGB officer to work for the Soviet secret service during a visit to East Germany, where his wife lived. As a courier, they had made use of one Erwin Tiebel, who, like them, had been born in Dresden and had served in the SS. These were the three who had now been arrested. Clemens stated that he had agreed to serve the communists out of his hatred of the Americans and to avenge the allied bombing of Dresden in 1945; Felfe gave the same reason. Over the years of his service Felfe had secretly supplied the Russians with regular copies of the BND's weekly digests, and the monthly reports of the BfV on its campaign against communist agents in West Germany; he admitted supplying some fifteen thousand frames of microfilmed documents and twenty reels of tape-recordings, and he confessed to receiving more than DM.310,000 (about £27,000). Since Felfe proved to be an incorrigible liar, the real extent of his treachery will probably never be known.

It may well have been less than he claimed. I understand that a volume of memoirs will shortly be published under Felfe's name, for which purpose the Soviet KGB has released material. From what I know of the facts, I have reason to believe that he did not work as successfully as Moscow had hoped and as no doubt the book will suggest. The 'watertight bulkhead' system I had introduced between the various sections of our headquarters had severely restricted his field of view at Pullach. That he was an incurable braggart was shown by his claim at his trial to have been one of Schellenberg's top agents in Switzerland during the war, and to have secured information on the Tehran and Yalta conferences 'out of the mouth of Allen Dulles' which had then been confirmed by 'Cicero's' reports ('Cicero' ceased sending reports in January 1944, a full year before the Yalta conference). Of course the West German mass media had a field-day when Felfe and his two accomplices were put on trial in July 1963. After a brief initial session in camera, the rest was unfortunately conducted in open court, causing just the kind of public damage to the BND that our Soviet adversaries would have wished.

The main public interest centred not on the traitor Felfe and what he had perpetrated – the court found that he had betrayed the names of no fewer than ninety-five BND agents to the Russians – so much as on what was described as the 'misguided personnel policy' operating in the service. The Social Democrats described it as a 'scandal without parallel' and attacked us for our 'lax standards' in recruiting staff: the Press made a great deal of Felfe's Nazi past (which he had concealed from us). The affair became a peg on which a large number of press articles were hung labelling the BND as a 'collecting point' for ex-Nazis. The fact was that Felfe had worked for two or three years after the war in the British Intelligence service in West Germany, and this seemed to us to imply a certain level of clearance. In addition, he was recommended to us by an official of the Ministry for All-German Affairs. State-Secretary Globke courageously defended the BND when it came under fire over this affair, and publicly affirmed that fewer than one per cent of our staff had ever worked for the SS (we had started the Gehlen organisation with only seven such officials).[1]

Felfe was sentenced to fourteen years imprisonment and a severe financial penalty; Clemens, the more truthful of the two, received a lesser sentence. When Gustav Heinemann became the socialist Minister of Justice in the Grand Coalition of 1966, he exchanged the other traitor, Alfred Frenzel, for a prisoner held by the Czechs; and, 'for reasons of humanity', moved heaven and earth to arrange an early release for Felfe too. He

[1] In my time the rule was that, apart from the Waffen-SS, no SS members were permitted to work at headquarters in Pullach unless they were special cases given clearance after checking the files at the Berlin Document Centre or at Ludwigsburg. There were grounds for believing that the BDC file on Felfe had been doctored by the Soviet authorities who turned it over to the Allies.

asked me to come and discuss with him the question of exchanging this prisoner for somebody from the east, but I would not hear of it and refused to see him, sending him a written memorandum to explain why. Nonetheless, in the summer of 1968, Felfe was exchanged by Heinemann for a number of people, including three students who had had nothing whatever to do with the BND but had been recruited by the Americans to spy in Russia, and a number of prisoners of the East Germans of whom one at most was an agent of ours. Clemens, who sincerely regretted his deeds, was not exchanged. He preferred to remain in West Germany.

In West Germany, our hands have always been tied when it comes to tracking down Soviet agents. It had taken us a year from the first breath of suspicion to gather enough evidence to pull Felfe in for questioning. In Britain, for example, it would have been much easier: he could have been grilled for three days until he broke down and confessed. I am a great admirer of the British Official Secrets Act – it is worded in a way which really guarantees national security. I had a copy of it translated into German and I put it to our Minister of the Interior as a model for a German law, but there was no response at all to my proposal.

With a staff of four to five thousand working for the BND, security was a constant anxiety. We did *experiment* with lie-detectors on the staff, but we made it a rule that they had to volunteer before they were subjected to it. The machine was really quite remarkable: in one case we applied the test to an agent who had some time before on our instructions joined the Socialist Unity Party in East Germany (we had had to extricate him prematurely for security reasons). The fact that he had been a member of the party was kept secret even at Pullach, although it was on his confidential personnel file. When he took the Polygraph test, I told him to deny it when asked whether he had ever belonged to the party. The result was a mighty leap in the detector reading – a result which deeply impressed us.

On the other hand, when we applied the test to another man whom we suspected might have a guilty conscience, the results were completely haywire. A secret committee of specialists considered this improbable result for some time; the medical members considered it possible that he had some tranquilliser or narcotic before the test was run. The evidence of lie-detectors is not accepted by German courts of law – but to a security branch it can at least provide a pointer.

At the conclusion of the Felfe affair, we circulated a comprehensive report of our findings to all the Allied Intelligence services in the west so that they could learn from our experience. After my retirement my successor prepared a popular history of the Felfe affair, which was to be published in West Germany under the title 'Moscow calling Heinz Felfe'. Horst Ehmke, Brandt's minister in charge of the Chancellor's Office, prohibited publication of the book after it had already been set up into proof at the publishers.

Scarcely any event cast a more turbid light on the federal Intelligence service than its apparent involvement in the controversial *Der Spiegel* affair. Eight years earlier, in 1954, the publication of my photograph on that magazine's front cover had been a word to the wise that there must be some kind of tie between Pullach and the Hamburg news magazine. It has always been my view that it is perfectly legitimate for a secret service to establish contacts with the Press. We had established this particular link shortly after the SSD campaign against us began. At that time I thought quite highly of Detlev Becker, the publisher of *Der Spiegel*. Obviously any such links with the Press and other mass media have to be handled very gingerly if there are not be be misunderstandings. This is a risk that will always have to be taken where the Press attempts to satisfy a public curiosity for information that can only be procured by using secret service channels.

There have been numerous versions of the *Der Spiegel* affair published in books and in the press. Colourful and over-dramatised as they are, they could hardly have gone further in their innuendoes, imputations and speculation. It was almost as though there was some hidden hand at work, bent on obscuring the true facts and discrediting the BND. That is why I feel it incumbent on me to break my silence on the affair.

At some stage in 1962 the magazine decided to publish a major attack on the defence minister, Franz Josef Strauss. It has been claimed that my relations with Strauss were strained, but in fact I have always thought very highly of him; he has a remarkable memory, and an impressive grasp of the essence of affairs. I consider him one of the most capable and active politicians we have. *Der Spiegel* had first attacked him over alleged irregularities concerning a commercial concern, Fibag, at a time when, to my knowledge, Strauss was completely unaware of the existence of such a company. What I did not realise at the time was that the magazine intended to deliver the *coup de grâce* in such a way as to implicate the BND as well, thus killing two birds with one stone. The 'stone' was to be a mammoth article on the recent manoeuvres, Fallex '62, about which top-secret documents had been fed into their hands by Strauss's opponents in Bonn. The article, which was written by Conrad Ahlers, was designed to expose alleged fallacies in Strauss's atomic weapon policies.

The manner in which the magazine sought to implicate the BND was this: they put to our Hamburg representative Colonel Adolf Wicht a written list of ten detailed questions a number of weeks before the planned publication date of their controversial article. I was away from Pullach at the time this list of ten questions arrived. They were handled in accordance with standard BND policy by my press liaison officer Winterstein. He checked which of the questions could be answered without violating defence secrets. *Der Spiegel* had informed us that the questions were being asked in connection with an article they were planning on the subject of the then Inspector-General of the Bundeswehr, General Foertsch. At no time did they tell us that the answers would be used in an article to be based largely on top-secret manoeuvre documents of a particularly high classification (documents which did *not*, however, emanate from the federal Intelligence service). In the event, the questions were answered from published material which by diligent research the magazine could have uncovered by itself. It is now clear to me that the intention in approaching the BND was solely to establish a 'lightning conductor' which would be used when the authorities took their revenge over the publication of the article.

The article was published in *Der Spiegel* on 8 October 1962. I was uneasy about the part the BND had played: when Winterstein showed me the list of questions and his harmless replies, I said that frankly I thought things might yet go awry. Strictly speaking, such questions should have been referred to Strauss's defence ministry for reply. Shortly afterwards I happened to be with Strauss, and he angrily informed me that he had turned the affair over to his legal experts, and was informing the Chancellor and the attorney-general that in his view the magazine ought to be prosecuted. Since the horse had already bolted, I saw little point in trying to lock the stable door and thought no more of the matter until, a few days later, the magazine's offices were raided, on the evening of 26 October, and its top editors were pulled in on treason charges. The publisher Augstein and several others, including Detlev Becker, were arrested in Germany on the attorney-general's instructions. Ahlers himself was in Spain, which brought his arrest into the ambit of the defence ministry. Strauss himself telephoned the military attaché in Madrid, and the Spanish police were called in.

All at once our Colonel Wicht was also arrested. Among Becker's papers the police had found a note which appeared to indicate that Wicht had tipped off *Der Spiegel* about the imminent swoop by the attorney-general. I do not know why it appeared expedient to the defendants, and acceptable to the prosecutors, to drag the BND into the position of an accomplice; but *prima facie* the evidence seemed irrefutable. With Wicht's arrest rumours swept the country, fed by people who claimed to know of my alleged antipathy towards Strauss: *Newsweek* magazine wrote, 'Most Germans are convinced Wicht acted on Gehlen's orders.' To those of us who knew the full story the accusation was absurd. Why should I have tipped off a magazine I was increasingly coming to recognise as a hostile instrument? But evidently it was taken seriously in Bonn. The truth was that the BND was entirely unaware of the article's contents. The allegation that we sanctioned its publication was designed to divert attention from the political figure who evidently *did* carry out the vetting of the article before it was printed.

It was not until I called on Adenauer for one of my regular briefing sessions a few days after the arrests that I learned of the suspicions being voiced against us. Strauss had evidently deduced from the note among Becker's papers that, after my conversation with him, I had immediately acted through Wicht to tip off the magazine. I was kept waiting in an ante-room for some time, and was then called in to see Adenauer himself (Globke was away – I believe he was ill that day). Adenauer had just seen Strauss, and he left me in no doubt as to his displeasure. It was clear he had been led to believe that the BND had played a dubious role – that we had both supplied the material for the articles and, through Wicht, tipped off the magazine as to the arrests. In fact, the arrests had come as a complete surprise to me. I stood my ground and demanded that a federal attorney should hold an inquiry into the affair. Adenauer agreed to this, and while he got on the telephone to Karlsrühe I contacted my deputy Worgitzky at Pullach and told him to catch the next train to Bonn with Horst Wendland and Winterstein immediately. They arrived next morning.

The federal attorney Kuhn, who usually dealt with the

BND's affairs, investigated the involvement of the BND in person.[1] He interrogated my three colleagues in the security office of the Criminal Police headquarters in Bonn, and then myself; the whole inquiry was conducted in an atmosphere of goodwill, the federal Intelligence service and I as its head were found to be blameless in the affair. In particular, Wicht was also subsequently acquitted: we were able to show that at the time he was alleged to have tipped off Detlev Becker about the coming arrests, nobody at Pullach had had the slightest inkling of them. We concluded that the document had been providently left lying around in such a manner that it was bound to be found in order to conceal the identity of the prominent defence ministry official who was the real culprit – the man who had supplied the secret documents.

The affair unfortunately caused considerable bad feeling within the service. While Wicht was still remanded in custody, Worgitsky – who had once held Wicht's office in Hamburg himself, and knew him well – insisted that I should make a public statement in defence of him. I refused, since this would have been construed as interference with the due processes of law, whereupon Worgitzky himself published such a declaration. Wicht was subsequently released without a stain on his name.

Unhappily, after this unpleasant affair, Konrad Adenauer changed his attitude towards us for some time.

In October of that same year, 1962, as the *Der Spiegel* controversy was occupying the front pages of West Germany's newspapers, the United States was dragged by Cuba into one of the most dangerous crises in the history of the post-war years. It was now that it was forcibly brought home to President Kennedy that he had let slip more than just a minor guerrilla victory in allowing the invasion of the Bay of Pigs to fail. Now

---

[1] Clearly, had the federal attorney-general thought there was any substance in the charges, he would have investigated the matter himself and not delegated the inquiry to Kuhn.

the Russians were blatantly preparing to exploit the situation by setting up missile bases within point-blank range of the east coast. The CIA succeeded quite early in detecting the construction work in Cuba itself by aerial reconnaissance, and there was still time to prevent the arrival of most of the missiles by sea from the Soviet Union. A number of transport vessels disguised as harmless merchantmen were already on their way to Cuba when Kennedy took his experts' advice and imposed a sea blockade on Cuba. Khrushchev was forced to climb down: confronted with this show of determination, which was coupled with an impressive demonstration of US naval strength, the merchantmen delivering the missiles turned back (although I suspect that part of the batch of missiles is still in Cuba). The malevolent cargoes were returned to the Soviet Union. Many people who watched with admiration this new-found resolution of the United States probably asked themselves whether the first barriers erected across Berlin in August the year before would have stayed up had the western powers displayed a similar determination then. But this was Kennedy's basic weakness. He was a man of half-measures; a president who wanted only the best, and frequently saw things in their real light, but was afraid to commit himself to the full to realise his aims.

We learned just how seriously the Americans viewed the situation at the time from statements of the then director of the CIA, John A. McCone, who described the crisis as one which 'could have sparked off a war, perhaps even a nuclear war'. We at Pullach were proud of the part our agents played in Cuba; they investigated the construction work in Cuba, and these reports were fitted into the over-all picture being built up by the CIA. I have always considered the CIA's Intelligence success on this occasion to have been one of its biggest accomplishments in post-war years.

The new year brought us the apotheosis we had so long worked for. For a long time France had no longer been our arch enemy, now she became our partner and ally for all time. In my eyes it was one of Adenauer's most spectacular triumphs, that he succeeded in winning General de Gaulle's faith in the new Germany. With the ceremonial signing of the Franco-German Agreement on 22 January 1963 in Paris, Adenauer had crowned his life's work.

For our own service, this historic event meant the formalisation of our long-standing and friendly relations with the French foreign Intelligence service SDECE;[1] long before our transfer to federal control, we had entered into informal agreements with our counterparts in France for collaboration in Intelligence affairs and the exchange of material. For a long time we had supplied the French with our 'Gehlen organisation' reports in exchange for nothing more than goodwill and the opportunity to build up West Germany's diplomatic status in French eyes. Although the role of the SDECE was not completely identical with that of the BND, there still remained a large area where we could usefully co-operate. I was always grateful that this relationship between the services was never affected by the strains which were occasionally placed on relations at the higher diplomatic levels. Regardless of the barometer reading on Franco-German relations as such, working liaison between the two Intelligence services remained constant and cordial.

If I made it my particular concern to cultivate our Intelligence relations with Britain, America and France, this should not be read as detracting in any way from the value of the many other ties we established. The fact that these three powers had accepted responsibility for the protection of West Germany was, in my eyes, one reason why they had a right to our support wherever it was possible. A further reason of no less validity was that I had the highest professional and personal regard for the directors of these Allied services, whom I knew and dealt with personally, on my visits to Washington, Paris or London.

[1] Service de Documentation Extérieure et de Contre-Espionage.

With the CIA's representatives what impressed me was the clear, sober and practical manner in which they tackled and overcame even the toughest Intelligence obstacles. With Britain's SIS it was the self-assured, almost superior manner of their extremely competent Intelligence officers – men who had been brought up in an almost legendary tradition, in short anything but the James Bond type. I had many private meetings with Brigadier Menzies, the first head of the SIS, and his successor; they invited me to their clubs in St James's, and I remember thinking that history might have been different had Germany had institutions like the Traveller's Club or the Reform; in the latter, they showed me the clock from which Jules Verne has Mr Phineas Fogg commence his 'Eighty Days Round the World'. In the representatives of the French service one senses an unshakable quality, that I can only loosely characterise as patriotism. Whereas we Germans can scarcely whisper the word *Vaterland* without risk of serious misunderstanding, a member of the French State service is and always will be a proud and willing 'servant of the State', with all that that implies, and is proud of it. This patriotism displayed by my French counterparts – indeed, by every Frenchman regardless of his beliefs – impressed me more than once. As a French colleague once said to me, 'The only person who will ever make a good European is one who started off as a good Frenchman, or a good Briton, or a good Italian, or a good German, and is proud of his country's traditions.'

While the trial of Heinz Felfe firmly occupied the centre of the newspaper stage, we at Pullach were more concerned with the important political events of the time. In Germany the chronic Berlin crisis was stepped up on 21 June 1963 by the erection of a new barrier around West Berlin to supplement the wall already existing between the two halves of the city and to prevent further escape attempts. The 'Crossing-Permit Agreement' signed six months later afforded only the weakest ray of hope.

The governments agreed the terms of a 'temporary regulation of visits of relatives of West Berliners resident in East Berlin', but hopes that this would lead to any easing of the tension were soon disappointed.

Particularly in the Mediterranean the year 1963 had brought a number of changes in key government positions. In Greece the resignation of Prime Minister Karamanlis on 11 June had touched off a chain of events which has disturbed this country – strategically so important for NATO's southern flank – ever since. As far as I could see, the Greek Intelligence service paid no attention to the changes in the government and continued to perform its difficult task with its customary skill.

A few days after Karamanlis's resignation, Israel's grand old man David Ben Gurion stepped down from the political stage as Israeli prime minister; he was succeeded by Levi Eschkol. One of Ben Gurion's great services to history was that he had paved the way for the reconciliation between the Germans and the Jews in his meeting with Dr Adenauer. I have always regarded it as something of a classical tragedy that West Germany had been dragged into an alliance with the State of Israel against the Arab countries with a remorseless inevitability from which there could be no escape. The struggle itself seemed to me so purposeless. I recall an Arab monarch telling me in 1953 that he knew only too well that the Arabs had to reach some kind of agreement with Israel – they ought to talk things over with Ben Gurion. 'But I would not dare to discuss such an idea even with my closest confidants,' he added, 'because if I did I would have no guarantee that I would survive another day.' The Arabs have always been too head-strong in their policies. I had always regarded their traditional friendship for Germany as being of immense value for our national reconstruction, and we at Pullach had done our best to inject expertise into the Egyptian secret service, supplying them with the former SS officers I have mentioned. But equally I recognised the political debt Germany owed to the Jews: we had to do what we could to contribute to the survival of Israel.

Leading figures of both camps did their utmost to build up and improve their bonds with the federal government, and, accordingly, with me as well. After the Suez war of 1956, we began to take a more professional interest in the Israelis. Nasser was becoming increasingly involved with Moscow, and we recognised that Israel was as much an outpost of the free world as West Berlin. In the end, the growing chain of political and military events, culminating in the renewed trial of strength in June 1967, obliged the federal republic to take up an un-ambiguous attitude in favour of Israel.

Later in 1963 there were far-reaching changes in the West German government. On 15 October Dr Adenauer resigned as Federal Chancellor, and was succeeded by Professor Ludwig Erhard.

More skilled pens than mine have written their appraisals of Adenauer's service to history. I can only add that a head of an Intelligence service will seldom have the good fortune to work under a head of government possessed of such an understanding of the uses of Intelligence, and of such a sound judgment. It is not meant in any way to detract from this if I add that Adenauer possessed in his state-secretary Dr Globke an incomparable and indispensable aide. Globke was replaced by a new state-secretary, Westrick, at the same time. I had found no cause to change my mind about Adenauer even when he momentarily adopted a critical and sceptical attitude towards the BND and myself over the *Der Spiegel* affair one year earlier.

With this changing of the guard at Bonn, a post-war era came to an end not only for the West German government but for us at Pullach too. I deeply respected Professor Erhard as an economics expert, but he could not provide the same active sympathy for the BND as had his predecessor. He did not recognise an Intelligence service as one of the basic props of government. It was anathema to his personal ideas. I could sense a certain hostility towards us among the civil servants at the Chancellor's Office.

To quench the public's thirst for knowledge about our activities, I decided with the government's approval to authorise the first major documentary film about our work. I was visited by two television producers, Günther Müggenburg and Rudolf Rohlinger, and I subsequently issued instructions that they were to be given access to anything they asked, within the obvious limits of national security. I need hardly add that there was no lack of warnings at the time: our security section was particularly concerned about the scores of shots that would have to be filmed at Pullach. We had the filming done at weekends so that our staff's faces would not appear. It may seem naïve, but 'rogues' galleries' of faces play an important part in espionage work: we unmasked the director of Soviet atomic espionage solely with the aid of one photograph (this man, Sergei Kudriavtsev is now Soviet ambassador in Cambodia). The two producers were as fair in their work as they were critical, and this confirmed the view I had always held that a responsible journalist will always respect and repay trust when it comes to treating sensitive subjects in a discreet way. The film was shown on West German television on 26 June, under the title: *From the Gehlen Organisation to the BND*. It had a huge audience, and went down far better than we had dared to hope.

Our main purpose in authorising this television documentary was to forestall a number of books and articles of dubious origins and doubtful tendencies that had already been advertised in advance. What I particularly wanted to get away from was the image created by modern espionage thrillers; I wanted to have the BND seen in its proper light as a modern and efficient foreign Intelligence service. Whereas in earlier years it had been the spicy sexual element that had pervaded the spy films, during the 1960s we were witnessing the new wave of sadistic strong-

General Gerhard Wessel (left), with the Federal Defence Minister Helmut Schmidt

Willy Brandt with certain of his colleagues in Moscow

The four stages of Gehlen's career

as Ensign

as Colonel

as President of the Federal
Intelligence Service

as old-age pensioner

arm types. This was what the layman now imagined when he tried to visualise the world of espionage. It may have been good for the box-office, but it did extensive damage to our reputation in the BND. This staid television documentary went a long way towards eliminating these prejudices and bringing home to the public the real nature of our work.

This is not to suggest that the real face of the Soviet KGB had changed since the early 1950s. One Sunday early in September 1964, a technician attached to the West German embassy in Moscow had been with a party of other diplomats visiting Sagorsk monastery, forty-five miles outside the city. As he knelt in prayer this man, Horst Schwirkmann, felt something pressed against his leg, and seconds later a damp patch appeared on the trouser cloth. When he looked up his neighbour had vanished. By the time the party returned to the embassy he was a very ill man, in severe pain and suffering from exhaustion. An American doctor in Moscow found skin burns caused by some kind of chemical poisoning. The Russians tried to detain Schwirkmann in one of their hospitals, but we managed to fly him out to a hospital in Bonn. Medical experts there ascertained that the burns had been caused by a sudden spray of mustard gas at short range – a poison of a special type that could kill within a few days without leaving a trace of the cause. He had been due to return home two days later.

Since Khrushchev was due to pay an official visit to Germany in the near future, the incident caused acute anxiety in Bonn, where Prime Minister Erhard called a meeting of the party leaders on the 11th. Eventually the government made a formal protest to Moscow, since the evidence was as clear as it had been in the Stashinskyi affair. After thirteen days the Russian government rejected the protest, and claimed that 'certain circles' in West Germany were trying to hinder any improvement in Soviet-German relations. At Pullach we were in no doubt as to the identity of the would-be murderers. Schwirkmann was one of our specialists, whom we had trained to ferret out

the hidden microphones planted by the KGB in our diplomatic
buildings round the world. They had tried to eliminate him
because he was on the threshold of unearthing their installation
in our embassy in Moscow (we later found over thirty microphones concealed in the building).

13. My last years in office

In our reports from Pullach we always made it absolutely plain that only the United States' intervention in Vietnam had prevented the loss of all Indo-China to the communists. I lent all my personal authority in support of the American decision to hold on to Vietnam whatever the cost, though I could never understand the methods applied by Washington out of ill-conceived regard for world and domestic public opinion.

To an officer fighting the communists in the field ever since 1941, the military strategy of the Americans was inexplicable. From the start they did everything in Vietnam by half-measures. They began with a force of thirty thousand, and when these were not enough they gradually escalated to half a million; in other words they have been trying to win a war by the one method every German staff officer was taught as an impossibility, and which not even Hitler made work. In staff college we were always taught: '*Nicht kleckern, sondern klotzen!*' – don't fiddle with the food, make a meal of it. With our wartime experience on the eastern and south-eastern fronts, we would have moved heaven and earth to avoid provoking partisan war, even if we had had to launch a massive airborne assault on the North Vietnamese headquarters to do so.

Under the adverse conditions their political leaders have created, the achievements of the American ground forces in Vietnam have been really remarkable. At the American commanders' disposal were every means for conducting military actions on the heaviest scale; behind them they had the resources of the United States, the mightiest nuclear power on earth. But these commanders could apply their military means only to a limited extent and in ineffective doses, while company after company of servicemen was swallowed up in merciless jungle warfare, fighting an invisible enemy who could merge with the jungle or the civilian population at a moment's notice, and who could change his tactics with a speed totally impossible in a democratic and bureaucratic power. In the circumstances it is difficult to comprehend why the Americans tried to adopt a mode of warfare which was bound to yield many casualties instead of exploiting the technical weapons at their disposal – helicopter units, modern artillery, tanks and rockets. Our own campaign against France in 1940 taught us that a massive and crushing use of force always costs less casualties (on both sides) than a gradual escalation such as we later tried in the Russian campaign.

The Americans started by leaving the French in the lurch in Indo-China; when the French withdrew, the Americans had to foot the bill. Early in November 1963, the Americans encouraged the overthrow of the Diem regime by a military junta. Diem's assassination was followed by a rapid succession of military revolts and changes of government, which crippled the government's authority to act and weakened the army. The expansion of the Vietnam conflict into full-scale civil war was the outcome. In the same month, November 1963, Kennedy was assassinated, and the BND had to remain in particularly close contact with our American colleagues ready to take immediate steps in case the Russians were tempted to exploit the emotional turmoil the assassination sparked off in the west.

The new war in Vietnam involved directly or indirectly the United States, Communist China and the Soviet Union, and remote though this new theatre of events was as far as the BND was concerned, we had to put the fighting in Indo-China into its larger context and investigate what its effects on other areas of the globe might be. We could only speculate whether the Russians, who had the greater influence on North Vietnam, would have permitted a Red Chinese aggression which would have led to the occupation of the whole of Indo-China as well as Thailand. From numerous reliable reports which reached us, we knew that at that time the Red Chinese leaders regarded the occupation of the areas of Indo-China and Burma bordering on southern China as merely the first stage in their expansionist strategy. In a second phase they were planning to eliminate the 'troublesome border positions' of South Korea and Taiwan (Nationalist China). The Chinese assumed that once they had achieved these two stages, the acquisition of the strategically vital island federation of Indonesia would automatically follow. In Indonesia there were over two-and-a-half million organised communists waiting for the hour of their 'liberation'.

As far as Vietnam is concerned, only the future will show whether the United States, by its years of bloody engagement in the south, has at least accomplished one thing: a reconstituted and fortified South Vietnam equipped with modern weapons and capable of defending herself after the American troops have been withdrawn. With present information, I cannot believe that this will be so. Once Red China has overcome her internal troubles she will resume her expansionist ambitions; unless, of course, the entire political situation is somehow changed. But the recent rapprochement between the United States and Communist China may lead to a temporary self-limitation of this expansionism and Washington's wooing of Peking, which has aroused alarm in Moscow, may also have a retarding effect on the south-east Asian interests of the Soviet Union.

Thus my own assessment is that, if Nixon succeeds in his political ambitions towards China, he may end American involvement in Vietnam in a way which would be in the interests of the west.

In 1964 the Soviet leadership had to contend with internal difficulties of its own, which were to culminate in the overthrow of the most powerful man in the communist camp. On 14

October 1964, Nikita Khrushchev, latest in the line of Soviet absolute dictators, went into political oblivion – stripped of his power under circumstances that even the most hardened Kremlin observer would not previously have thought possible. Even the most influential Soviet officials doubted up to the last moment whether the coup would succeed when the dictator was summoned to answer their accusations. But Khrushchev did unceremoniously vanish from the political scene after those few dramatic hours in the Kremlin, leaving party leaders in the communist countries as unprepared and nonplussed as the western governments. As usual there was no lack of reproach from the western Intelligence services, including the BND, that we had not clearly predicted Khrushchev's overthrow.

In fact, we at Pullach had continually reported that there were growing differences of opinion at top level in the Kremlin. Our information tallied in its essential details with what the other western Intelligence services found out. According to our sources major disputes had arisen during 1964 out of what had originally been minor differences of opinion. The younger members of the government had accused Khrushchev of responsibility for just about everything that had gone wrong with their plans outside Europe – the growing internecine conflict with Red China, the 'humiliating climb-down' over the Cuban missiles, and certain mishaps they had suffered because of premature operations in Africa. In internal debate, the policy of 'peaceful co-existence' was labelled a complete failure, and Khrushchev condemned as the hapless promoter of that policy.

Numerous reports identified as his possible successor a leading member of this younger generation, none other than Alexander Shelyepin, former boss of the KGB. His hour, however, had still not come. The old guard of Kremlin officials denied their younger colleague their allegiance. The final outcome was equally unexpected for the renowned Kremlinologists of the west. Khrushchev was succeeded by a *troika*, a triumvirate of leaders whose long survival has proven an almost greater surprise than the fact that such a compromise was adopted in the first place. In numerous BND summaries I stressed that the *troika* was in reality a three-horse team, in which one horse would always have the most pulling to do. It was with this leader that the west would always have to bargain. This *primus inter pares* was the dynamic party leader, Leonid Brezhnev. As the strongest of the trio he could formally take over absolute power in this collective at any time he desired; but so long as his two colleagues, the jovial State President Podgorny and the adroit Prime Minister Kosygin, continue to play their part as they have done up to now, Brezhnev has no need to force them out.

Two days after Khrushchev's downfall, the Chinese exploded their first atomic bomb and thus joined the other nuclear powers – a development which in no way took the western governments by surprise.

The western Intelligence services had been concerned about the problem of the Chinese bomb for some time, and had tried to establish how powerful it was. As facts were hard to come by, Intelligence analysts had had to work overtime to complete their calculations. At the time, we predicted quite accurately that without the assistance of Moscow, Red China would never succeed in catching up with the two big nuclear powers. This prediction has been borne out by subsequent events. One glimmer of hope remains for Peking as a second-rate nuclear power – that the major powers will tie their hands by a Non-Proliferation Treaty and weaken themselves in so doing. It is obvious that under the existing circumstances Red China is not going to sign any treaty limiting the development of nuclear weapons.

Early in 1965, the West German government's attention reverted from the Moscow-Peking axis to the situation in the Middle East. The Bonn government, which had hitherto sat firmly on the fence, was forced by the long-feared exacerbation of German-Arab relations to come out into the open and take decisions which ruled out all prospect of reaching a compromise solution.

There had long been a division of opinion in West Germany over the expediency of exporting arms to Israel. These exports provoked violent controversy and led to threatening reactions from the Arab states. It is true that Bonn discontinued its support for the Jewish state in February 1965 in so far as it discontinued its arms deliveries, but by then the train of events, once set in motion, could no longer be halted.

On 24 February Walther Ulbricht, the East German leader, arrived in Cairo for a week's visit to inflame still further this growing conflagration. The communist leader was welcomed as an honoured visitor and was lauded at every stopping point of his extended tour as the antithesis of the 'imperialist West German government, the promoters of Israel's power'. But behind the glittering façade erected by Cairo for the East German visit, it was clear from many reports reaching Pullach that Nasser had suffered many disappointments, principally because East Germany was in a far less satisfactory economic position than the west, and was therefore not able to satisfy by any means, all the Egyptian requirements. There was a further problem, in Nasser's view; the Arab *reis* has always displayed a sensitive 'nose' when it comes to sizing up a business partner, and now Nasser showed frequent distaste at having to deal with the East Germans – not so much with the prim and lifeless Ulbricht as with the numerous communist functionaries who came hawking their wares round Cairo as the years passed.

But by 1965 it was *Realpolitik* alone that mattered. This was no time for the Arabs to be guided by personal dislikes, contemptuous though Cairo may have been of the East German officials. Professor Erhard's government had decided to announce its establishment of diplomatic relations with Israel in May that year. I could have told Erhard that the Egyptians had an Intelligence team that knew precisely what weapons had been supplied to Israel, and would certainly not be satisfied with less themselves. We had repeatedly advised Bonn that granting diplomatic recognition to Israel would result in the majority of the Arab states immediately breaking off relations with Bonn.

On 13 May 1965 formal diplomatic relations were established between Bonn and Israel. An important element of the foreign policy formulated by Adenauer had been brought to its completion; but at the same time West Germany lost many traditional friends of long standing in the Arab world. These ties have remained broken to this day.

The West German government was reminded harshly of its own domestic problems that spring. We received several reports that the East Germans and the Russians were planning to disrupt the German parliamentary sessions scheduled to take place in West Berlin early in April. At the same time Berlin and Bonn were swamped with communist-inspired rumours designed to spread panic among the West German population. The resulting furore in the political parties and government agencies created an atmosphere in which it is remarkable that we were able to produce any level-headed analysis at all.

In our analyses from Pullach, we adhered to our old assessment of the Berlin situation. This encouraged the parliament and other political authorities to ignore the clumsy communist attempts at intimidation and proceed with their sessions in West Berlin. From Intelligence reports, we deduced that whatever Moscow and East Berlin might think up by way of propaganda and agitation, they would stop a long way short of the actual use of military force or anything that might make a confrontation with the western powers inevitable. Their sole purpose was to force Bonn and West Berlin to cancel the scheduled sessions and thereby concede indirectly that the federal republic had no business to be in West Berlin. The climax of this coercion campaign was reached on 4 April, with the blocking of the access corridors across East Germany, and particularly the autobahn from Helmstedt to West Berlin. While the military traffic of the western powers was allowed to pass unhindered, the West German parliamentary deputies had to fly (as most of them had already decided to do). There were fears that a civil airliner laden with these deputies would be forced down on to the East Berlin airport of Schönefeld, but these proved unfounded; the only other incident was when *Russian* fighter aircraft buzzed the assembly hall at low level.

Both the Berliners and the parliamentary deputies kept their nerve. What East Berlin had hoped might lead to the expulsion of the West German Parliament for ever from Berlin had the opposite effect: the steadfastness and solidarity of city and federal republic were demonstrated for all the world to see.

Not many months after the level of hostilities in Vietnam had been stepped up, we saw indications that widespread preparations were being made for a communist insurrection in Indonesia. Most remarkable for us was the complicity in this of the President himself, Soekarno. This irresolute leader had held on to power for several years by playing off the growing communist party of Indonesia against his army officers. Now, with his tacit approval, the party had established powerful cells all over the country and planned suddenly to murder the leading generals so as to remove the army as a pillar of the state and tilt the balance of power in the party's favour. For a long time we had received indications that Soekarno was secretly making common cause with the Chinese communists who were behind these preparations: he felt that he had been let down by the powerful military clique, and the communists had offered him the leadership of an Indonesian 'People's Republic' if the coup succeeded. (In reality they were planning to eliminate Soekarno too, and to transfer power to the leader of the Indonesian communist party, Aidit.)

The insurrection began after dark on 30 September 1965: communist squads murdered a number of the most important army officers in particularly bestial fashion; but the coup as such was a failure, because the other key assassinations were prevented. The popular military commander-in-chief, General Nasution, and the present Indonesian head of state, General Suharto, crushed the uprising with the help of loyal troops. Among the senior officers whom the communists had managed to murder were two particular friends of Germany, the army's Commander-in-chief General Yani, and the former military attaché in Bonn, Brigadier-General Pandyaitan. We in Pullach were in the fortunate position of being able to furnish the Bonn government with prompt and detailed reports from Indonesia, thanks to one particularly reliable (and hence sacrosanct) source there. It was he who had advised us much earlier of the deteriorating situation. No words of mine will do justice to the importance of the Indonesian army's subsequent success in eliminating the communist party in its entirety. The liquidation of the communists, including Aidit who was executed, was carried out with a harshness and thoroughness typical of the Asian mentality.

I have refrained so far from discussing either the development of the BND's organisation and staff or its changeable relations with the federal government after Adenauer's retirement. The attentive reader may well have guessed from my occasional asides that this relationship was not always devoid of misunderstandings, and on occasion it underwent what might be called a degree of strain. It is in the nature of an Intelligence service that it must receive encouragement and support from the government of the day; if the government lacks interest in or expert understanding of its Intelligence service, not even the best such organisation will succeed in overcoming the prejudices against it.

The real controversy over the future of the BND started in

1966, the last year of Professor Erhard's term of office. A number of newspapers published articles debating the future structure of what they referred to (misleadingly) as 'the three Intelligence services' – meaning the BND, the BfV and the Military Intelligence Service (MAD), the last controlled by the defence ministry. A number of qualified writers discussed the situation, but there were also unqualified journalists who claimed that there were 'catastrophic conditions' in the three services and put forward suggestions of their own. A number of self-proclaimed experts on the secret service fired broadsides at us from their comfortable paper jungles, or broadcast on wireless and television, offering us their advice. To the uninitiated it must have appeared that there had never been any co-ordination between the three services, and that we were all at each other's throats, concerned only with expanding our private empires at the expense of the others.

I regretted at the time that the government did little to counter these usually baseless allegations. This official silence in turn was grist to the experts' mill, and it encouraged them to publish even wilder conjectures about us. Eventually, in many journals, including some of considerable standing, the old proposal was aired that the three services should be merged. Often the proposals were so vague that it was difficult to distinguish whether they advocated merely bringing the organisations together under some superior co-ordinating authority or were thinking in terms of the complete amalgamation of the three agencies (one foreign Intelligence and two security) into one 'super service'.

My own view was that the existing degree of loose collaboration was ideal; it would have been impossible for them to be brought together under one person. The three services had such distinct fields of operation that an amalgamation would not have served any purpose whatsoever, particularly from the political point of view. The BND, as a foreign espionage organisation operating *outside* West Germany, was obliged to

remain absolutely non-political; but the BfV and MAD were
security organisations, exercising counter-espionage and defensive functions in the civilian and military planes respectively,
and as such were necessarily more political in character. The
clear distinction between their duties ought to be apparent even
to the layman.

This sort of irritating public speculation was able to grow and
blossom into a luxuriant undergrowth during the Erhard
administration, but with the formation of the Grand Coalition
under Kurt Kiesinger in December 1966 the situation changed.
Quite apart from the fact that the Chancellor's Office kept as
tight a grip on 'its' Intelligence service as did the other two
ministries on theirs, the very nature of the Grand Coalition was
such as to evoke little enthusiasm for a 'Ministry of State
Security'; and I know of no indications that other opinions have
since come to the fore.

My last complete year of office, 1967, brought the BND one
more triumph – one which has been frequently referred to since
then, at home and abroad. We predicted the Israeli attack on
Egypt down to the very day. A few days before hostilities broke
out in the Middle East, I had committed myself in a written
Intelligence appreciation to the view that, in the first days of
June, an Israeli preventive attack on Egypt was to be expected.
I and my colleagues were so convinced of the inevitability of
this that we briefed a group of parliamentary deputies, who
happened to be visiting Pullach, on the threat. During the week
preceding the attack, I had to attend the parliamentary budget
committee for its regular hearing on the BND, and one of the
deputies also asked me whether there would be war in the
Middle East. I replied that I thought the Israelis would attack
'next Monday'.

We were right, even though – as an angry American journalist
pointed out on Werner Höfer's television programme long
afterwards – at the time of my prediction the Israeli's themselves

had not made the decision. Our prediction was a typical example of what can be achieved by close collaboration between espionage and experts in military and economic analysis. In this particular case the latter were able to draw upon a large number of individual reports from our Middle Eastern sources. Even so, it was a bold prophecy, as is evidenced by the fact that there was a complete lack of confirmation from the other western Intelligence services. Even the CIA, which had far and away the best contacts with the Israeli secret service, was convinced right up to the last minute that the United States had succeeded in preventing the outbreak of a war. Unfortunately, our prediction also fell on deaf ears: the deputies to whom we made it admitted at the time that, convincing though our arguments were, they believed it was just another instance of undue Intelligence-service pessimism.

We had first observed the gathering signs of Egypt's preparation for war with Israel through our Intelligence channels after Gromyko's four-day visit to Cairo ended on 1 April. Our sources clearly indicated that he had made no attempt to subdue the belligerence of his Arab friends; on the contrary, we received pointers that, in his discussions with Nasser, Gromyko had deliberately refrained from putting frankly to him the latest verdict of the Soviet secret service on the military strengths of the two opposing countries. The Russians were privately convinced that the Arabs would never manage to match the quality of the (numerically inferior) Israeli armed forces. We can only speculate why Gromyko actually encouraged the Arabs to fight in a situation so hopeless.

The Israeli Intelligence service *Shin Beth* – which has become one of the most efficient in the world in the two decades of its existence – lived up to its reputation. It was able to follow the preparations of its Arab neighbours with extreme accuracy, as was shown by later investigations, and it provided the Israeli military authorities with all the material they needed to decide where and what to attack. In view of the numerical superiority of the Egyptian air force, the Israelis had to tilt the balance as early as possible, so they used their own magnificently equipped air force to deliver a pre-emptive strike on the Egyptians in lieu of a declaration of war, the same tactics as Hitler had used in Poland, France and Yugoslavia. This forestalled the Arab air assault which would otherwise have proved fatal to the little country. The Israelis were able to strike at the most important Egyptian air bases with surprise air attacks launched from the Mediterranean, and the majority of the Egyptians' operational aircraft were wiped out on the ground. Concentrated tank attacks followed hard on this initial victory, and the Arabs' fate was sealed. In a blitzkrieg lasting only six days the Israelis won victory without the use of atomic warheads.

The major powers intervened and hostilities ceased. Since then, Israel has hung on to the Arab territories she has occupied, and is holding them in pawn for a later peace settlement. But the Russians have undertaken not only to replenish the material losses of the Arab countries, but to guarantee them *superiority* in modern weapons too. By means of these arms deliveries (on which the western Intelligence services have been keeping close check) Moscow has secured for itself an increasing influence on Egypt, just as Gromyko planned. The outcome suggests a brutal rationalisation of the Soviet scheming: the Arabs, once defeated, would be forced to give up all aspirations to independence. Whoever won, the Soviet Union was bound to emerge the victor in an Arab-Israeli conflict in 1967.

In the wake of the Arab defeat, Soviet aid to Egypt has multiplied: over the last three years thousands of Soviet advisers and technicians have flooded into the country. There can, however, be no doubt that while the proud and patriotic Arabs welcome the Russians as helpers, they will never treat them as friends. Between the foreign instructors – despised for their arrogance – and their 'trainees' there has recently been friction that has led to blows. To Nasser and his senior officials the defeat was a disgrace, which the Soviet patronage has only served to prolong.

In the five and a half years between Adenauer's retirement and my own, my presidency of the BND came under increasingly heavy fire. While I was rewarded with the esteem of Adenauer's successors, Professor Erhard and then Kurt Kiesinger, as well as of their state secretaries, in the fulfilment of my duties, my work at Pullach was burdened in an increasingly unpleasant manner by the sniping of a number of senior civil servants who – ignorant of the ways of an Intelligence service – had persisted in entangling us in red tape and ill-informed criticisms, so that I had repeatedly found that when I tried to settle important problems I had the responsible parliamentary sub-committees and the all-powerful chairman of the Audit Committee on my side, but the ignorant bureaucracy of the civil service firmly up in arms against me.

A new security affair now threatened to break within the BND – one on which I cannot enlarge since it has not been disclosed by the authorities: suffice to say that one of the disaffected staff members claimed there was a new Felfe in the BND, and that I was not investigating the case with proper diligence. (In fact the man he named was the historian and analyst who had first thrown suspicion on to Felfe six years before, but only I knew that.) I learned from one of my loyal staff whom I had infiltrated amongst the dissidents that they were demanding my early 'retirement', so I advised the Chancellor's Office that we proposed to investigate the affair internally.

It was at about this time that Professor Erhard resigned and on 1 December 1966 the Grand Coalition was formed in Bonn under Kiesinger; our proposal for an internal investigation was overruled. There followed no less than nine months of upheaval at Pullach. It was an intrusion which made our Intelligence work in a vital period of conflict in Europe and the Middle East exceptionally difficult. Eventually, however, the attorney-general was ordered to take over the inquiry, and soon after he advised the government that there was no substance in the allegations against the analyst concerned (the man is still employed as a trusted official at Pullach).

I had anticipated that with the dawning of coalition government, the federal Intelligence service might become an object of political controversy. In my first conference with Kiesinger after he became Federal Chancellor I had recommended to him that since I would reach normal retiring age in 1967, I ought not to remain more than one year beyond that. Otherwise the question of my successor would have to be settled in the hectic atmosphere of an election year (scheduled for 1969). There were really only two candidates with Intelligence experience: the first was Major General Horst Wendland who had acted as my vice-president since Worgitzky's retirement; the second Lieutenant-General Gerhard Wessel,[1] my former colleague who was now a Bundeswehr general. I would have preferred the former, but he was already a sick man and this may have weighed against him. My senior colleagues at Pullach favoured Wessel, an enthusiasm I could not share, for while I had found him an outstanding 'Number Two' I doubted if he had the necessary *Format* for a real position of command. I hope later events will prove me wrong in this respect. When word went out about my intention of retiring in 1968, a number of others began jostling for the position, but when the time for decision came, the choice fell on Gerhard Wessel.

Wessel succeeded me as president of the federal Intelligence service on 1 May 1968. In a short ceremony attended by some

[1] Lieutenant-General Gerhard Wessel, my successor, was born on Christmas Eve, 1913; he joined the General Staff in 1941, and served under me in Foreign Armies East from 1942 until the end of the war, succeeding me as its chief in April 1945. He joined the Gehlen organisation in 1947, transferred to the embryo Bundeswehr and supervised the setting up of the military counter-espionage organisation (*MAD*).

sixty officers and men, Professor Carstens delivered a farewell speech, and introduced my successor to the senior members of the service. Wessel spoke a few words, followed by myself, and then it was all over. The warmth of Carstens's words about my work on behalf of Kiesinger and the federal government, and the award some days earlier of the highest medal the West German republic can bestow went some way towards compensating me for the last years of intrigue. 'Obviously you have had to swallow disappointments and suffer setbacks,' Carstens said. 'But taken as a whole we can only regard your achievement as exceptional and vital for the future of our country; it was an achievement that had to be accomplished behind closed doors. I can only quote the words of President Kennedy as he took leave of his former secret service chief Allen Dulles at the end of November 1961 and handed the office of Director of the CIA over to my old friend John Alex McCone. He remarked, "Your triumphs remain unsung, while your mistakes are trumpeted to the skies." ' About that I myself have no complaint: the head of a Secret Service must learn to take criticism in silence.

My going, and the new appointments that were made to the BND, brought tragedy in their wake. General Wendland, who had been in the service since its beginning and who had been my chief of personnel and then my acting deputy, learned that he was to be by-passed by a politician for the post of vice-president (eventually the socialists appointed their party manager in Hamburg, Dieter Blötz, to the post). Perhaps the stress under which all the BND senior staff had laboured in the cause of Germany had proved too much for him; or perhaps it was his general ill-health. When I spoke to him before flying to Istanbul to take leave of my old colleagues in the Turkish Intelligence service, I thought he seemed depressed; in Istanbul I received a telegram reporting that Wendland had shot himself in his office at our headquarters on 9 October 1968.

Part 4

The future of the West

14. Soviet foreign policy and communist ideology

In previous chapters I have described the origins of the service, and how it developed, but in doing so I have tried to keep clearly in view the red streak that has permeated the whole story so far. Virtually all the incidents I have described were caused in some way by the great conflict existing between the free and the communist world. It has influenced our lives for many years already, and it will continue to affect the future of our country for decades to come. Of this I am in no doubt at all. It is this that compels me to devote the chapters that follow, the concluding section of this took, to a personal credo, a statement of my own beliefs about the future.

An unceasing conflict of ideologies takes place at every level of human life, and in every field of activity. On our own side we still have the support of a massive phalanx, the democratic west, resolute and determined to fight for the maintenance of liberty. We are fighting in the first instance with weapons of the mind, against the destructive influence of communist ideology, especially in those areas where communism is marching onwards towards its new objectives.

What I must particularly emphasise is that the theoretical and ideological premises of communism are unchanged. They are as fundamental in deciding practical political actions as they ever have been. By way of example I will try briefly to describe the international communist approach to their un-changing goal, which is to bring about 'world revolution', or to 'bestow the blessings of Socialism on mankind'. I will then end by putting in perspective the achievements of Soviet power politics during the twenty years of my office, from 1948 to 1968, and by analysing the present world situation.

For myself and my colleagues the situation at the end of the Forties – which coincided with the foundation of the federal republic of Germany – brought with it new and important responsibilities. Whereas until then we had been concentrating our attention on the military planning and potential of the Russians and their satellite territories, our mission was now enlarged to embrace the surveillance of Soviet power politics in all their aspects, including their short-term operations, their medium- and long-term planning and their broad-based preparations of a strategic and geo-political character. On top of this, we had to devote as much attention to the domestic situation within the Soviet frontiers as to the expansionist policies of the Russians beyond them.

The consequences of Yalta had already indicated that terror and destruction would accompany communism wherever it made its way towards world domination. Within a few years we had the final proof that this would be one of the consequences of Soviet foreign policy: the violent overthrow of Beneš whereby Czechoslovakia was converted to a communist 'people's democracy' in June 1948. Twenty years later, as my years of office drew to an end, the Czechs and Slovaks were prevented by the Russians from going their 'own way towards Socialism'. It was an unchallengeable confirmation that Soviet policies have remained the same, that both the beginning and the end of the period in which I directed our foreign Intelligence organisation were distinguished by violent coups designed to impress upon a virtually defenceless country that its fate was inescapable.

What has happened to the Czechs and Slovaks, and what happened to the Hungarians, the Poles and our own fellow countrymen in East Germany, evoked a degree of condemnation in the west that should have brought people to their senses. But today, barely three years after the dramatic military invasion of Czechoslovakia in August 1968, it has been all but forgotten. The undisguised use of brute force is now dressed up by skilful communist propaganda as a measure which anybody can surely understand was necessary to 'preserve essential interests' in the eastern bloc.

Starting from scratch, it was not an easy task for us to piece together a complete picture of the most important political developments in the Soviet bloc, or to trace the initiatives and directives emanating from the Soviet hemisphere. Our potential enemy controlled a gigantic machine, a veritable 'instrumentarium' affording him an unlimited selection of operations and an inexhaustible arsenal of weapons and tactics.

Convincing though our service's analyses were, they were not always to the liking or taste of every political personality in West Germany. It is true that we managed to detect virtually every major trend of any significance in the Soviet bloc, often months or years in advance, and that in most cases we correctly appreciated the consequences as well; but we were forced to realise again and again that any foreign Intelligence service which reports disagreeable facts, even if only occasionally, very rapidly attracts a reputation of being narrow-minded if not actually perverse. More than once I found myself cast in the role of a Cassandra when I was obliged to warn that the facts did not support certain illusions entertained by Bonn. This was particularly true in the late 1960s, as more and more of our country's politicians rediscovered Russia's 'love of peace', attractively packaged in the Soviet offerings of co-existence and détente. It fell to our lot at Pullach to be labelled 'cold-warmongers'. I will leave it to history to pass judgment on whether we promoted the cold war or not.

The purposefulness of Soviet foreign policy has frequently escaped notice. One surprising factor we had to contend with was the opinion of many leading politicians and senior government officials that Soviet policies were inscrutable and indeed irrational. I could never see how anybody could believe this. I have always maintained, and I still do, that communist policies in general and Soviet foreign policy in particular are distinguished by their consistency and single-mindedness. Furthermore, communist statesmen are often so convinced of the rectitude of their beliefs that they announce their aims and intentions with almost brutal frankness. It is a curious feature they have in common with Adolf Hitler, who also made no secret of his aims. The trouble is that these announcements are seldom taken seriously by our side, or they are robbed of their significance by the fact that people who are unfamiliar with the subject-matter only select those passages that appear suitable to them. These are invariably those that tie in with their own opinions.

The dominant role played by Soviet ideology is largely forgotten or disbelieved. I am convinced that only a broad and accurate knowledge of the enemy can protect us from faulty decisions. What is needed is a knowledge of the mentality of the Soviet peoples and their Allies, and a knowledge of the doctrines of Marxism and Leninism, which the communists see as a means not only of explaining the world about us, but of changing it as well. However violently this may be disputed by 'experts' to-day, communist ideology is still the basis on which all important decisions in the communist empire are taken. It is and always will be the manual on which all their actions are based.

In the west, many political analysts maintain that the 'age of ideologies' is over; that the theory of world revolution is on the decline as well, if not already extinct; that all communist foreign policy now pursues aims totally independent of its ideology. This permits us to conclude that our relations with the communist states, above all with the Soviet Union, may yet be 'normalised'. This basic argument clearly depends on the conviction expressed by a host of western Sovietologists that the two social systems are becoming increasingly *convergent*; and it gainsays the virulence of the Marxist and Leninist teachings of world revolution as a factor in Soviet foreign policy.

The communists, on the other hand, maintain that the highly developed capitalist countries of the modern industrialised consumer society have reached a significant stage in their development. This new Capitalism is characterised by the accumulation of capital and hence power in the hands of the state and major industrial corporations, with the result that the Capitalism of old has now become a Capitalism of state monopolies. But this new Capitalism harbours within itself the same malignant contrasts as before and is therefore doomed to destruction. The communists admit that this Capitalism of state monopolies is highly potent, and by encouraging scientific research and by social reform it is capable of raising the living standards of the working classes. But while this will admittedly improve their *absolute* position, it will not halt the *relative* progressive pauperisation of the working classes. This new kind of Capitalism is not just the result of the technological revolution, it has been brought about by pressure exercised by the socialist camp. In consequence, every reform in the capitalist social structure must be seen as a predictable phase in the continuing process of world revolution. The Capitalism of state monopolies is what Lenin himself predicted would occur, as the 'important preliminary development phase' in the transition from Capitalism to Socialism – which we can describe as the communist version of the theory of convergence.

In my view, the controversy as to whether Soviet foreign policy is still rooted in ideology, or whether it serves the primarily nationalist interests of the Soviet Union, is a barren and pointless one. Soviet foreign policy services both interests equally. If we accept that ideological objectives are a facet of political strategy – as the communists do themselves until they take over power within a country – all the apparent contradictions vanish of their own accord. It would scarcely be possible to find an action or 'development phase' in the relations between communist and non-communist countries which does not conform with communist ideology; the Treaty concluded between Moscow and Bonn on 12 August 1970 is a case in point. Nor does the Soviet Union's support for the United Arab Republic conflict in any way with the long-term, ideologically aligned plans of Moscow, even though in Egypt the communist party is still prohibited and its members have been persecuted. The waxing influence of Moscow in the Middle East, with its principal focus in Egypt, will – the Soviet leaders argue – convert Arab-style 'Socialism' to the pure version represented by Moscow more rapidly than if the United Arab Republic were to be left to its own fate.

Before I turn to the policies of communism in general (and Soviet policies and their consequences in particular), however, I feel that a few basic comments on the relationship between communist theory and practice are called for. I do not regard it as my job to embark in these pages upon extensive ideological observations or to enlarge upon the immense volume of material already available on this subject. Better brains than mine have examined this theme from every conceivable angle; they are still doing so and will continue to do so, frequently without finding the audience they deserve. I therefore intend to limit my own modest contribution to those matters in which the relationship I have emphasised between communist theory – in other words their ideology – and practice – as represented in politically significant events – can be identified beyond all doubt.

The first thing to recognise is that the relationship between policy and objective implies that the active politician will be influenced by subjective influences whenever he sums up a situation. He will investigate whether and how the desired objective can be achieved, and from a number of potential solutions he will identify those which in his considered view seem to serve that purpose best. But the Intelligence analyst – the officer responsible in wartime for assessing the enemy's situation – must in general take his own side's situation and intentions into account only as a secondary factor. In appraising the enemy's situation he will therefore frequently be more objective than the responsible politician, assuming that he is capable of penetrating the enemy's mind. In other words, an Intelligence appraisal will almost inevitably view situations with a sharper and clearer eye even than that of an experienced politician, who is frequently burdened with a multitude of other problems of his own as well. The politician who realises this and does not act as Hitler did – accepting only what accorded with his own subjective ideas – will form the right decisions, free of all illusions.

As with every other kind of activity, politics takes certain fundamental values as its premises. These premises consist in part of constitutional edicts like our basic law, international law, and conventions like the United Nations Charter; but they also derive, although we are not always conscious of them, from religious convictions, from our *Weltanschauung* and current ideologies.

So long as all the actors on the stage of international politics are following the same premises, these limitations assume a lesser importance: in the free interplay of forces the same norms and laws hold for everybody. But once different premises and values apply, this parity of interests is bound to disappear. Since the Soviet revolution of October 1917 leading politicians have been obliged to accord their own actions with the norms and values currently approved by their own country, while at the same time judging the actions of the adversary by the different norms valid for them. In doing so they must repeatedly recognise that the enemy's tactics and actions conflict with their own norms. Were this not so, our own politicians would not continually have to throw our highest values, like Liberty and Democracy, into the scales of argument to justify our actions, or to expose the baseness of the enemy's arguments.

It is obvious in my view, therefore, that the sets of values conditioning political decisions in east and west are different.

As long as we are faced with this, in other words as long as communist parties, whether in or out of power, adhere to the communist dogma, politics will continue to be significantly beset by the ideological element. It would be a good thing if we could all come to terms with this harsh fact, just as all communists are convinced that the struggle with 'imperialism' is inevitable.

We can find the ultimate values and objectives, which serve as the Pole star for the Soviet Union, its satellite countries and every communist party, in what is claimed to be the scientifically-based *Weltanschauung* of Marxism-Leninism. It is there for all the world to see – in the institutions of learning, in written constitutions, in party programmes and statutes as well as in countless basic documents which, I can only keep emphasising, represent the Soviet manual of attack and will continue to do so.

If I now adduce the experience and wisdom of all the major western Intelligence services to establish that Soviet aims have remained constant throughout the years, I am not blind to the objections that will be raised. The same people who have learned nothing even from the most recent communist 'lessons' and like to refer to the Intelligence services as 'incorrigible', never tire, it seems, of pointing out that, within the Soviet bloc there have been developments over the past few years which have restricted the practical application of Marxism and Leninism to an ever-smaller area. These changes are there for all the world to see, they say, it is just certain 'pessimists' who refuse to accept the evidence of their own eyes. Of course, I fully recognise that modern Marxism and Leninism is as remote from the 'classical' teachings of Marx and Lenin as modern Christianity from the teachings of Our Lord. This does not alter the fact that in countries where modern communism is in power, it insists immutably on the predominant role of the party. The all-powerful party in turn moulds the doctrine so as to suit the state of affairs existing at any moment. That is how the non-ruling communist parties in France and Italy can call *inter alia* for the conversion of their countries into 'socialist' societies, without, of course, altering their true programmes one iota.

Until such time as the opposite is proved true – and this can only occur when some country, organised hitherto on socialist principles, adopts on its own initiative, and unimpeded by its Allies, some other form of government – we must assume that communist ideology will continue to be the dominant factor conditioning communist policies. Therefore any discussion of Soviet policies, including my own, is bound to take as its starting point the fact that the definitions of political and social concepts are understood differently by communists and non-communists, and are frequently the precise opposite of each other.

There seems to be a distinct reluctance to face squarely the consequences of this, so at this point it seems vital to make semantic distinctions.

At the very heart of the Soviet idea of the nature of foreign policy are two terms whose interpretation is indispensable for an understanding of the practical politics of the Soviet state: 'Ideology' and 'Co-existence'. The concept of Ideology has undergone many different metamorphoses in its long history. Originally it was a word of purely philosophical content, but it is now used to describe an obscure mixture of theoretical, pragmatic, ideological and praxeological propositions. The ideology of Marxism-Leninism, assumes that any ideology is false when it consists of idealistic or bourgeois notions; it is true only when it echoes the notions of dialectical materialism and the proletariat. Two criteria distinguish true from false thinking: a philosophical element (the distinction between materialism and idealism) and a class element (or class distinction). All learning that is politically neutral with respect to society is rejected as ideologically false, as it is claimed to be capable of grasping only the surface (or the outward appearance) of reality.

This is one reason why the definition of Co-existence as understood by the Soviet government and the eastern bloc is different from the interpretation preferred by the non-communist world. The communist version of Co-existence can be summarised as being a transitory state somewhere along the road towards the establishment of a socialist society. It is characterised by 'peaceful' competition in every sphere between the two great camps, while avoiding military confrontation. Seen in this light, it is wholly intelligible that Moscow continues to pay lip-service to the theory of the avoidability of nuclear war, even if it no longer suggests it is actually impossible. It must be clear to even the most belligerent Soviet marshals that there can be no victor in such a war. But it precludes the Russians neither from supporting violent revolutions, nor from intervening in certain circumstances which may lead to conventional war – what we refer to as localised wars and the Russians term 'national wars of liberation' (prefaced with the adjective 'just' if they tally with the underlying trends in Soviet foreign policy; otherwise classified as 'imperialist'). The conclusion to be drawn from this is that the Russians will always avoid a direct confrontation with the United States where they can, and will take good care that localised wars like that in the Middle East do not get out of hand.

At the purely ideological level, however, which delineates the intellectual area of conflict, there can be no co-existence. The communists have made no secret of this fact. Of course this Soviet understanding of the word 'co-existence' is fundamentally different from what the non-communist world means by the word. We regard co-existence as a permanent state of living together, or at least of living in harmony as neighbours with the prospect of living together at some time in the future. In our definition the term excludes the political aggression of using clandestine methods of subversion from behind a smoke-screen of ostensibly peaceful cohabitation.

Co-existence is a state of affairs particularly desired by the communists, for it enables them to overcome the natural barriers of anxiety and fear, and it enhances their prospects of penetrating the minds of the working classes as well as of the intellectuals within the capitalist countries. In the communist sense of the word, therefore, co-existence is a prerequisite for the gradual ripening of revolutionary conditions. A typical example of the conversion of a country to a socialist (i.e. communist) system by peaceful means can be seen in Chile, the first great triumph of the Russians in South America, where a Marxist government has been democratically elected to power.

Détente – a tension-free state of affairs – is understood by the communists to be a purely relative concept, or at least one of only limited duration; the détente – and this fact seems to me of particular importance with regard to the euphoria in which Germany is now wallowing – will last only so long as it serves communist interests. The harsh reality of this is frequently brought home by the persistence – indeed the intensification – of the ideological conflict and of its associated agitation and propaganda campaigns. In the communist meaning of the word, détente is a weapon to be wheeled out of the arsenal of political tactics – one which can be exploited like its heavier-calibre brother, co-existence. Among its many functions it creates a better climate for 'penetrating the minds' of the capitalist peoples. In this context it is noteworthy that, in the more important basic documents, the communists speak to the peoples as such, and not to their respective governments. This well-considered distinction derives from the expectation that, when their minds have been aroused to what 'peace, progress and socialism' can offer, the people themselves will ultimately force their governments to concede the communist demands.

Soviet foreign policy is conducted at two distinct levels, that of national government and that of international communist movement; but it keeps the two levels of activity as separate as possible. While the former operates strictly within the limits and concepts of international law, the spider's web of links between the international communist parties makes it possible for them to influence the domestic policies and the political mind of other countries in various covert ways. In this connection it is worth noticing that every communist party organisation maintains a bureau solely concerned with liaison with other communist parties.

This duality of political behaviour is only part of the potential available to the communist bloc. Intercourse with foreign states was formerly a matter for diplomats; and other kinds of intercourse beyond the frontiers, like trade or cultural exchanges were regarded as non-political activities. The recent statement of our Federal Chancellor in connection with some projects in underdeveloped countries that, as far as possible, politics must be kept out of trade, is wholly in accordance with this attitude.

The communists put a completely different interpretation on things: for them there is no area or activity free of ideology or free of politics. To demonstrate this from communist teachings, we need refer only to Lenin's dictum that all actions must be 'partisan'.

The doctrine that every human activity and action must have an ideological and political content produces an astonishing multiplicity of methods open to the communists in their relations with other countries. On the one hand, for example, the Soviet Union makes constant attempts to keep up the diplomatic dialogue with the United States, at the same time it continues unabated its campaign of hatred against this bastion of the west. After all, the 'addressees' are quite different people: the diplomats deal with the Foreign Ministries while the 'unorthodox' methods are aimed at the man in the street – to receptive social groups like the 'friends of peace' and other fellow-travellers, as well as to the broad fields of economics, learning, technology and culture, by-passing the government as far as possible. The favourite targets for this kind of campaign are parliamentarians and public personalities in the widest sense – people whose interest is roused and whose sense of personal importance is flattered, frequently with great subtlety. An important part is played on the Soviet and communist side in this continuing struggle by psycho-politics and *desinformatsiya*. A literal translation of this – disinformation, or false information – does not fully convey the meaning of the word. In fact it refers not only to false information, but to any stream of information designed to influence the recipient in a certain, predetermined manner.

The most glaring example of this is the monotonous Soviet call for 'total disarmament'. Of course the Russians and their friends realise full well that this demand can never be realised. Nor would they ever like to see it realised, for this would jeopardise the security of their own power system and rob the Russians of the ability to nourish the fires of conflict in every corner of the globe by their arms supplies. But the effrontery of the demand, with its apparently strong humanitarian overtones, puts the western hemisphere in the awkward position of having to reject it as impracticable. At the same time we can only produce counter-proposals which must inevitably seem feeble in comparison with the Soviet 'offer' and – at least in the eyes of neutrals – point up an apparent lack of good will. It casts the communist bloc in the role of 'peace lover', while the United States can be pilloried as 'warmonger' and aggressor. There can be no question but that the persistent Soviet references to the 'warmongering and belligerent' role of the United States have found their mark in the western hemisphere.

I could list many more examples of the systematic psycho-political methods applied by the Russians, where we in the service repeatedly warned of the deeper connotations. The burning question of Berlin is an example which will serve here to speak for many others. My own impression – which is founded on my own knowledge of a mass of reliable Intelligence

G.M.—L

reports – is that the Russians are trying and largely succeeding, by means of various separate measures which taken in isolation seem completely unimportant, to build up West Berlin in the public mind into an independent political entity. In doing so, the Russians are making alternate use of blandishment and bluster, and allowing neither the ideas of Ulbricht (which do not always conform with their own) nor the countless protests from our own government to disturb them.

It is perfectly clear that the Russians can already consider it a considerable victory that the Bundestag has now not been convened in Berlin for several years. Apparently many politicians on this side of the Iron Curtain (and on the other) have forgotten that, according to Article 23 of our basic law, which was drawn up by the Four Occupying Powers, Greater Berlin (which, of course, includes East Berlin) has been part of the area subject to the basic law from the very outset – in other words part of the federal republic. Perhaps they were anxious to overlook this fact in order to present as accommodating a face to the Russians as possible.

I have never ceased to regret that the West German government – out of deference to public dislike of any operation which might smack of the methods of the Nazi Propaganda Ministry – has refrained from reacting vigorously to the communist smear-campaigns, and has failed to reply in the same vernacular.

I am perfectly aware that our constitution in particular and the democratic system in general circumscribe the extent to which we are able to conduct a methodical propaganda campaign. The vital freedom of opinion and freedom of the Press anchored in our basic law prevents us from harnessing the mass media to the same extent as is done in the communist bloc. Nonetheless, it could have been possible, as a few particularly successful acts of initiative have shown, for us to put a stop to a lot that has happened. We could for example have prevented the distortion of the popular attitude towards Berlin, and we could have challenged the incorporation of East Berlin into the

East German state, a move which even Ulbricht long hesitated to make.

My aim in writing these last pages has been to refute the widespread contention that there have been substantial changes in the aims the communists have set themselves. Whatever changes there may have been in the *methods* they employ there can be no denying that communism itself is as dangerous as ever. Communism still menaces the free-world – it still wants to win over our peoples and to incorporate us into its own power-system. There is not the slightest indication that these ambitions will change in the foreseeable future.

While the Soviet leaders have long recognised the dangers inherent in a world-wide military conflict, they are seeking (and finding) their successes by 'other means'. It was the purpose of this chapter to point to a few of these successful communist methods of influencing and undermining other peoples. Thus these concepts, of ideology and co-existence of normalisation of relations, and of the struggle for peace, and demands for détente and for total disarmament all stand arrayed against us, all doing their bit for 'creative further development' in the 'continued struggle'. The mind-boggling variety of these concepts is matched only by the variety and quantity of the organisations and agencies established throughout the world with the sole task of putting these communist theories into practice.

15. World communist operations and infiltration

Before I turn to any examination of international communist activity, I must comment briefly on the consequences of the profound tensions existing between Moscow and Peking in so far as the over-all development of international communism is concerned. Intensively though Peking has tried to dispute the Soviet predominance and to construct a second stronghold of world communism which, in the Chinese view, is vastly superior to and more progressive than the Soviet Union, the exertions of Red China can be regarded as having come to nought. Her strength and national potential has proved insufficient to secure and to hold on to important, and above all, permanent, strongpoints outside Communist China. The clash between the communist super-powers has moreover resulted in internal problems throughout the structure of international communism, penetrating right down to the individual communist parties. This strain was compounded on the one hand by mishaps within the Soviet empire in Europe, culminating in the invasion of Czechoslovakia; and on the other, by the insistence with which Red Chinese leaders lay sole claim to being the only apostles of the 'true' communism. I will examine the conflict between Moscow and Peking in the next chapter; but I attach importance to stating here that, while we in the service never underestimated the effects of the severe internal communist dispute on their world-wide programme, at the same time we at no time regarded this as seriously impairing the Soviet claim to leadership in the communist world. In saying this I do not exclude the possibility that, at some time in the future, we shall see a Red China freed of internal strife and fully recovered, injecting new impulses into the body of international communism, defining fresh objectives and spreading its teachings throughout Asia. Where Peking failed in Indonesia in 1965 she may yet succeed in some other Far East country with the help of its Chinese-controlled communist party, with a resulting extension of Red Chinese influence and an expansion of the Chinese empire.

Although the cracks appearing between Moscow and Peking – which some experts go so far as to call a 'schism' – figure prominently in many current analyses of international communism, I am myself inclined to see greater dangers to Moscow in other developments. These are occurring above all in Europe. Some of them we have already seen. Others are on their way – above all, the bitter fight Moscow is having to wage against separatist trends and the increasing tendency of 'deviators' to go their own way in the European empire.

The principal evidence of gradual decay within the communist camp is that, since the dissolution of Comintern in 1943 and Cominform in 1956, there has been no institutionalised central control of the world movement. Many events of recent years, and indeed certain terms used in communist policy documents, indicate moreover that Moscow's claim to the predominant role is being increasingly challenged.

In the opinion of the Yugoslav communist Milovan Djilas there are centrifugal tendencies in international communism. This seems a very valid point to me. But it is important not to succumb to wishful thinking. My own view is that at some time in the future, instead of the one uniting world movement, there will be a number of what we might call 'national communisms'. Then the communist countries – if I may misquote Stalin here – will be communist in form but nationalist in essence. But this development will take decades, if not a century. Nobody can predict where it will end, so we cannot take it into account in our political calculations. Obviously it is the duty of every

Intelligence service to bear the possibility of such a development constantly in mind; and it seems equally obvious that one ought to keep a constant look out for ways in which the free world can encourage such tendencies. This is quite different from launching an offensive anti-communist crusade; all I put forward is that the west should employ all possible means, including psychological warfare, to maintain its position; otherwise we will be accused by posterity of having failed to act with resolution to halt our gradual decline and fall.

Nor can we exclude the possibility that, over the next few years, both sides will again make common cause and we shall see a fresh (even if perhaps only temporary) rapprochement between Moscow and Peking. This might occur, in particular, if, after the present generation of leaders in the east retires, younger forces can prevail with their opinion that worldwide victory by communism can be achieved only if all communist forces pull together. I know that Tito, for one, is grimly aware that after his demise Moscow may succeed in pulling Yugoslavia firmly into its grip again, and this would be an important victory for the solidarity of the orthodox communist front.

At any rate, at the present time, it is Moscow's brand of Communism that represents the real challenge to us. This is the force with which we must do intellectual and political battle in the widest sense.

In the previous chapter I touched on the role of the legal communist parties as supporters and exponents of the 'official' foreign policy of the communist countries. This is, however, only one aspect of the opportunities open to the legal and illegal communist parties. Whatever country they operate in, and diverse though the effects of their work may be, one thing unites all the communist parties – their constant, unchanging mission. The first phase is to subvert and to recruit the people who will make future leaders; the second to bring influence to bear on every sector of public life; the third to put pressure on the government until the communists are allowed a share of the power; and the final phase is to take over all power themselves.

Given this progression, it will be seen that communist parties in many countries have proven incapable of overcoming the resistance of freedom-loving citizens so far as to complete even the first phase of their mission. An example will illustrate this point. In the course of our inquiries before the parliamentary elections in West Germany in 1953 – the last in which the German communist party took part before it was banned not long after – we detected attempts by the authorities in Moscow and East Berlin to put their weight behind a certain pro-communist party wholly separate from the official German communist party, and hiding behind bourgeois colours. Their aim was to penetrate the bourgeois camp using eminent public figures to provide 'window dressing'. For this purpose, according to Intelligence reports we received from East Berlin, the League of Germans made an election alliance with the 'All-German People's Party', a neutralist party launched in November 1952 by Helene Wessel and Gustav Heinemann (a convinced opponent of West German rearmament, who is now Federal President). The League of Germans was officially branded a communist-front organisation by our security authorities, the Office for the Protection of the Constitution, but the All-German People's Party ignored the warnings and submitted a joint list of candidates together with the League. The parliamentary elections were duly held on 6 September 1953: neither the communist party nor the new tandem-party came within sniffing distance of the obligatory five per cent of the electorate needed to qualify for seats.

In other countries of the free world, however, the party has already made considerable progress. The second phase of the communist progression has already been reached. The vanguard are the communists in those countries where they have succeeded in establishing popular front governments, the transition before the final phase in which the communists take over all power and pave the way for their country's ingestion into the communist empire.

In 1970 there were almost fifty million (49,800,000) card-carrying members of about two hundred communist parties and splinter-groups of party status; but of these, 46,700,000 belonged to the so-called 'ruling' parties, and only 3,100,000 were members of communist parties in the eighty-five countries of the rest of the world. If we distinguish between the Moscow and Peking brands of communism, we can describe 22,600,000 as being 'loyal to Moscow' (of which 13,500,000 are party members in Soviet Russia) and 21,400,000 as being 'pro-Chinese', of whom no fewer than 21 million are residents of Red China itself. From this compilation it will be seen that 5,800,000 communist party members are 'floaters', neither bowing to Moscow nor scraping to Peking.

It is possible to draw many conclusions from this kind of data. I have no intention of joining in a numbers-game, but I can state without hesitation that Peking's attempt to gain influence on communist parties outside her sprawling empire has unquestionably failed for the time being. In western Europe, in particular, we have seen recent Chinese attempts to form splinter groups within the existing communist parties gradually dwindle to insignificance. In my view only the three huge, over-staffed Red Chinese missions maintained at The Hague, Paris and Berne are of any note as outposts of Communist China in western Europe.

Of the Soviet-aligned communist parties in western Europe the Italian and French parties are particularly conspicuous by virtue of their large membership – 1,500,000 and 300,000 respectively. They represent a factor to be considered in the domestic policies of these countries.

The improvement of West Germany's relations with France obliged us to pay somewhat closer attention to the role of the French communist party. Through the operatives we were able to infiltrate into that party, we kept track of the influence it wielded over domestic affairs in France and also obtained advance notice of the smear tactics used by the French communists to disrupt the Franco-German rapprochement. We were able to watch their collaboration with the German communists in this campaign as well. From our own standpoint – and no doubt my old French colleagues shared this view – it took a great load off our minds when the French communist party was riven by internal dissension over the military intervention of Russia in Czechoslovakia in the summer of 1968. The French communists lost a number of their best known intellectuals and the party itself lost much ground. Only the next few years will tell whether the transition from their previously flexible approach to a new dogmatic, rigid and unwavering party line will benefit the French communists or not.

By way of contrast, the Italian communist party must be regarded as the most virile communist party in Europe at the present time. It is working purposefully towards its goal of setting up a popular front in Italy, but at the same time it manages to maintain rigid loyalty towards the broad party line laid down by Moscow. Numerous Intelligence reports showed that the occupation of Czechoslovakia shook the Italian communist party no less violently than the French, but at the time I was convinced, even when the noises of protest grew quite insistent, that the Italian communist party leaders would under no circumstances allow an open split between them and their headquarters in Moscow.

Every communist party in western Europe is confronted – and will continue to be confronted for the foreseeable future – by something of a dilemma. For the time being they can scarcely expect to come to power legally or under their own steam; but they cannot see much hope of gaining their ends by violent revolution. This is why the communist parties in virtually every country of western Europe see themselves obliged to establish cells in the most diverse sectors of public life, if they are to gain influence, and to engage in intensified propaganda and subversive activities. The most instructive example here is the numerically small communist party in Great Britain, which numbered only some 32,500 members in 1968. The party is not officially represented in the House of Commons, it concentrates its efforts, not without success, on the infiltration of the leadership of the various trades unions. As the unions are the props of the Labour Party and moreover the principal source of that party's finances, the communist foothold in the unions affords them powerful opportunities of influencing Labour Party policy.

As the 1971 strike in the steel-industry showed, there is no doubt that West Germany is one of the key areas under attack in Europe. Whatever the reasons certain people may have for playing down the current importance of the Communist Party in West Germany, the fact remains that its fighting power is multiplied by such a plethora of auxiliary organs and agencies like the communist-inspired League of Conscientious Objectors that it will only be a matter of time before the party begins its final assault on every section of the public mind. In West German industry, voices have already been raised in alarm, and these must not be ignored. They call for an intensification of measures for the protection of factories and buildings against communist-inspired attacks, and a campaign to thwart further attempts at infiltration. My own impression is that the steps that have been taken so far in this direction are wholly insufficient.

The reader will recall that I have already referred to the two-tier nature of the functions of the diplomatic missions maintained by communist countries abroad: they are both organs for the propagation of official foreign policy and bases for local communist campaigns. This dual role of communist diplomatic missions is worth studying more closely, particularly since it is incompatible with the conventional status of diplomacy. There are countries in which even the Russians would not entrust senior members of their missions with duties beyond the pale of 'classical' diplomacy; in these cases the covert missions are performed by lesser staff like chauffeurs or junior clerks. In other capitals the Russians have not hesitated to employ even senior members of their embassies on this kind of work. Thus there have been incidents in various countries, including West Germany, in which Counsellors of the Embassy (i.e., the next senior official to the ambassador himself) have been required to perform acts which have caused their 'host countries' the gravest injury. There are even cases known to me in which the heads of mission themselves managed to couple their functions as senior diplomatic representatives with those of undercover agents. I am thinking in particular of the Soviet ambassador Solod, who overstepped the mark so far in Guinea at the beginning of the 1960s that even the 'progressive' head of state, Sekou Touré, was obliged to declare him *persona non grata* on account of his subversive activity. Taking advantage of his position as a diplomat, Solod had tried to subvert the Guinea National Youth and to establish communist cells throughout the country.

In addition to the diplomatic missions, whose attractions as camouflage and supply bases have never been lost on the Russians, the other communist missions and agencies abroad can also be exploited to cover illegal activities. A subversion expert in a doctor's overalls can operate as effectively from a Soviet-financed hospital, gratefully accepted by an African country, as can the Czech teacher operating from some school in an Arab capital. The approach can be adapted to the particular circumstances holding in the theatre of operations and especially to the security situation. It is a primary requirement that there should be a continual supply of suitable communist agents of both sexes, people who have been given a thorough training and specially prepared in their native communist lands for operations in the target countries. Even though these highly-trained specialists may ultimately surface at their destination groomed as 'diplomats', their individual training has little in common with the training for an orthodox diplomatic career. It is true that knowledge of the country concerned, its mentality and its languages is needed equally for both careers; but the most important part of the preparatory work of these people consists of mastering certain illegal arts. In many cases the specialists sent out to carry out subversive activities work closely with the 'residents' or other members of the communist secret services based in that country; not infrequently the two fields are controlled by the same specialist.

This book has no chapter on the Soviet secret service as such. It is true that its tactics are a basic element of many of the affairs I have described, but they can play only a minor part in a study which has as its main subject the West German Intelligence service and its work. The things I and my colleagues witnessed in our fight against the KGB[1] would suffice to fill a book on their own, and perhaps one day it can all be told. It would inevitably be very different from anything that has been written in Germany or elsewhere about the Soviet secret service and the Intelligence services of other communist countries. As far as I can see, the serious histories so far published deal with the more distant past, for security reasons there have not been any significant accounts of more recent years. Be that as it may, my own narrative can hardly go beyond a discussion of the KGB tactics in the communist campaigns I have dealt with so far.

At least forty per cent of the staff of the embassies, trade missions and other agencies of the communist countries belong to the KGB or the other secret services of the communist countries concerned. Scarcely a week passes in which members of these staffs are not requested to leave western countries as *persona non grata;* sometimes a public fuss is made, sometimes

[1] The Soviet State Security Commission.

it is not. In West Germany, in most cases over the last few years, the most that the public learned was a casual mention that another Soviet 'diplomat' had been obliged to pack his bags and leave without ceremony, having been caught spying. There is unlikely to be any change in this in the future, since it is obvious that higher interests are at stake.

For example, I recall that during my own period of office more than a hundred espionage incidents were revealed from January 1957 to autumn 1963, involving Soviet diplomatic missions in thirty-six countries. Some of these diplomats were kept under observation and no direct action was taken; in the other cases about 160 Soviet Intelligence agents were unmasked, declared *persona non grata* and ordered out of the country.

During my time, for example, a very senior member of the Czech trade mission at Frankfurt-am-Main was a member of the Czech secret service. Again, when the travelling exhibition 'Fifty Years of the Soviet Union' was held in West Germany in 1967 and 1968, one of its chief officials was also a member of the KGB. Among the members of every delegation put together in the Soviet Union for trips to the west there are always two or three members of the Soviet Intelligence or security services, partly to keep an eye on their own colleagues and partly to pursue their own inquiries. These may be interesting sidelights for the reader, but they are considered commonplace in the Intelligence and security agencies.

Communist 'influencers' and other specialists are seldom required to leave a country; in most cases they are not even recognised for what they are. They adapt their tactics and approach chameleon-like to the opportunities afforded them. The experts infiltrated into a country to disseminate *desinformatsiya* are the ones particularly worth watching. While the co-ordination of the whole information programme is in the hands of a sub-division of the Secretariat of the Communist Party's Central Committee – the Agitation and Propaganda

Division – the KGB has established for its active *desinformatsiya* operations a vast and magnificently equipped department. By 'influencer' the KGB understands people who, by virtue of their position, can multiply the impact of the information fed to them and give it the widest possible distribution.

A specific and curious example of disinformation was a book published by a French author[1] on the *Rote Kapelle* communist espionage network. No doubt the author was completely satisfied that his information was correct. The implication of his work was, however, that what the Germans referred to as *Rote Kapelle* was merely a resistance group of patriots based primarily in Nazi-occupied Europe. In reality it was one of the many arms of an octopus existing long before the war in Germany, Britain, Scandinavia (where Ernst Wollweber was the resident, succeeded by Herbert Wehner) and many other European countries. Only the anti-Nazi arm was destroyed, the other arms survived to continue the fight against the Allies after the war. The British SIS defector Philby was probably recruited by the British arm. His post-defection 'memoirs', supplied by Moscow with the object of discrediting the British SIS, were an unusually inept piece of disinformation: they had been so clumsily translated from the *Russian* language that *vokzal* or 'station' had been rationalised into 'Vauxhall station' in the English text. Nor are the British the only targets. About a decade ago we recruited an SSD agent in East Germany to work for us as a double-agent; of course he had to carry out his East German missions in our country as before, and one of these, he duly reported to us, was to supply certain documents to *Der Spiegel* from East Berlin.

Often the influencers do not realise that they are merely playing a game to rules drawn up by the KGB. Mr Cyrus B. Eaton, the respected and philanthropic founder of the Pugwash conferences, and his friends are probably regarded by the

[1] Gilles Perrault, *L'Orchestre Rouge*.

Russians as influencers too, though without their knowing it. In many cases, I should like to make plain, the work of the influencers is perfectly legal; it is this, and their completely unsuspecting natures, that make it impossible even to estimate how many influencers there are, let alone to pinpoint them and neutralise their effect. In West Germany it has not proved possible to identify more than a few isolated cases. These influencers have been prevented from doing further harm; but conditions here are so favourable for the communist Intelligence services that it is clear there must be many hundreds at work in our country, in addition to the thousands of regular communist espionage agents.

I would like to conclude this chapter with an extract from the 'Rules for Political and Psychological Subversion' laid down by the Chinese Sun-Tse about five hundred years before Christ:

There is no art higher than that of destroying the enemy's resistance without a fight.

The direct tactic of war is necessary only on the battlefield; but only the indirect tactic can lead to a real and lasting victory.

Subvert anything of value in the enemy's country.

Implicate the emissaries of the major powers in criminal undertakings; undermine their position and destroy their reputation in other ways as well, and expose them to the public ridicule of their fellow citizens.

Do not shun the aid of even the lowest and most despicable people. Disrupt the work of their governments with every means you have.

Spread disunity and dispute among the citizens of the enemy's country. Turn the young against the old. Use every means to destroy their arms, their supplies and the discipline of the enemy's forces. Debase old traditions and accepted gods. Be generous with promises and rewards to purchase Intelligence and accomplices. Send out your secret agents in all directions. Do not skimp with money or with promises, for they yield a high return.[1]

These rules comprise a set of principles which in my view still hold good, virtually without change or reservation, for every one of the aspects I have mentioned of world communist activity and subversion.

[1] Translated from *Encyclopédie Française*, 1959, vol. ix.

16. Twenty-five years of Soviet power politics

In this final chapter I propose to show the most important consequences of Soviet power politics since the end of the Second World War, and the probable effect of these policies on the 1970s, on whose threshold we now stand. In doing so I will consider Soviet policies towards Germany first and deal in some detail with the present state of Soviet-German relations in the light of the West German government's new *Ostpolitik*. In so doing I propose to lay bare the unaltered essence of Soviet power politics, a driving force which is too often camouflaged and hidden from view. I want to show the iceberg in all its immensity, not just the minute tip that shows above the surface.

Communist policies can at present be seen in their most perfect form in the Soviet version. There is much truth in the dictum that what is of benefit to the Soviet Union cannot be of harm to the communist movement and, conversely, that the triumph of communism in any corner of the globe must also benefit the interests of the Soviet Union as an imperialist world power.

The goal is the revolutionary transformation of the world into a Utopian-seeming communist 'ultimate society'. Adherence to the strategic goal of a communist ultimate society is not some kind of outdated and inconvenient ballast which (as many people in the west seem to think) the communists are going to offload at the first opportunity they get in order to enhance their freedom of action. Errors of judgment on this decisive point could only lead to the most fateful consequences. We

were presented with one urgent instance of this when the former
eastern affairs adviser of President Johnson, the otherwise
sensible and highly qualified Zbigniev Breczinski, proclaimed
to anybody who would listen that the era of dis-ideologisation
had finally dawned. This pronouncement of a widely accepted
expert (who has since revised his opinion) could have had
untold effects on American foreign policy and hence on our
own. He turned out to be wrong, a fact which our own conscientious inquiries confirmed time and again.

I have always regarded Soviet policies as a uniform whole,
and they must be judged as a whole if dangerous errors of
judgment are not to arise. I accept that the communists are not
a monolithic bloc in any way. Of course there are signs of
tensions and there are divergent theories within the communist
system: there are errors of judgment, mishaps and setbacks so
that the communist world movement as a whole sometimes
appears as disunited and crisis-prone as the Atlantic alliance.
Communist politicians are also human beings; they are fallible
and they show it. Moreover, the communist bloc houses a
quantity of dry tinder, and if this were ever ignited it could bring
disaster for Moscow and her satellites. I will take the opportunity later in this chapter of indicating where such prospects
might be sought.

The Soviet Union has seen nearly all the Tsars' dreams of
expansion realised as a result of the Second World War; the
Baltic states were again incorporated within her boundaries and
Finland came *de facto* within her sway. In the Far East part of
the Kuril islands had been occupied, and the losses she had
suffered in the Russo-Japanese war of 1905 were thus avenged.
To the triumph of Soviet arms was soon added the transformation of the eastern and south-eastern European countries into
'socialist societies'. Via Yugoslavia and Albania, the Russians
had secured routes of access to the Adriatic and thus to the
Mediterranean. Germany which – *pace* Lenin – was the key to
world revolution was now at least half within the communist

grasp; and the prospects seemed auspicious for the triumph of communism in West Germany as well.

The communist parties in Italy and France had survived their years of repression remarkably well; within a short time they were again operational and had won a share in the government of their countries. The turmoil of war had also exacerbated social tensions in Latin America. In the rest of the world, the British and French colonial systems were creaking at the joints. In consequence of the aid afforded them by the United States – more for philanthropic and moral reasons than out of political farsightedness – it seemed only a matter of time before the chaos stirred up by the independence movements outside Europe paved the way for communism. Finally, it was also clear that the days of Chiang Kai-shek's Nationalist China were numbered, and that Mao Tse-tung was certain to succeed him. The triumphs of communism on a world-wide scale seemed just around the corner.

Scarcely any of my readers will disagree with me when I suggest that this colossal increase in the power of the Soviet Union ought to have alarmed every person concerned with the future of the non-communist free world. But the truth was that the warning voices went unheeded by almost every government; a glaring example of how a potential adversary and his plans and objectives can fail to be identified in time. While the Soviet Union restocked Hitler's depleted munitions dumps in eastern Europe, the western Allies destroyed the arms factories and industrial installations in their zones of Germany. The United States demobilised her armies post-haste, thereby inflicting on herself a military weakness which was to cost her dearly in Korea a few years later.

Favourable though her starting-point was, however, the Soviet Union proved incapable in the early post-war years of accomplishing the strategic objectives she had set in many countries. Stalin found to his cost that the 'decadent imperialist Capitalism' still had astounding fighting power. When China fell to the communists in 1949 there arose not only a crippling economic burden for Stalin, but also a major rival for the leadership and domination of the communist world.

In Czechoslovakia the communists managed to seize power in 1948, but for the time being the other attempts to expand the communist power base were frustrated. The Russians failed in their attempt to put pressure on Turkey to open the Straits for their naval vessels; moreover, the Russians had to relinquish the previously occupied northern provinces of Iran. The communist revolution in Greece collapsed. In Malaysia it became apparent that the local communist strength was insufficient to open up the territory as a base for the Soviet Union in southeast Asia. What happened in the industrial countries of western Europe was particularly disappointing for Stalin. Everywhere the communist parties were squeezed out of government, and in several cases they lost all their parliamentary seats as well. In West Germany the western Allies prevented the Russians from exerting any kind of influence on the restoration of political and economic life. The attitude of the western powers at the time of the Russian blockade of Berlin proved moreover that they were resolved to prevent the communist movement from scoring any further successes in Europe.

In my view, the Berlin blockade became such a *cause célèbre* of the Cold War that I ought perhaps to focus on it at greater length. When Stalin took his decision to order a blockade of West Berlin, he did not do so just because of Lenin's dictum that he who holds Berlin is Lord of Europe and thus of the world: he wanted to force the west to give up West Berlin as a forward position behind the Iron Curtain and permit its incorporation into East Germany as a necessary preliminary to the eventual inclusion of the whole of Germany in the Soviet empire. It was only when his blockade failed to reduce West Berlin, and, when years later he realised intensive communist attempts to take over West Germany from within were proving equally fruitless, that Stalin resigned himself to an interim period in which the partition of Germany should be stabilised. His new concern then was to confront the West German federal republic with a powerful and stable East German state so as to make a fusion of the two halves of Germany impossible without Soviet acquiescence. I remember that we received reports of utterances by Khrushchev in which he stated bluntly that even if West Germany were to become wholly communist, Moscow would still keep the two German states apart in the interests of Soviet security. This principle has been echoed by Khrushchev's successors.

The collapse of the Berlin blockade and the failure of the communist advance into South Korea signalled the end of an epoch in which the political strategy and tactics of the communist world movement was devoted to the aggressive expansion of its empire. Stalin adjourned the strategic offensive *sine die* and began to consolidate and strengthen his own empire. Since the beginning of the 1950s communist policies have been characterised by the attempts of the non-ruling communist parties finally to overcome their isolation and to achieve a degree of co-operation with 'progressive' forces. Their aim is a new popular front, whereby the United States will be inched out of Europe and isolated on a world-wide scale, while all major risks are carefully avoided. As far as her own empire is concerned, the Soviet Union's primary aim is to complete the assimilation of her satellites and to promote the political solidarity of the masses by means of an accelerated programme of social, political and ideological education. The course of this does not, of course, run smooth. There have been and will continue to be disruptions in the eastern bloc such as in East Germany on 17 June 1953, the uprisings in Hungary and Poland in 1956, and the Czechoslovakian crisis of 1968. But this is the general line that has been rigidly followed to the present day.

The endeavours of the non-ruling communist parties to prove they were capable of government were vitiated as long as the

Cold War period lasted. The historical incidents I have mentioned like the communist seizure of power in Czechoslovakia at the end of the 1940s and similar coups in the early 1950s can hardly have acted as an inducement to other parties to allow the communists a share of the government. Nothing could better illustrate the strategically offensive nature of the policy of peaceful co-existence than the fact that it is only since its introduction (after 1955) that the non-ruling communist parties could hope for any success in their dialogues with the 'progressive' forces. This new brand of popular front was achieved in a somewhat weakened form in Finland some years ago, and it has recently been accomplished with a much more Marxist flavour in Chile as well; the new brand is distinguished from the popular front of the 1930s by the fact that it permits the collaboration of non-Marxist elements (Christian organisations, for example). In permitting this, the communists are satisfied that, as time passes, they will take over all the power themselves, by virtue of their own superior organisation.

As a particular example of this kind of détente the Russians repeatedly refer to the Cuba crisis of 1961. In the west we have repeatedly heard that the Cuba conflict proves that crises in which both super-powers are in direct confrontation need not necessarily lead to war, and that this was confirmed by Khrushchev's dismantling the Soviet missile bases. It has long seemed obvious to me that this inference needs urgent correction. What we are being asked to regard as a Soviet 'defeat' has, in fact, left the Russians with an unrivalled opportunity for exploiting Cuba as an all-purpose base for international communist activity and subversion.

Attempts at détente (which have at times bordered on the hectic) have characterised the western political posture since then. The Russians have responded by pressing various plans for disengagement or disarmament. Most were destined to fail since the communists always refused to allow any opportunity for inspection of their own military potential. Nonetheless they were psychologically effective, for they focused public attention on the apparent 'peaceability' of the socialist camp. Of these plans – apart from the demand for total disarmament and the two nuclear test-ban treaties – the Russians have been capitalising for many years on the Rapacki Plan as a propaganda ploy. Adam Rapacki, a post-war Polish foreign minister, called for a neutral zone free of atomic weapons, extending across northern and eastern Central Europe as a buffer between the Soviet Union and the west. To the naïve, it was probably a very attractive proposition; it was indeed difficult to answer without knowledge of the background and of the objectives the Russians were pursuing.

The modern variant of this general line was the doctrine decided on at the Rumanian communist party's congress on 4 July 1966. This proposed a European security system consisting of only the European powers, and called for the dissolution of the two military alliances, NATO and the Warsaw Pact. If accepted, the outcome would be a withdrawal of all United States forces across the Atlantic, while Soviet forces could still mass at will along the Russo-Polish frontier – hardly an attractive proposition for western Europe. This doctrine has been repeated in all the important declarations of the communist countries and parties since then, most recently at the summit meeting of party leaders and heads of government of the Warsaw Pact countries in East Berlin on 2 December 1970.

It is natural that the aggressive nature of the Russian policies of 'peaceful co-existence' and 'détente' must primarily affect their relationship with the most powerful nation in the free world, the United States. This was demonstrated most explicitly by their injured disruption of the Paris summit of May 1960 after the U-2 incident. Over the previous months we in the service had gradually pieced together an Intelligence picture which indicated that the Soviet Union was losing interest in the Paris conference at a rate which was in direct proportion to the gradual emergence of a united approach by the three western powers under American leadership. The U-2 incident was merely a fortunate circumstance affording Khrushchev a welcome opportunity to stage the desired scene in Paris before the eyes of the world. We were in the fortunate position of being able to provide advance warning that Khrushchev had decided to break up the conference.

An aim of Soviet policy is the isolation of the United States and its eventual withdrawal from Europe. This has always implied that the United States must remain permanently embroiled in crisis situations outside Europe, but also that for the time being any direct confrontation with the major western powers must be avoided. There will definitely be no change in this policy so long as the potential of the United States remains superior to, or equivalent to, that of the Soviet Union. This simple fact alone, which was confirmed by countless Intelligence reports prior to my retirement from the service, shows that the Soviet Union cannot have the least interest in seeing the United States released from her involvement in Vietnam, and will therefore never put pressure on the North Vietnamese to end the war.

Of course the Russians could bring pressure to bear on North Vietnam any time they wished, but they will do so only if the United States should decide to abandon South Vietnam to its fate. President Nixon's wise attempt to normalise his country's diplomatic relations with Red China may open up the path to a solution of the Vietnam problem which, while not completely satisfactory, will at least be tolerable.

I should like to consider the causes of the present situation in Vietnam. One of the principal American errors was to support the liquidation of President Diem. Quite apart from the moral objections to political assassinations, which I have already voiced, his removal plunged his country into a domestic conflict and gravely weakened it at a time when the country was fighting for its very existence. The political climate was so cleverly manipulated by the Soviet and Chinese secret services that the Americans obviously lacked an accurate or complete picture of the internal situation. Admittedly Diem was no great champion of democracy; but to try to introduce democracy in the middle of a war would have been an unjustifiable hazard. This was a view, I might add, that I already held when the first Intelligence reports of an approaching crisis began to come in.

It would be foolish to cherish the illusion that the Kremlin will not try to serve up fresh 'Vietnams' for the United States wherever it can in future. It will force the United States to become involved in further conflicts which require no great exertion on the part of the Russians; the kind of conflict which can be extensively exploited for its propaganda value in the eyes of the rest of the world.

As with Vietnam, the Soviet Union is not *directly* involved in the other most dangerous crisis area extant at the beginning of the 1970s, the Middle East. Unlike the remote conflict in Vietnam, however, the Middle East dispute is situated in one of the most important zones as far as Germans are concerned, and it is endowed with a significance far transcending the simple dispute between the state of Israel and the Arab countries. For Europe this is a region of vast importance: both bridge and pivot. It confronts the southern flank of NATO and borders on the Mediterranean which it has always been one of Russia's ambitions to dominate. Here are Europe's vital oil reserves, without which it cannot survive for any length of time.

For the Soviet Union, the Arab region is not merely a conglomeration of countries that have passed the phase of national revolution and are already well on the way to becoming socialist societies. They see the Arabian sub-continent as a springboard for the assault on Africa, and at the same time, unlike for the major western powers, the Suez Canal is critically important to the Soviet Union for her sea routes to south-east Asia.

The growing interest of the Russians in the Arab world has

been apparent to us since the mid-1950s. That was why, as I have indicated, we decided to establish a network of contacts in the area to provide a continuous flow of Intelligence reports. The Russians centred their interest and their operations on Egypt. From the Soviet standpoint the other countries merited particular attention only if their social transformation was sufficiently far advanced or if they displayed a willingness to provide bases for the Soviet navy and air force. Their role is to contribute to the network of air bases and anchorages built up by the Russians over the eastern end of the Mediterranean, where the Soviet naval squadron is already a dangerous adversary for the long unchallenged and formidable American Sixth Fleet.

Unlike Vietnam, however, there is always the possibility that should the conflict in the Middle East again flare up the Soviet Union may be forced to intervene actively to prevent an even greater defeat than that which the Arabs suffered in 1967. The explosive situation is particularly highlighted by the presence of thousands of Soviet technical advisers in Egypt, and by the stationing there of Soviet aircraft flown by Soviet pilots on a constant stand-by basis. This Soviet military presence obliges Moscow to keep the situation permanently under a tight rein. This degree of control is particularly important in view of the fact that the senior Soviet advisers, headed by the Middle East specialist Ambassador Vinogradov, have apparently failed so far to couple the considerable arms deliveries with the necessary safeguards to protect the Russian position.

Nor do the long-term treaties the Russians have signed alter this uncomfortable situation. From my own knowledge of the Arab mentality I believe the Russians will find it extremely difficult to convert their enormous military and economic aid into a political currency. Despite every public assurance to the contrary, I am inclined to regard President Sadat's vigorous steps against his opponents among whom were the most outspoken supporters of Moscow as being proof that he is continuing Nasser's unremitting fight against every kind of communist activity in his country.

Given these dual Russian aims – of tying down the United States and NATO while maintaining and increasing the dependence of the Arab countries on the Soviet Union – it is clear that there is little hope that the Palestine conflict will soon see an early or final solution. Even if the next few years see a peace settlement, which under present conditions can be reached only at Israel's expense, the Middle East will remain the world's most crucial crisis area for a long time to come. The United States and western Europe would do well to grow accustomed to this fact.

The danger of a direct confrontation between the United States and the Soviet Union is obviously greatest in Europe; by Europe, I mean Germany, and that in turn means Berlin. This is why Moscow is doing all it possibly can to prise Europe out of the arms of the United States.

It particularly impressed me to see the perceptiveness with which de Gaulle predicted this in 1961 and 1962, as I knew from my discussions with French colleagues. At that time de Gaulle assumed that, voluntarily or involuntarily, the Americans would sooner or later have to withdraw from Europe. He foresaw with mounting foreboding the day when a disunited Europe would have to withstand Soviet imperialism on its own. This would arise, or so de Gaulle believed, in the latter part of the 1970s; the important thing was to prepare for it while there was still time. De Gaulle saw the new Paris-Bonn axis as the bulwark of an independent Europe – and in his language that meant a Europe 'capable of self-defence'.

In this connection I am reminded of a conversation I had with General Ollié, a close confidant of de Gaulle and a former commander-in-chief of the French forces. He visited me early in October 1962 at the general's request and adumbrated to me the latter's innermost thoughts for unofficial forwarding to the

Federal Chancellor, Dr Adenauer. The chancellor told me he agreed that the general's ideas were right in every respect, but for various reasons he was unable to adopt them in their entirety as exclusively as the French president had perhaps expected. Whatever other considerations there were, Germany's special position and our heavy reliance on the United States had to be considered above anything else.

I have referred in various contexts on earlier pages to the unchanging and consistently pursued aims of Soviet foreign policy, and particularly of their policies towards Germany.

The 1969 change of government in Bonn, with the emergence of a socialist coalition government under Willy Brandt as chancellor, was exploited by the Soviet Union as an ideal opportunity to modify their methods in Germany while retaining their long-term aims. The new government launched immediate, and almost insistent, attempts to break the log-jam in their *Ostpolitik*. In view of these overtures, which soon became public knowledge, the Kremlin hastened to tie down the West German government to a treaty which they designed from the outset to be nothing less than a formal confirmation of the partition of Germany. The treaty concluded in Moscow in August 1970 reflected the West German acceptance of the two-State theory, ceremonially documented just as the Soviet government would have wished. Thus the solution of the German problem the Russians had contended for in vain for so long had been startlingly thrust into their laps.

At the time of writing, the Soviet-German treaty is still the subject of powerful controversy and awaiting ratification. While its supporters – predominantly Brandt's government and the majority of his coalition's deputies – lauded this as an event of historic importance, its opponents not only called attention to its disadvantages but questioned the very essence of such treaty documents. The federal government then went further and amplified the Moscow treaty, with its confirmation of the partition of Germany, by an agreement with Poland signed in Warsaw on 7 December 1970, an agreement that put the seal on the final surrender of Germany's ancient territories to the east of the Oder and Neisse rivers. Thus they formally acquiesced in the communist policies of aggrandisement in central and eastern Europe.

The opponents of this treaty hold the view that the Russians never have and never will sign a treaty in which their own interests do not come first and foremost. Nor, so far as I am aware, has there been any historical instance of the Russians' attaching any importance whatever to establishing a genuine, let alone a permanent, rapport with a neighbouring country. I would refer those who still doubt this to the memoirs of the former American ambassador in Moscow, George F. Kennan, who warned most urgently against swallowing Soviet proposals or offers of treaties without first making sure of the necessary safeguards for one's own position.

I believe that the view repeatedly expressed by the West German government, that there is no alternative to the *Ostpolitik* of the socialist and liberal coalition, is a mistaken one. It may well be that the Soviet Union itself will force us sooner or later to swallow an alternative. The hardening line expressed by the communist press during 1971, and the un-ambiguous statements of loud-mouthed generals and leading communist officials, particularly those in the East German government and communist party, underline this possibility. So also does the increasing frequency with which they demand the recognition of the German Democratic Republic.

An exceptionally undesirable consequence of these treaties with the communist governments has been that there is now widespread distrust of the federal republic in the western world. This western distrust has been aroused and expressed in so many different ways that neither the official words of encouragement and commendation mouthed by western statesmen, which are beginning to look as hollow as they sound, nor the soothing assurances of the West German government and its spokesmen can conceal it. For example, I understand that western Intelligence services with whom I always enjoyed the utmost co-operation are now reluctant to exchange their more secret information with the present federal Intelligence service.

The treaty negotiations between Moscow and Bonn would not have been conceivable had there not been a series of preliminary conversations conducted by close confidants of Willy Brandt, the then Foreign Minister, in Rome, long before he formed his socialist liberal coalition government in the late autumn of 1969. The ice had been broken by the editor of the Italian communist newspaper *Unitâ* in a visit to a number of leftwing German journalists in Bonn in September 1967. After this discussion on the two Germanies, a leading member of Brandt's circle travelled to Rome and met the secretary of the leader of the Italian communist party, Luigi Longo, and late that November a three-man delegation from Willy Brandt's Social Democratic party arrived in Rome for unpublicised meetings with leading communist officials in the Hotel Cavalieri Hilton.[1] Secret knowledge of these exploratory talks placed the federal Intelligence service in an awkward position for some time. We were still attached to Chancellor Kiesinger's office and I was directly responsible to him. When our sources in Italy – who kept the communist party there under surveillance with the knowledge of the leading Italians – sent us their reports I was obliged to shelve them for obvious political reasons. Fortunately the Italian Democrazia Cristiana party had also kept watch on the secret meetings. We obtained copies of their reports, translated them and supplied these to Kiesinger.

Some details of these 1967 talks between Brandt's SPD officials and leading Italian communists subsequently leaked out in public. One thing is certain: it was in these Italian

[1] A full account of these was given in the Italian weekly journal *Vie Nuove* in November 1970.

conversations that the foundations were laid for the 'new *Ostpolitik*' the federal government was to adopt after Willy Brandt came to power in 1969.

The profit to the communists in finally gaining acceptance for their theory of two, or rather three German states (if Berlin is included) lies mainly in the psychological effect this will have on the East German population. I cannot emphasise this too much. These people have remained far closer to our own country, through all the vicissitudes of humiliation and disappointment, than many would now like to believe. Now they are forced to recognise that their present status is going to be with them for ever, that they have been irrevocably sacrificed to the communists. And what is true of the psychological effect on the East Germans is equally true *mutatus mutandis* for the people of the other communist satellite countries who are just as unsympathetic towards communism. In my view the Kremlin can thus expect to reap a further reward – the consolidation of its satellite empire, which it has always striven to achieve. Now the process of Bolshevisation can really begin.

Finally, the Russians attach no less importance to the psychological value of the Soviet-German treaty on the West German population. They are not the only ones to anticipate that more voices in the federal republic will demand that this new-found *modus vivendi* with the Soviet Union be built upon and expanded. Thus the internal stability of NATO will be subjected to new strains. The Kremlin will secure an added (and once again, a unilateral) advantage in its campaign to undermine the west.

These remarks on Soviet policy towards Germany would be incomplete without a mention of the role of Berlin. I am more puzzled than ever before as to what kind of 'normalisation' the Brandt government envisages for the situation of West Berlin. Not even the internationalisation of the road and rail corridors linking Berlin with the west and the disappearance of East

German controls which this would permit – neither of which either the Russians or the East Germans will ever accept – could ease the exposed position of West Berlin as an outpost of the free world. Every single one of the concessions that may be made by the communists, like easier access of West Berliners to East Berlin and East Germany, can be cancelled without a moment's notice: there will always be reason enough.

If the west and the federal republic do not remain constantly on guard, piecemeal Berlin settlements will only serve to make the divided city's long-term position more hopeless than it is. In any case, Berlin's usefulness as a political 'lever' will not be done away with by any agreement; it will remain as a bludgeon in the arsenal of the Russians and East Germans, to be produced from time to time to test the nerve of the western powers and the federal republic.

This is no time for the informed – and there are many, for it is not only I who can scent the Brandt government's irresistible urge to make concessions over West Berlin – to still the voices of warning. We must not cease to give voice to our justified anxiety, if we are to prevent still further concessions from being made without equivalent returns and gestures by the other side.

The basically aggressive character of Soviet strategy entails some problems and risks for the communist empire. The policy of détente inevitably pierces holes through the hermetic seal which has hitherto separated the communist countries from the west. As they seek to expand their trade, technical and cultural exchanges, there results an intensified contact not only at the official but also at the personal level between citizens of east and west. The satellite countries have displayed a tendency to reap what rewards they can from the 'golden west'. This will almost inevitably increase. For this reason the Russians are obliged to play down the policy they have purposefully adhered to since 1966, namely of calling for a European security system, within their own communist empire.

Within the Warsaw Pact there is still no foreseeable danger that member-countries will lose their political allegiance to Moscow. The Brezhnev doctrine can leave none of them in any doubt but that Moscow is determined to prevent any repetition of events like those in Poland and Hungary in 1956 or any communist reformation like that attempted by Alexander Dubcek in Czechoslovakia. Western journalists ascribed the invasion of Czechoslovakia almost entirely to military considerations. Clearly such considerations will have played their part in the decisions that were taken, but far weightier than these was the realisation that Dubcek was in danger of losing control of the situation, and that a landslide might shortly begin which would end in a new brand of communism, or even in some kind of 'Social Democratic' order

Nobody should forget how Dubcek was forced to capitulate. When he could not live up to his promises, the Russians took the necessary steps. The invasion itself was designed not only to preserve the Soviet empire but to safeguard the European policies which the Russians intended to continue to pursue. In Czechoslovakia that August every hope of attaining a modest degree of national sovereignty and intellectual freedom was ruthlessly crushed. Once the floodtide of liberty had ebbed, there remained only the residue of resignation and apathy. The passive fatalism of the eastern European population, which is manifested in their unsatisfactory morale, remains meantime the main problem in pursuing Russian policies of détente. I remain absolutely convinced that the communist system is flatly rejected by the broad mass of the Polish, Hungarian and Czech populations, although they will obviously not openly admit it.

As far as East Germany is concerned, it is known that among its citizens there is still no real sense of belonging to the German Democratic Republic, apart, of course, from the narrow circles of party officials and beneficiaries of the system. This in no way detracts from their justifiable pride in their hard-won accom-

G.M.—M

plishments as a new industrial nation; but the bulk of the population will always be indifferent towards communism. Just how false the public façade of support for their régime really is was demonstrated only too clearly when our Federal Chancellor Willy Brandt visited Erfurt in East Germany for talks in March 1970. Neither I nor my former colleagues were in the least surprised that this solidarity with the west was given such conspicuous and audible expression at Erfurt: the feelings are there, and they will be spontaneously kindled each time the occasion arises.

Perhaps it is this, more than anything else, which ought to make it an irrevocable duty for every West German government to respect this deep-seated emotion in East Germany, and to refrain from committing any action which might serve to perpetuate the partition of Germany. The incidents at Erfurt also show, moreover, that no communist government – least of all that of East Berlin – can afford to introduce measures of liberalisation. To do so would be to jeopardise its very existence, which is based on the unhampered and unchallenged rule of force. Any suggestion that such measures can be encouraged through concessions by the west are pipe-dreams, and nothing else.

Monolithic though the communist empire established by the Russians in eastern Europe may be, Moscow is troubled by continuing disunity on the broader communist front. I have already touched upon the major deviators – Red China and Yugoslavia – in examining the ideological differences between them and the Soviet Union. Albania is not a significant factor in all this. In these pages I propose to mention a few of the elements I have learned about the pursuit of different paths to communism.

As far as Moscow's East European satellites are concerned, the recalcitrant Yugoslavia remains the missing link in a chain which – as the Russians see it – must be closed one day. From many sources we know that the Soviet leaders do not see any possibility of change so long as Tito, Yugoslavia's head of state – who without doubt is one of the great political personalities of the century – is in a position to decide the fate of his country. The Soviet Union has its eye, therefore, on the period immediately following Tito's departure. His going will, the Russians anticipate, release the dyed-in-the-wool communists who have been pining for closer contact with Moscow, and at the same time create opportunities to force this territory under Moscow's sway. The Soviet Intelligence service has already begun, under careful cover, to set up plans for this in Yugoslavia, and the separatist disturbances in Croatia late in 1971 are probably to be interpreted in this light.

Of far greater importance to Moscow and to the entire communist camp is, of course, the squabble with Red China. Since their objectives of world revolution are identical, it is their ideological differences that first meet the eye; but most probably the real tension is primarily built up by conflicts in power politics. While I have no intention of minimising the bitterness of this conflict I do suggest that the rivalry between the two communist super-powers has been exaggerated, and that while it is not as yet possible to fathom the political motive underlying this exaggeration, it is clearly influenced by subtle Russian propaganda. I see that a study of 'New Trends in Kremlin Policy' recently published by a European and American joint study-group takes the same view.

I am as reluctant now as I was over ten years ago to regard the split between Moscow and Peking as irrevocable and final. After all, what is 'final' in politics? In any case, the communist and socialist movements have shown nothing but schisms in their 125 years of history, without having suffered undue injury.

Nor have I been able to share the hopes of my western friends that this dispute might yet force the Soviet Union to come to terms with the west. It is obvious that the dispute with

Peking is a nuisance for the Russians, but it does not put them at any serious risk at present, nor will it in the foreseeable future. Given the immense Soviet military superiority, outright war between the two powers is improbable for several years. It would be bound to end in defeat for Peking, while at the same time placing an almost intolerable burden on Moscow with the necessary provisioning and administration of the conquered territories. Nor do the Ussuri river incidents of March 1969 alter this judgment in any way: they were local in character, and were deliberately played up by both sides. Should I be wrong in my analysis, and should it in fact turn out that the Russians really do wish to secure their rear in the west for fear of Red China, then I can only hope that we will refuse to grant them any support so long as the Kremlin continues to deny its satellites independence.

As in the case of Yugoslavia – though under wholly different conditions and circumstances – the Russian leaders who are still fighting for a global communist movement are counting on sweeping changes in Red China once the Chinese dictator Mao Tse-tung has gone. But while I am inclined to put quite high the Soviet chances of assimilating and perhaps even annexing Yugoslavia to the Soviet Union once Tito goes, I judge the Soviet prospects in China after Mao's death very much less favourably. The Prime Minister, Chou En-lai, can be regarded as one of the architects of consolidation, and he will not offer the Russians any hope that China will submit to the unchallenged hegemony of Moscow. But nor, on the other hand, will either they or anyone else prove able to carry on the almost sacred cult of personality surrounding Mao. Chou is probably realist enough to try first to restore to the interior of his country the stability vital for an effective foreign policy. A stable and consolidated China will then be able to play a hand in international affairs very different from that of the giant nation at present, emasculated as it is by domestic disorders.

In stating my belief that in the long run we are more likely to see a rapprochement between Russia and China than a continuation – let alone an aggravation – of the present conflict, it has, of course, been necessary to take the Soviet leadership into account as well. It seems probable that future changes in the Soviet command will be of greater significance in all this than is generally accepted. In Khrushchev, the legendary figure of Stalin – utterly implacable and obsessed with the politics of power – was succeeded by a showy personality whose sudden tactical whims frequently provoked acute dismay amongst his own entourage. In Brezhnev and Kosygin we have seen Khrushchev replaced by pragmatic and hard-bitten politicians, wielding power with Podgorny in a triumvirate which was widely predicted to have little life-expectation.

At the time of writing there are recurring press reports presenting Leonid Ilyich Brezhnev, the 65-year-old Secretary-General of the Soviet Union's communist party, as the 'new Stalin'. I cannot believe that Brezhnev will manage to outwit his partners and climb the last rungs of the ladder to absolute dictatorship. This is a mantle that will fall to one of his successors. But I share the view of many prominent experts on the Soviet Union that one particular personality will attain absolute power in the Kremlin in the not too distant future and that he will then master-mind both the struggle for dominion within the communist empire and the external conflict with the western world. Of all the top-level Soviet officials we have seen over the last few years one man has stood head and shoulders above the rest – Alexander Shelyepin, whose work in the secret service, in the youth movement and currently as leader of the Soviet trades unions has guaranteed him a following of incomparable breadth. Should Shelyepin succeed in improving his relations with the military commanders and Soviet marshals, he may well become the 'new Stalin'. He has been defeated once already by the resistance of the old guard officials; but he is shrewd enough to wait until the moment is ripe. Of one thing there can be no doubt: his own supporters credit him with all the necessary ambition and ability necessary to reach for the mantle of absolute power.

Important though this analysis of the future conduct of Soviet power politics may be, it is not the end of the story. With twenty-six years' experience in analysing the Soviet estate, I would be inclined to predict the Soviet objectives for the 1970s as follows:

They will try to consolidate their own empire in Europe, including all their wartime and post-war conquests, where necessary by force of arms. This is the Brezhnev doctrine, of which an example was the occupation of Czechoslovakia, to which I would add that, in my opinion, the Soviet Union will not hesitate to intervene with the same ruthlessness in Poland or Rumania, for example, should need arise.

They will intensify their attempts to dissolve the western system of alliances in Europe and replace it by a 'European peace settlement' (as the Russians understand the concept of peace). The hinge of these efforts will remain West Germany, which they will try to undermine, isolate and intimidate as a preliminary to transferring her to the Soviet sphere of influence.

They will also establish strongpoints in the Mediterranean, in the Arab world and in the Indian Ocean. They will extend their influence in Scandinavia, from Finland to the Barents Sea. They will expand their strength in Cuba, as a base for the ultimate war with the United States that may later come. Meantime negotiations with the United States, coupled with certain concessions on the Soviet part, will be pursued only where overwhelmingly favourable results will accrue from them for the Russians.

Finally, they will make provision for the inclusion of Red China in a communist world empire under Soviet hegemony once Mao Tse-tung has gone, without resort to armed conflict if possible.

If the west continues to play its present passive political role, the 1980s will probably see a grave worsening of the international situation, once the present generation of leaders in Moscow and Peking has been replaced by a new one. The question of who will take over power within the Kremlin is of particular importance in this connection. During the 1980s the world will probably see the elimination of Red China as a rival contender for the dominant role in world communism by force of Soviet arms, should it have proved impossible to draw her into the fold by other means short of war. The communists will then intensify their activity in the key areas of western Europe and the Mediterranean, coupled with an attempt to draw western Europe itself and the countries bordering on the southern Soviet Union into the communist empire. And the communists will then make their final dispositions for the ultimate clash with the United States of America.

Given these political objectives, the west's chance of survival will depend on whether we succeed in confronting the Soviet Union with a concerted strategy born of the knowledge I have tried to set out in these pages. Of course, there are numerous experts, even in the United States, who see these dangers in the same light as I do; but the vast majority of the public has still to recognise the dangers. Above all they still fail to grasp that the west can fight this virus coming from the east only by a strategy of *political offence*.

If we are asked, 'Has the Soviet Union become less dangerous?' I can only reply emphatically that she has not. The Soviet Union is not a static power, solely concerned with the maintenance of her possessions in good order; she is a politically dynamic and aggressive world power which will stop at nothing to secure her aims. There is no basis whatever for the hints dropped in recent months about a 'genuine change' in Soviet policies; this is the purest speculation. The methods and tactics of Soviet campaigning have been refined; but the will to attack everything we hold most dear, and particularly our freedom of thought and action, remains unchanged.

We should not refuse to treat with the east, provided we pursue the negotiations over a long period of time, devoid of any illusions and without proposing any concessions on our own part. The Soviet mentality will never understand any treaty dealings in which we fail to formulate clear counter-demands against them: such dealings will always be regarded with the utmost mistrust. The correct way to negotiate is always to start off by listing the maximum demands, while at the same time bearing constantly in mind what are the minimum demands – that is, the demands whose non-acceptance must be followed by a breaking-off of the negotiations.

We must hope that these facts will come to be accepted, for there is only one way for the free world as we know it to survive – and that is if the whole of the west can put its parochial interests in second place and recognise that the supreme need now is to unite into one political entity, capable of combating the aggressive Soviet 'peace policies', with their unchanged ambition of bestowing on all mankind the 'blessings of Socialism'.

Even more important than the unification of Europe is the Atlantic alliance. Here too, ways must be found of establishing a rigid community of purpose between this reborn Europe and the American continent. While there are obviously many issues that divide Europe and America, a settlement of these differences must nonetheless be reached. One step must be taken immediately. NATO's south-eastern hinge in the eastern Mediterranean must be given the massive political and military attention it deserves if this NATO flank is to be defended. There ought to be far closer collaboration between the NATO countries and Turkey and Greece, and if possible the diminutive but politically and militarily virile Israel should be included too. There is no time to be lost.

One thing must be certain: we must prove that Manuilsky, the head of Cominform for many years, was wrong when he wrote in his basic declaration in 1931:

... The capitalist countries are so stupefied and decadent that they will merrily toil away at their own destruction. They will be betrayed by their own anxiety for friendship. And as soon as their guard is down, we shall smash them with the mailed fist.

As for the Intelligence services of the free world, they must work in close unison and with the greatest possible energy to defeat these communist intentions. In so doing they will have played their part in securing a future for the free world, and in ensuring its freedom and security.

Appendix

Gehlen's memorandum to Adenauer on the future Intelligence service

21 May 1952

1] *The need for a federal Intelligence service*

One of a sovereign nation's most important sources of the materials on which its political actions are based is its Intelligence service. It will be seen that this embraces two distinct kinds of work, which are different in both their objects and their jobs, and it will be most practical for these to be kept organisationally separate as well.

a] As far as internal affairs are concerned, the German federal republic already possesses in the offices for the Protection of the Constitution the Intelligence organisation it needs for obtaining data on the domestic political scene;

b] Hitherto there has existed no Intelligence organisation for obtaining data on the external scene in the political, economic, military and counter-espionage sectors. With the establishment of the German federal republic's autonomy a need arises for the creation of such an organisation, i.e. a federal Intelligence service which will work beyond the federal republic's frontiers, and operate within the federal republic only where necessary for the setting-up of control points for its work abroad, and for the protection of its own Intelligence communications.

It will be necessary for these two distinct state agencies to co-operate closely with one another as the Office for the Protection of the Constitution will have the best opportunities for frustrating the enemy's attack on the inland establishments of the federal Intelligence service, and the federal Intelligence service for its part will be well placed to detect the enemy's points abroad for launching attacks on our domestic government institutions.

2] *Duties and organisation of the federal Intelligence service*

In laying down the duties and organisational structure of the federal Intelligence service the main concern must be to avoid at all costs the errors and shortcomings of the past. So it is not a matter of resuscitating the old *Abwehr*, but of creating something basically new, bearing the following points in mind:

a] Unified control of all German Intelligence work beyond federal frontiers, in the sectors of foreign policy and of economic, military and counter-espionage. Thus the role of the federal Intelligence service will be total Intelligence data procurement of every kind abroad. As in Britain and the United States the procurement of Intelligence and other data must be run on wholly non-partisan lines, in the national interest alone. It will be an institution working with scientific methods, and in general it will have nothing in common with the picture of the Intelligence worker common in cheap popular literature, or suggested by the dubious activities of the Kemritz case.

Unified control will enable the federal Intelligence service to function economically, because frequently the same agents and the same controllers will be able to operate in several diverse sectors; it will also obviate the risk of duplicated or conflicting efforts such as we have witnessed at Germany's expense in the past. Every other non-German country of any importance is in the process of reorganising its services along these lines.

b] It will be found most practical for the unified federal Intelligence service, which is ultimately a matter of common interest to all the other government bodies, to be directly subordinated to the head of government (a solution adopted by post-war France and the United States).

Without prejudice to this direct subordination to the Federal Chancellor, the unified federal Intelligence service must also be firmly anchored in the various requisitioning authorities (the Foreign Ministry, the Economics Ministry, the Defence Ministry, the Ministry for All-German Affairs and other federal agencies with an interest in the Intelligence data obtained), to enable the federal Intelligence service to accomplish to the full the requirements asked of it by these requisitioning authorities.

To ensure this it will be necessary for each of the ministries concerned to appoint a 'special adviser' (*Sonderreferent*) to the Minister; he will be the plenipotentiary of the Minister in all Intelligence matters. He will simultaneously be the liaison officer to the federal Intelligence service and will formulate his minister's Intelligence requirements to the federal Intelligence service. At the same time he will receive on behalf of his minister the analyses and reports of the federal Intelligence service relating to that particular ministry's field, and within the ministry's sector he will ensure that the work of the federal Intelligence service is given all possible support.

The terms of service of the head of the federal Intelligence service must be such as to exclude any encroachment on the right of the minister to express to the Federal Chancellor opinions on Intelligence data produced by his own department. Equally, the head of the federal Intelligence service must be enabled to refer to the views of the minister concerned in formulating his own over-all analysis of the situation.

c] All German groups already operating on their own initiative in this field – insofar as they are not operating impermissibly under foreign control – must be embodied in suitable form in the federal Intelligence service to be set up.

3] *The setting-up process*

Experience suggests that to set up an Intelligence service and overcome all its teething troubles takes at least five years before it becomes fully operational as an efficient instrument. During the post-war era an Intelligence organisation staffed and controlled entirely by Germans has been built up on the initiative of General Gehlen, founded on the idealised concept of defending the western way of life and Christian culture against communism. This 'Gehlen agency' (*Dienststelle Gehlen*) operates in every Intelligence field against the eastern bloc countries. Hitherto it has been financed by the Americans on the basis of a Gentleman's Agreement reached by General Gehlen, in which the purely German character of the service is formally recognised and he is expressly conceded the right to owe allegiance exclusively to the German authorities concerned. In consequence, General Gehlen took up contact with the Federal Chancellor after the federal government was set up and asked him to authorise the continuation of this work. As the expert opinion was that this is an organisation whose achievements are of international standing, it is proposed to use this organisation as the matrix for the construction of the federal Intelligence service.

Over the last few months there has therefore been a minute investigation of the organisation by the Federal Chancellor's representatives, as to its political, personnel, administrative and capability aspects. This investigation has shown that it would be desirable to exploit this organisation in setting up the federal Intelligence service, especially since the Americans, in the interests of strengthening the federal republic's defensive capability against communism, are prepared to transfer to the government the technical equipment available to the organisation, including approximately 200 vehicles, and to continue with a financial subsidy in return for the provision of the eastern Intelligence data obtained. There is no danger of any unhealthy dependence on a foreign country inherent in the personnel of this organisation, and General Gehlen has moreover stated his intention of disbanding the organisation should the federal government not take it over.

It is proposed to set up the federal Intelligence service in the following stages:

a] Clarification of the issue of a future federal Intelligence service with the representatives of the major parties;

b] After the German Agreement takes effect, the transfer of General Gehlen with a small staff to government status, as 'Office for the federal Intelligence service', with the task of creating the federal Intelligence service from the existing organisation and other groups and suitable persons according to general directives to be laid down by the Chancellor's Office;

c] Simultaneously to the setting-up of the Office for the federal Intelligence service, the appointment of the special ministerial advisers in all the Ministries concerned;

d] Programmed transfer into the federal Intelligence service of the existing organisation according to the procedural rules to be laid down and to the existing German civil service regulations, in such a manner as will not interrupt the flow or quality of the current Intelligence reporting; and

e] simultaneously with [*d*]; Incorporation of other suitable groups into the service, or the co-ordination of their activities.

Glossary

Abwehr. (German: 'defence') Intelligence service controlled by prewar and wartime German defence ministry.

BfV. *Bundesamt für Verfassungsschutz* (German: 'Federal Office for the Protection of the Constitution') The approximate equivalent of the FBI or of the Special Branch in Britain: the investigatory arm of West German counterespionage and counter-subversion activities, without however any executive powers (i.e. of arrest).

'Blank Office'. (*Amt Blank*) The West German government agency set up in 1950 as a forerunner of the defence ministry.

BND. *Bundesnachrichtendienst* (German: 'Federal Intelligence Service') The successor to the 'Gehlen organisation', which it absorbed upon its creation in April 1956, headed by Reinhard Gehlen from then until April 1968 and thereafter by General Gerhard Wessel.

Bundestag. (German: 'Federal Diet') The elected West German parliamentary assembly.

Bundeswehr. (German) Official title of the West German armed forces.

CIA. Central Intelligence Agency established in the United States by National Security Act of 1947.

CIC. Counter-Intelligence Corps, units attached to the US army of occupation for the protection of troops and installations.

Cominform. Communist Information Bureau established by Soviet communist party as an organisation embracing all the communist parties of the world.

EDC. European Defence Community.

FBI. Federal Bureau of Investigation.

FDJ. (German: 'Free German Youth') Youth organisation in Soviet Zone of Germany.

FHO. (*Fremde Heere Ost*) (German: 'Foreign Armies East') 12th branch of German army's General Staff, controlling Intelligence activities on eastern front.

G-2. US army Intelligence.

Gestapo. German abbreviation for *Geheime Staatspolizei*, the secret state police controlled ultimately by the SS and Heinrich Himmler.

Ia. Staff officer, operations.

Ic. Staff officer, Intelligence.

Ic/AO. Joint military Intelligence and counter-espionage officer on a military staff.

KGB. (Russian) *Komitat Gosudarstvennoy Bezopasnosti:* Soviet committee for state security established in 1953.

LDPD. Liberal-Demokratische Partei Deutschlands: East German Liberal Democratic party.

Luftwaffe. German air force.

MAD. Militärischer Abschirmdienst (German: 'Military Screening Service'). Comparable with the CIC in function, protecting the *Bundeswehr* units from espionage and subversive activities.

Ministerialrat, Ministerialdirigent, Ministerial-Direktor. Ranks within the German civil service, in ascending order of seniority.

NATO. North Atlantic Treaty Organisation, created in 1949.

NDPD. National-Demokratische Partei Deutschlands: East German National Democratic party.

Neues Deutschland. Official organ of the East German communist party, the Socialist Unity Party.

NTS. (Russian) *Narodnyi Trudovoy Soyuz*, an anti-communist 'National Labour Union', whose initials were also sometimes taken to stand for 'we bring death to the tyrants'.

OKW. Oberkommando der Wehrmacht (High Command of the Armed Forces). Initially designed as a controlling authority for the armed forces, but during the war it became preoccupied with conduct of military operations on all fronts except the eastern.

OKH. Oberkommando des Heeres (High Command of the Army). Comparable with the War Department.

ONI. Office of Naval Information (Intelligence agency of the US navy).

OSS. Office of Strategic Services, wartime American Intelligence agency disbanded late in 1945.

Reichswehr. (German: 'Reich defence'). Official armed forces of the Second Reich permitted by the Treaty of Versailles of 1919; forerunner of the *Wehrmacht* and *Bundeswehr*.

RSHA. Reichssicherheitshauptamt ('Reich Main Security Office') Formed in 1939, comprising the Gestapo, the criminal police and the *SD*, and controlled ultimately by Heinrich Himmler and the *SS*.

SED. Sozialistische Einheitspartei Deutschlands ('Socialist Unity Party of Germany') East German ruling communist party.

SHAPE. Supreme Headquarters, Allied Powers in Europe.

SS. Schutzstaffel (German: 'Guard Brigade') Himmler's powerful para-military organisation created in 1929 and expanded ultimately into a fourth armed service.

SD. Sicherheitsdienst (German: 'security service'). Intelligence and espionage arm of the *SS*.

SSD. Staatssicherheitsdienst: East German state security service; political police.

State-Secretary. (German: *Staatssekretär*) Highest rank in the German civil service, akin to the British Permanent Under-Secretary, except that his is not a permanent, but an essentially political appointment.

UAR. United Arab Republic.

USFET. United States Forces, European Theater; successor to SHAEF.

V-man. (German: *V-Mann*) a better class of agent, enlisted for patriotic or idealistic motives. (Literally, *Vertrauensmann:* a trusty.)

Wehrmacht. German armed forces of all three services from 1933 to 1945.

Biographical data

3 April 1902	Born in Erfurt, Germany. Parents, Lieutenant-Colonel (ret.) Walther Gehlen, publisher, of Breslau, and Katharina Margarete, *née* von Vaernewyck.
1 April 1920	Matriculation.
20 April 1920	Joined up in the provisional *Reichswehr*.
Summer 1921	Officer candidate, No. 3 artillery regiment.
Autumn 1922	Ensign.
Autumn 1923	Ensign First Class.
1 December 1928	Promoted lieutenant.
1 February 1928	First Lieutenant; until early 1933, adjutant of No. I detachment of 3 artillery regiment.
10 September 1931	Married to Herta Gehlen, *née* von Seydlitz-Kurzbach.
1 May 1934	Promoted to captain.
1 October 1933	Staff college until 1935.
July 1935	Posted to General Staff, serving in various positions including as adjutant to deputy Chief of Staff (*O.Qu.I*) and simultaneously in the operations branch and in the fortifications branch of the General Staff.
10 November 1938	Commander, 8th battery of 18th artillery regiment.
1 March 1939	Promoted to major.
1 September 1939	Upon outbreak of war, operations officer (*Ia*) of 213th infantry division, until 6 October 1939.

10 October 1939	Chief of Fortifications Group of War Department, until May 1940.
May 1940	In succession, liaison officer to the Commander-in-Chief (von Brauchitsch) to the Sixteenth Army, to General Hoth's Panzer group and to General Guderian's Panzer Group, until the end of the campaign in France, June 1940.
1 July 1940	Adjutant of General Halder, Chief of the General Staff, until October 1940.
7 October 1940	Chief of Eastern Group of General Staff's operations branch.
1 July 1941	Promoted to lieutenant-colonel. (GS).
1 April 1942	Appointed head of General Staff's branch, 'Foreign Armies East'.
1 December 1942	Promoted to colonel (GS).
1 December 1944	Promoted to brigadier-general.
9 April 1945	Dismissed as head of Foreign Armies East.
22 May 1945	Surrender with my principal colleagues to American forces at Fischhausen, on Lake Schliersee.
26 August 1945	Flown to United States with four of my colleagues.
1 July 1946	Departure from United States for Europe.
12 July 1946	Discharged from prisoner-of-war status. Formal birth of the 'Gehlen organisation'.
1 April 1956	Transfer of 'Gehlen organisation' to West German government; birth of Federal Intelligence Service (*Bundesnachrichtendienst*). Promoted to lieutenant-general of reserve in the *Bundeswehr*. President of the *BND*.
30 April 1968	Retirement from Federal Intelligence Service.

Index

Index